## Horatio C[...]

Horatio Clare was born in 1973 and e[...]
York. He trained as a journalist and j[...]
ment, where he researched and produced on many programmes,
including *Front Row*, *Night Waves* and *The Verb*. A contributor to various newspapers, magazines and travel anthologies, he now writes for
a living.

## Praise for *Running for the Hills*

'The joy of *Running for the Hills* lies in its seemingly effortless richness
and precision. No matter what Clare seizes on he brings it to the page
bursting with its own actuality. It is the prose equivalent of a collection of poems by Ted Hughes – or Wordsworth' *Sunday Times*

'Enchanting . . . without a trace of sentimentality and with much love,
Clare recalls a not-so-long-ago childhood of unimaginable richness
and wonder . . . His delightful reminiscences of a rural upbringing
make you ache with regret for that harmony between man and nature
which vanished as technology sent us spinning out of control' *Daily
Mail*

'His poetic, beautifully written memoir pieces together fragments to
tell the story of his unconventional upbringing on a Welsh hill farm
and of his parent's doomed marriage . . . Despite its portrayal of hardship, *Running for the Hills*, is lifted by a sense of joy and spiritual freedom' *The Economist*

'Exquisitely pieced-together memories of a childhood spent in the
Welsh countryside . . . Among the hard grind of wet winters and sheep
sickness, the young Horatio finds a rhythm and pace that stays with
him even after his struggling parents split up' *Good Housekeeping*

'Clare brilliantly captures his parents' initial love affair with the idea of escaping London for the hills, despite the ramshackle isolation and lack of heat and water . . . A marvellous memoir about the blessings and hardness of nature and relationships' *Publishing News*

'Beautifully written, particularly in its detailed observations of the natural world . . . Despite its nostalgic subject matter, the descriptions avoid the pitfalls of a rose-tinted rural idyll . . . This bittersweet account of a rural childhood in the not-so-distant past resonates with lessons for today . . . A thoughtful insight into a world that many dream of but few understand' *Guardian*

'This insightful memoir carefully considers the impact of a unique place on its inhabitants' *Waterstone's Books Quarterly*

'An intriguing portrait . . . strikingly told' *Times Literary Supplement*

'The quotidian details of farming, the feel, taste and smell of living on the land among animals, are beautifully rendered . . . But he also manages to evoke those moments when self-important humans are suddenly made aware by dramatic landscapes of the comparatively small place they occupy in the natural world, and there are passages here that remind one of Wordsworth's recollections of his Lake District boyhood in *The Prelude' Daily Telegraph*

'A deeply personal story related in graceful and sensitive prose' *Bookseller*

'Charming . . . It's the smallest things, the textures and colours, that mark the child's memory. Clare digs deep to bring us evocative details . . . with an impressive honesty and delicacy' *Independent*

# Running for the Hills

*A family story*

## HORATIO CLARE

JOHN MURRAY

© Horatio Clare 2006

First published in Great Britain in 2006 by John Murray (Publishers)
A division of Hodder Headline

Paperback edition 2006

The right of Horatio Clare to be identified as the Author of the Work has been asserted
by him in accordance with the Copyright, Designs and Patents Act 1988.

3

A CIP catalogue record for this title is available from the British Library

ISBN-13 978-0-7195-6539-7
ISBN-10 0-7195-6539-1

Typeset in Monotype Bembo by Servis Filmsetting Ltd, Manchester

Printed and bound by
Clays Ltd, St Ives plc

Hodder Headline policy is to use papers that are natural, renewable and recyclable
products and made from wood grown in sustainable forests. The logging and
manufacturing processes are expected to conform to the environmental regulations of the
country of origin.

John Murray (Publishers)
338 Euston Road
London NW1 3BH

To my parents and Alexander

# Contents

# Preface

THIS IS A story about my childhood and a farm on a mountain. I have tried to tell it truthfully though it begins before I was born, with the meeting of my parents. To reconstruct their history I have put together what they told me and what I know of them, and what they wrote (they let me have their diaries), and supplied the rest from my imagination. It is not a documentary, but it is a truthful description of my picture of what happened.

The children of separated parents are raised on incomplete histories, fragments of a main tale which begins mysteriously and ends in failure. My brother and I were lucky: it was not as though our mother and father were looking at the same thing and calling it different names. Rather, their perspectives fell like two beams of light on the opposite sides of a ruined castle, illuminating different faces of its collapse. We compared their images and formed our own impressions of what the edifice had looked like, and why it had fallen down. It was always a stormy, changeable picture; hard to look at and difficult to see.

Yet it was a vital story for me. I did not want to spend my life hoping to understand its beginnings. I knew there had been thrilling and beautiful times, as well as desperate and difficult ones: I needed to try to see the world as it was then, through the eyes of the young couple who tried to make it turn for them.

I felt driven back up the mountain where it all happened, and hoped, by telling the story, to understand it better. That is why it begins at the end of the 1960s, in a place called the House of Tongue.

# I

# In the Eye of the Sun

THEY MET AT the House of Tongue, at the tip of Scotland, near the furthest point north. As she walked into the room he was the only man to stand up. They exchanged bright smiles, the kind that come from shyness: neither was comfortable in the grand drawing room, under the glassy stare of shot stags and the crossed swords of long-conquered Scots.

Like a spy in a boys' adventure story, the young man's manners were too polished, his unaccented speech too English. Robert was born in Shanghai and raised in Kenya and South Africa. He was not at home in the chattering party which surrounded him; he was too quiet, too watchful, too polite.

Jenny was also self-conscious, but she flushed and bubbled with it, buried it under avalanches of enthusiasm and laughter until, in the middle of dinner, someone sneered something about a 'bloody homosexual' in Parliament. In a trice she reacts.

'But what on earth does it matter? I don't think it makes the slightest difference! So what if he's queer? So what?'

The other speaker halts. There is an embarrassed silence. Robert raises his head and for the first time looks beyond the pretty, skittish surface of the girl on the other side of the table. He says nothing, but she catches this sudden, steady look, and beyond the agreement in his spreading smile, she sees another thing: the assessment of another intelligence, another will.

'Hmmph!' she thinks, and reaches for her wine.

After dinner they spread out around a great fire with cigarettes, cigars and spirits. The host, Max, sat down with Robert to play chess. They were friends and rivals; similarly ambitious, agitating young journalists. They had been in Nigeria together, covering the Biafran war. Most of those at the House of Tongue that night were journalists of some sort: Jenny was the *Standard*'s Assistant Literary Editor.

Max was following Winston Churchill's *My Early Life* as a manual for grand success. He liked to win his games, and he had played Robert before. Jenny sat nearby and watched. Her presence added an edge to the contest. Robert thought for a time, sometimes a long time, before shifting a piece. Max bit his fingernails, the effort of each bite clipping across his face. The game slowed and intensified, the pieces clotting on the board in gently bloody confrontation. Jenny sat watching the men, following the game, and at some point (she remembered, decades later) realised that she wanted Robert to win. On his turn Max moved quickly, defiantly; he pressed, he attacked. His game was good, aggressive and alert, but, in the end, Robert won.

The next day was misty, the grass as wet as the sky and the loch deep green below the pelt of bracken. After breakfast Max handed out rods, guns and bright cartridges. The women made jokes and mocked distaste and went along with it anyway. Jenny denounced it all and went for a walk. She may not have been as easily confident as the others, but she knew her own mind, and never concealed a conviction.

'I think it's disgusting. Foul!' she cried, over her shoulder, at Max and his laughing crew. She said of him later, 'I could never love anyone who insists on killing things the whole time.'

Robert walked too, he left before breakfast and went miles. He did not shoot or fish. He looked out to sea and put up grouse. There was nothing, not even a croft along the shore. He packed a meditative pipe and smoked, sitting on a cold rock.

Jenny went across the moor, slipping and sliding in high boots of inappropriate green leather which soon became blackened with peat slime. Every pop of the guns behind her confirmed her resistance to Max.

Later, in a warm evening with no wind, the loch dreamily still and the old sandstone house glowing red, Max took her out in a rowing boat. The creak and drip of the slow oars seemed to amplify the glassy peace; Jenny felt that the herons and even the midges were listening. They moved out into the middle, drifting into the lacquered green reflection of the col. Max seemed calmer than he had been, not chasing her any more, thinking about other things. They eyed the water.

'My God, someone's coming in!'

Jenny stared at the pale figure, which was even then throwing itself forward in a shallow dive, a great fish flopping.

'Well, that is quite mad. It must be absolutely freezing.'

'It's Robert,' Max said, narrowing shooter's eyes.

Robert pulled towards them, breast stroke, gasping huge breaths. Ten yards away he took an extra deep one and plunged under, shimmering to the side of the boat and surfacing with a sputtered cloud of vapour. Jenny saw his shoulders were brown and flecked with sunspots and moles. Kicking beneath him, shrinking and growing, his feet were white.

'Isn't it freezing?' she cried, shivering.

'Very refreshing,' he said, exaggerating the shudder in his voice. He turned, ducked under, set off.

'Loopy,' said Max.

'I can't stand cold water! Ever since my mother used to make us swim in the freezing sea I just can't bear it. Being an adult is never having to get into the water,' Jenny said, watching Robert swim.

There was a girl there called Anne, another of Max's friends. Jenny noticed Anne looking at Robert. As she followed Anne's gaze Robert glanced up, not at Anne, but at her.

'I think I've fallen in love with Robert,' Anne announced.

'Have you? Golly. Do you know him then?'

'He's going to be my problem, ' said Anne, thoughtfully.

Jenny decided she would go back to London when she looked out of a window and saw the lawn covered with mackerel. Max was laying them out, dozens of bright silverblue fish.

'What are you going to do with so many, Max?' she demanded.

'Oh Lord, Jenny. Don't tell me you don't like fishing either! This is Scotland, for God's sake!'

'I think it's fine to kill things for the table. But how on earth are you going to eat all of these beautiful mackerel?'

It was a long way to the station and she called a taxi. She was waiting for it, saying goodbyes, when Robert appeared, carrying his bag.

'I'm going back too,' he announced. 'I'll come as far as Newcastle with you.'

This train journey fascinates me. For the first time they are alone together. Robert gives her to understand there is someone, a woman, in Newcastle. But when the great station arrives he does not get off. They cross the Tyne together. What do they see as they gaze across the compartment at the other? She looks on a beautiful young man. His hair is fair, his skin is browned, his face broad and handsome. The nose is straight, the jawline firm. His voice is authoritative, with that near-arrogant crispness that public schools and colonies breed, but he speaks softly, gently.

He has a habit of tilting his head back slightly as he listens, green eyes locked on hers, and nodding forward as he responds. His humour is quick and dry and never far away. He is not fixed; there is a fragility about his quickness, as if he believes in his own intelligence and is uncertain of all the rest.

He is familiar with the company of beautiful women but has never encountered anyone like Jenny. She leaps from her seat, crying out her delight at the dark magnificence of Durham cathedral. She snorts with giggles when he is witty. She rolls her eyes at the other passengers, responds to the stolid ticket inspector like a naughty schoolgirl performing for her class; she seems to find authority provocative and ridiculous. Her hair is fine and dark, her eyes are bright and light brown. She has the elfin air, smile and sass of the Chelsea girl she was not long ago. She smokes cigarettes carelessly and talks continuously, veering wildly between innocence, mischief and insight. Their fingers touch as she hands back his matches, and he notices how cool hers are. I see them smiling across the compartment, charmed and laughing with nothing to lose in that blissful conspiracy of ignorance and curiosity with which love affairs begin.

They begin to unfold their lives to one another. Robert talks of his childhood, of following his father's postings to Kenya and South Africa, of being a student in Cape Town, of his marriage, of opposition to the regime, of friends imprisoned and murdered, of his flight to Britain with his young wife and their little daughter, of the failure of that marriage, of divorce.

Jenny listens, responds with sketches of her own upbringing in Shrewsbury, and her boarding school in Kent, where she was the only girl who was not the child of missionaries. She tells of her flight from what her mother always insisted was 'upper middle class' Shropshire, of her happiness at Cambridge; she mentions adventures in America and Thailand, teaching in the East End, of how much she hated working in television.

When the train reached London they separated, but in helping her with her bags Robert somehow kept hold of the one containing her soiled green leather boots. On the following Monday evening he finished earlier than usual and waited for her outside her office in Fleet Street. When she emerged, hurrying as usual, he gravely presented her with the boots. She barely recognised them. He had worked the leather for hours, with spit and rags and carefully chosen polish, and now they shone and gleamed.

'Heavens, Robert,' she cried, 'they're beautiful! How sweet of you!' He gave her a watch not long after that, saying 'I notice you never seem to know the time,' with one of the sidelong looks which always made her laugh, but nothing moved her like the polishing of the boots, which seemed to her a pure kindness.

Robert would not come out to play at lunchtimes or after work, he shunned the wine bar crowd in which she had many friends. He was never fond of the laughing Diary boys, the gossip and booze. He was always working, and quiet in the company of men, except Max.

They were well matched to their jobs. Jenny was pretty and bright, and awkward and open all at once: the combination swept her past the wary fences of the writers and academics she interviewed. Her subjects trusted her immediately and talked freely as her tape recorder turned, and she missed nothing. At the office package after package of books arrived to be opened and considered. She sampled them, tested them against taste and instinct, read and re-read them, and – though it took her much longer to believe than to acquire it – developed an expert eye.

In the din and dinge of old Fleet Street she was an unlikely presence. 'You'll never make a journalist, dear girl, you're not nearly tough enough,' said one.

'It's not what you write,' grated her senior one day, 'it's not even how slowly you type it. It's the pauses while you search your keys for the right letter!'

Robert blazed at his work. He had a passion for it; he went for the heart of the story as if angry headlines and cool paragraphs could slay the tormentors of the world.

They saw each other often, and one day his kettle appeared in her kitchen, and she knew that he had moved in.

Then one night they went to a restaurant in Notting Hill. Red tablecloths, dark walls. Robert listened while Jenny, inspired, laid out her dream.

'I don't want to be stuck in London,' she declared. 'I think we should buy a house in the country. Imagine a lovely old place somewhere away from all the wretched fumes.'

'You're serious?'

'Yes, yes! Do you want to go to work on the tube for the rest of your life? Wouldn't you love to have mountains to climb?'

'We can do that at the weekends.'

'Yes, but we could have a house too. We could have a house and fields. I miss the country. I miss nature. Come on, Robert darling! Let's find somewhere beautiful.'

She picked at her food and giggled as he couched his objections in jokes, but she was glowing with something else, something impatient. Years later, when I asked him about it, he said, 'Oh, she was absolutely determined. She had made up her mind to do it. I loved her and she presented me with a decision she had already made.'

— * —

So they began to hunt. They would hammer up the motorway on Friday nights to Jenny's sister Ursula, happily married to Geoff and living in the Forest of Dean, on the Welsh border. From there they launched themselves in every direction, and round and round they went, from estate agents' windows to cottages and farms, to small houses and to large, up hillsides and down muddy tracks, back to estate agents' windows, and they could not find it.

They combed the windy edge of Wales, dropping off the ridges into hidden valleys, winding down to villages ignored by everything but the weather. Years later Jenny would see signposts to places and say, 'I think we went there when we were looking for the farm. Yes, we did. Miserable place.'

The journeys back down the motorway were long exercises in resignation for her. She thought she would never find it, and mulled over what she had seen. Behind the wheel Robert wondered how long they would have to keep looking. He loved the country and walking, was glad of the missions for the space and the exercise; the way people lived on the border with the past seduced his reporter's eye. He looked for their means, their crops and flocks. He looked at what their livelihoods had made of them, and planned his next campaign at work.

One evening, following a fruitless day around Abergavenny, a small glum town in the rain, when they were just about to turn for London once more, Jenny remembered an estate agent they had missed. Robert waited while she ran back into town. Russell, Baldwin & Bright were about to close.

'I don't suppose you've got a little farm somewhere beautiful . . .'

'Something came in today, actually.'

The envelope contained an untidy summary of a place for sale, and detailed directions. Robert scanned it.

'Smallholding and outbuildings, seventy-two acres, hill rights. It's a working farm.'

'Where?'

'The other side of the Black Mountains. Blooming miles.'

'Oh! Real Wales!'

'Really faraway Wales.'

'We might as well look at it. It'll be an expedition.'

The vendors would expect them at three o'clock. The departure from London was delayed by a hunt for the car keys.

'I had them, I put them somewhere. I'm so sorry, darling, let me just think a minute. Oh, here they are! How did they get in there? In the grill!'

Robert rolled his eyes. 'Where else?'

As they crossed out of England, over the bridge, the sun drowned in veils of sky the same colour as the Severn mud. Making the turn at Newport the rain descended, netting them, rattling over the car. Forty minutes north they climbed the rise into a little town.

'Oh what a pretty place,' Jenny cried. 'Isn't it charming!' Georgian lines proportioned the little High Street, shops adjoined like ladies in their best, neatly lined up for tea. It seemed abandoned to the wind and rain.

Robert nodded, following Jenny's directions under the looming walls of an invisible manor, north up the tightening valley, right at a fork, into further hills. To the right the mountains vanished into the murk; in every direction cloud hung sullen over rising ground.

'Turn right there. Good. Now, right at house, steep pitch.' It was very quiet beyond the car; when it slowed they could sense the peace, almost hear it.

The car paused, gathered itself and assaulted the gradient in first gear. 'Crikey!' Robert laughed, as they were tilted back in their seats like fighter pilots, climbing straight up the side of the hill.

'My God, look at this. It's a pitch all right. Right at fork, through wood half mile.'

'My God, look at *this*,' Robert said calmly, hauling the car up and around a bend so steep it seemed to fill the windows on his side with wet road. The engine panted and gasped with relief at the top, flipping them over another rise into a soaking wood.

'My God, my vertigo,' Jenny cried. 'It's an abyss!'

The right side wheels spun over leaf litter banked against a straggle of rusted fence, which offered no protection from the cliffy drop into the trees. To the left the wood gathered in thick scribbles, tapping the roof above their heads and dropping sudden tears on the windscreen. The road proceeded on and up through a waving tunnel.

'Where is it taking us? We'll be swallowed in the mists like the Ninth Legion!'

'If we don't roll over backwards like a beetle. Hold on, it's another pitch.' Robert swung the car round and up, as to the right flickered fields, more wood, cloud and bracken.

They rose over the crest. Below, the fields sloped more gently and before them, across three meadows, the mountain, untamed and sudden, climbed into the sky. At its foot, nestling in the crook of a gully, was the house, sheltering under a stand of larch trees. They could see three descending roofs, white walls and dark windows. It was a longhouse dug into the curved flank of the mountain, a little tumbledown manor at the head of its own valley.

The track was a double path of stones and red earth separated by a block of grass which brushed the undercarriage menacingly, threatening to rear up and ground them. Robert took it slowly. Sheep stared with blank frankness from under the shelter of thorn trees and thin gasps of smoke blew away from one of the chimneys.

As they neared the house half the track became a stream, pooling muddily at the yard gate. They stopped beside a high barn wall. The yard was a rough cobble of mud, muck and protruding stones sloping steeply up to the front door. The stone-tiled roofs were green with moss and rain. A huge midden slumped against the stable wall. Black cattle like buffalo hung around the lower end of the yard and the savage barking of dogs hesitated when Robert switched off the engine, then resumed with discouraging vigour. There were little orange cats running about in the mud.

'Ah-ha! The vendor . . .'

A short round figure in a soaked black tweed jacket, a mud-checked cap, red cheeks and bright eyes came down the yard to meet them. Robert shook his hand.

'How do you do? I'm Robert and this is Jenny.'

'Emrys,' said the vendor. 'How do you do? You've come a long way.'

'Yes, thank goodness,' said Jenny. 'Thank you for having us up your mountain.'

'Well. It's a pity you can't see the view.' Emrys shouted when he was shy. 'There's a good view there, when it's visible.'

'You're pretty high up, here?'

Emrys led them up the yard to the house.

'A thousand and something, I think it is. Geeyet outofit! Fly!' Emrys shouted at a white whiskered dog's nose, poking under the barn door and barking. He was smiling, though.

'There'll be tea in a minute. We've been watching the television. You can't get much signal except when it rains.'

The door opened to wet flagstones and a dim interior. The wall, Jenny noticed, was almost two feet thick. To the left a dark wooden screen hid the uphill end of the house. They went in. There was a tiny fire in a choked grate: the vast hearth Jenny looked for was blocked up. At the foot of a narrow flight of stairs, in a corner beside the fire, was a place out of the draughts where Emrys had his little daughter's cot. He led them through to the kitchen which was stuck on at the back. It was a big step down to huge flagstones resting on earth; there was no flooring, and the smell of damp was incredible, like nothing they had ever experienced, a wet dripping damp, wetter and damper and darker than any cellar.

Jenny loved it. Really: she fell passionately in love with it straightaway. Someone had told her that you can fall in love with a place as much as a person, and now she knew it to be true.

They rattled away along the track. It was bitterly cold at the far gate. Jenny opened and shut it and climbed back in, shivering.

'What an amazing place!'

'No bathroom. No water! Chemical lavatory in that shed in the yard . . .' Robert was thoughtful, but there was an excitement in the car.

'Think of the view, though. You'd do your business with a view across the whole valley.'

'Ye-es . . . dug into the hill at one end, terribly damp. We'd have to excavate it.'

'God, it was damp! We'd have to have washes with the kettle in a tub. There must be the most enormous fireplace just waiting. We'd have to put a bathroom in. We could put a big bathroom in over the stable, and another bedroom.'

'We'd have to put a water tank in first. Carrying those drums from the stream – you'd get pretty fit! And it needs a new roof.'

'Golly. That wouldn't be cheap.'

'I could get a book on it. It can't be that difficult.'

'Wasn't Emrys sweet? What a nice man! And isn't it amazing? It hasn't been touched. It must be 1600s.'

'You'd never manage these steep bits in the snow, even in a tractor.'

'You'd have to leave the car at the bottom and walk, with your supplies on a dog sled.'

'The fences are all falling down.'

'And the sheep are wild!'

'Would we keep the sheep?'

'Oh yes,' Jenny cried. 'We'd have to have a few sheep!'

'So we'd be farmers at the weekends, would we?'

'Well, darling, I don't know . . . let's come back and look at it again, when it's not raining.'

\*

Jenny went to a lunch held by a small anti-establishment magazine. The entire establishment seemed to be present. She was seated next to an economist of high renown and low charm, a man with a bacon face who had always considered himself one of the best people. In a grand and public way, he was as sweet as possible to the girl sitting next to him, until she told him about her plans.

'Farming in Wales? What on earth do you want to do that for?'

'Oh well! It's so beautiful and wild! And I don't want to spend the rest of my life on the Central line, thank you very much. It just isn't me. And if I'm going to have children I don't want them to live on exhaust.'

'And how are you going to make any money?'

'I'll have a few sheep, and I can carry on reviewing books.'

'My dear girl, you'll never make any money out of sheep. I mean absolutely nothing. Farming's a dead duck.'

'Is it? I thought there were pots of money coming from Brussels.'

'Well, that's right. Without the subsidies the entire industry would collapse, certainly sheep farming, which is the lowest of the low in terms of yield, and as for hill farming in Wales you'd be better off going down a coal mine!' He swept a popping eye around his listeners. 'I mean it. In twenty years' time there won't be any sheep farming left, and the hill farmers will be the first to go. I can show you the figures if you like.'

'No thank you,' Jenny cried, loud enough to turn heads. 'You'll just have to come to the rescue. If it's all horrible, I hope someone will come and help me.'

— * —

'We're going to see the view this time,' Jenny said, to distract herself from the strain as the car wrenched itself around the cruel bend at the top of the first pitch. It was a clear August noon. London had been cool and still in anticipation of a hot day and Wales was bright and windy, cloud shadows bowling over the hills. After the wood came the second pitch. Topping it, they saw the mountain for the first time, like a huge capsized sailing boat with its keel slicing the sky. The hillside was mauve and green and dark grey; great screes of stones in wild fields tumbled motionlessly down its high hull.

Jenny gasped and grabbed his arm as Robert slowed the car, the engine noise shrinking away in the sudden, vast space. They stared, thrilled. 'Look at that,' she breathed, 'just look at that!'

The land dropped away from them, fell into woods and levelled out far below in a patchwork valley of countless fields, ribboned with streams and hedges, scattered with stacked hay bales, barns, and here and there farms, little monarchies on the climbing slopes of the facing hills. Beyond them, rising out of the valley and into the further bowl of the sky were the mountains, great sweeping ridges, high crests, ice-cut shoulders and peaks, old dragons rolling across the horizon.

They found Emrys at the back of the house, scanning the mountain.

'What is it, Emrys?' Robert asked, hands on hips, chin lifted, searching the hillside.

'Fly – taking the sheep up.'

'What's she doing?'

There was a disturbance in the bracken a hundred yards above them and Jenny could see white bundles of sheep dashing suddenly through the dense fern.

'She's bringing them from the gully where it's steep. She'll push them along, then up over the tump, above the bracken, see.'

Clouds marched along the skyline and Jenny felt the foreign difference of Robert and herself, his old flares, her polished boots, up from London and proposing to buy all this, as though it could be bought, as though it could be owned.

Robert was thinking about walking up there, on an August day, pushing a few sheep ahead of him, with the whole of Wales below and views for miles and miles from the top. So much. He could see them there, his beautiful Jenny and him, on the mountain. He could just see them, far away but visible nonetheless.

*

The sale by auction was advertised in the *Express*; the Wellington Hotel, Brecon, custard yellow and pedimented, was the venue. The function room held a stout, curious crowd, elderly tweed jackets stretched across broad shoulders. Everyone wanted to know what the place would fetch, so high and far away from the road, cut off in the winter. Many had heard there were Londoners interested, and some didn't like the sound of that. Farms should go to farmers, young couples starting out. It wasn't the best land, but there were some tidy little fields up there, and plenty of water. It was a shame to think of it all being broken up and left empty most of the year. Mind, if that was how it was going to go, there were a few there who would rent the ground. And perhaps they'd sell? The speculators cawed and nodded, hands hooked in the belts of smart trousers, smiles on wind-red faces, winks and prices passed back and forth. There were a few with a beer, but the notorious thrift of the hill farmers wasn't going to put a real smile on the Wellington manager's face. Most of these men were Chapel, as were their wives, and their money was not meant for drinking.

Everyone knew who was going to bid, of course, and most had a fair idea of how far he would be able to go. Derwyn Norster had been born there. His parents had bought it during the war and he'd grown up there. They had moved round the hill and down to the other side of the wood for better land and better access. Derwyn was Emrys's neighbour and he and Ira had had their eye on the farm ever since they married. Derwyn never really felt he had left it, living so close, with adjoining fields, and as far as Ira was concerned they had a right to it. Their boys, Aled and Alwyn, knew nothing but farming. Aled was thirteen already and Alwyn was sixteen and he at least needed somewhere to live. If only they could have the farm back it would be like having the whole mountain. Derwyn had made Emrys an offer for it up by the hill gate only a couple of days after it went round that Emrys was planning to sell. Emrys had turned him down and there had been a row. Derwyn had a terrible temper. Emrys hadn't had reason to mention any of this to Robert and Jenny. When Robert asked him about the neighbours he'd merely said

Derwyn wasn't such a bad old boy. It was what anyone would have said.

Robert found a place to park outside the Wellington. He had timed it to the minute, as usual, which never ceased to amaze Jenny, who had spent much of her life in desperate and doomed attempts not to be late.

'Right then,' he grinned, collecting his pipe from the glove compartment and fitting it into the pocket of his jacket. He leaned over and gave Jenny a kiss.

She kissed him and peered distractedly at her reflection in the driver's mirror. 'Phew, I'm nervous,' she gasped, and laughed. He paused, reaching for the door handle, as the rain rilled on the windscreen and the roof.

'Oh, darling, it's very exciting but you don't have to be nervous.' He twisted back towards her and took her hand, stroking it slowly with his thumb.

'How far shall we go?' she said, slightly horrified at the uncertainty and the thought of money she did not have just running away with them.

'I don't think we should worry about that too much. The question is, do you really want this farm?'

'Yes! Yes I do!'

'Right then.'

He locked the car after them and took her arm. He was looking forward to it. Competition with other men was strong in his nature, and he relished it.

There were chairs set out in front of the auctioneer's table but most people were standing around the back and down the sides of the room. The auctioneer was already out, talking to Emrys. Emrys, his wife and their little daughter were all done up in their best and they had three seats in the first row. They looked beautifully smart, composed and very nervous. Little Anwyn's hair had been brushed so that it shone. Jenny smiled at everyone who looked at her. Robert kept his eyes down until he had found somewhere for them to stand, in the middle, just to the right of centre, then he took one very careful look around. Emrys gave him a nod and a smile. Robert smiled back.

'Ladies and gentlemen, thank you,' called the auctioneer, an avuncular man with a shiny nose and tiepin, who looked at them all as though he had met them each personally, not so very long ago, in slightly disreputable circumstances.

'Thank you all.' He cast an eye around the room and it fell completely silent.

'Today as you all know we have a special sale for you, a very special sale indeed. Emrys Pryce has honoured us with the commission to sell his beautiful farmhouse and seventy-two acres of prime farm land. The commission includes the barn and stable, other outbuildings, grazing rights and hill rights for over two hundred stock, and as I said, seventy-two of the best acres you will find anywhere. The land is well drained and every field has access to one of two springs that have never been known to dry. The farm and land are of course within the protected area of the National Park. The situation is as perfect as anything we at Russell, Baldwin & Bright . . .'

'Russell, Baldwin and Not so Bright,' Robert hissed in Jenny's ear.

'. . . have ever seen in many years of working in this area. The stunning views are quite unsurpassed in my experience, and I have no hesitation in describing what we are selling today as a piece of heaven on earth, a house in the eye of the sun. I know you would all hope to see a good price for this farm, the right price.'

He paused. His assistant, a young man who aped his air, took the top off his fountain pen.

'And now without further ado I propose to get this sale under way. Please make your bids clear. I've got a pretty good view, but I don't want to miss anyone.'

Emrys looked over his shoulder. Jenny thought she understood and smiled comfortingly at him. But he kept looking anxiously back.

'So ladies and gentlemen, for the house, the buildings and seventy-two acres, let's not dally around. For the house and land I'll start at five thousand pounds, who'll give me five thousand pounds?'

'Five thousand pounds on my right, five thousand I'm bid. Six thousand at the front? Six thousand five hundred, sir.'

Robert had not moved. Derwyn Norster was the man on the right, and he was looking at the rows of heads in front of him for the man who was bidding against him. He nodded again.

'Seven thousand on my right, seven thousand and it's with you, sir, do I have eight thousand?'

Robert nodded. The auctioneer was too smart to smile, but there was a distinct thickening of his voice. 'Eight thousand I'm bid, eight thousand to my left!' Heads turned. Robert's smooth face was almost expressionless, but his chin was tilted up expectantly. Derwyn nodded, making a sign with his right hand. The auctioneer turned fractionally towards him, 'Eight thousand five hundred – ' and Robert nodded sharply. 'Nine thousand!' Robert nodded again.

'It's still with you, sir,' the auctioneer told him, then looked at Derwyn, who twitched his head. 'Nine thousand five hundred! Nine thousand five hundred pounds. Do I see ten at the front?' Two heads, a man's, dark, and a woman's, grey, were leaning together in silent conference, then the man's head moved. 'Ten!' But instantly, emphatically, Robert nodded. 'Ten thousand five hundred and it's back with you, sir, ten thousand five hundred, who'll give me eleven?'

The heads at the front were staring at the floor. Ira Norster was glaring about her with bulgy eyes. Derwyn made his sign, and the auctioneer, grave now, looked at Robert, announcing, 'Ten seven fifty – ' before he was interrupted by another eager nod. Jenny's heart was pounding, Robert seemed to be bidding faster than the auctioneer could call.

'Eleven thousand pounds! Eleven thousand pounds I'm bid, eleven thousand pounds and it's with the gentleman on my left. Are we all finished at the front? Eleven thousand pounds?'

He switched from the seated couple to Ira, who stared back unblinking. Derwyn was very flushed. He hung his head.

'Are there any more bids?' the auctioneer demanded of the silent room. 'Then I'm going to sell this farm, I'm going once, for eleven thousand pounds, I'm going twice, going three times and SOLD! to Miss Williams, for eleven thousand pounds, sold to you, madam.'

Jenny screeched and flung her arms around Robert and he hugged her. Emrys had one arm round his wife, who was crying over her smiles, and with the other he shook the auctioneer by the hand.

Jenny squeezed Robert's hands with all her strength. 'Oh well done, well done! So quick!'

He smiled, pushed his nose against hers. 'You've got a farm on the mountain, Jenny.'

Legend had it that even as the auctioneer was going once, Ira had been digging her husband in the ribs for another bid, and even as he had been going twice Derwyn had decided to do it and even as he had been going three times Derwyn's hand had been going up – and then 'SOLD to Miss Williams!' Legend had it that the auctioneer had wanted her to have it.

And there was something else, too. Emrys had been looking over his shoulder for a reason. For Emrys had shown someone else around the farm, someone else who had fallen in love with it. She was an American lady, Emrys said, very classy, very rich. So rich she was going to buy the farm because she loved it, and visit when she could, and live in it in the summer time and at the end of her life. But the farm was sold on a Friday. On the preceding Monday, history says, President Richard Nixon devalued the US dollar, and the American lady was never seen in the valley again.

Emrys took Robert around the farm. The house sat at the top of its own narrow valley; the fields sloped up steeply from a deep stream and rolled over into two wide arms of land, which spread out, beneath the mountain, from the house. The acres fell into two rough halves, and on each side their contours were similar: steep fields below the hill fence flattened into meadows, below which the ground fell sharply to the wooded stream. Each field was named. Emrys led Robert out behind the house, along a green lane to the Hill Fields. These ran for a quarter of a mile below the hill fence to a cluster of larch trees. From the larches the men worked their way down to thick woods, where there were badger setts and woodland birds, grey squirrels and fallen trees wrapped in moss thick as wool, growing fungus like great troll's ears. Below one mighty drop, tangled in giant bracken and crowds of nettles, was the wreckage of a vehicle, rounded blue panels smashed into the earth.

'That's my old Austin,' Emrys explained. 'Ran her off the top there.'

'Easier than the scrap heap?'

'Aye, and cheaper.'

There was something shocking about the shattered carcass of the car, a frozen explosion gradually sinking into the wood. They crossed the stream and climbed up the other side, to the foot of steep fields. Emrys told him the names as they went. Below the Hill Fields, the Rough Field was full of docks and burrs. Beside it, the L-Shape was in fact a stair-shape, and dropped into Pritchard's Wood, which would be full of bluebells in the spring. Climbing up the other side, they had passed the badger setts in the Horse Fields, and the rabbit warren, and the mighty steep bank where anything which slipped would fall to its death, except foxes. Then, circling back towards the house, they had come to the Lower Meadows, where they were now, which were the steepest of all. They trudged up to the top of them, and there were the meadows, the best pasture. Of these there were three: the First Meadow, nearest to the house; the Middle Meadow, and over towards the road where they had first seen the view, the Far Meadow. Along the top of them ran the track. Above the track, overlooking the meadows were 'the Quoikers', as Robert heard it, big sloping fields, southwest-facing, like the house, and wide open to the view. The Quoikers climbed up to the hill fence. The far Quoiker had been divided across the middle into two; it had a line of oaks, alders and ash trees halfway up. The top half of it and the near Quoiker were prone to gorse. Emrys had ploughed it a couple of years before but the bushes had come back. (Robert checked and found the sound came from two words 'Coed Cae' – 'wood field'.) Last, they came to the Patch, which was nearest to the house, just below the yard, beyond the pens: it was flattish on the top, where the land rolled over to the track, and then it plunged down to the stream. Emrys kept a few old things in the Patch, and the pony, and there was a bright green sludgy bit in the middle where the run-off from the yard accumulated.

When they got back Robert went to Jenny and put his arm around her. 'You have absolutely no idea what a wonderful farm you've bought.'

Emrys understood but did not share their enthusiasm for the land; to a farmer it was 'banky': too steep and too thin-soiled. After the walk he said, 'Come with me, Robert,' and they went off into the big barn where Emrys had his cider.

As it got dark they stood underneath one bulb, which hung from a long flex stapled to a beam. The upper half of the barn was full of bales, the lower half was empty, the floor a bed of hay. In the middle was a race: great stone flags on their ends, staked and framed with posts to make a corridor four feet high across the width of the barn, where you could pack sheep in tight, or back a cow up, or make a pen for new lambs with a couple of bales. Emrys had the cider in great glass bell jars; it was roan-red and fizzy. With few words and many smiles he refilled their glasses. They had a couple and then a couple more. By the time they emerged their cheeks were flaming and they had to drop their shoulders to change course. Robert went down to the bottom of the yard and pissed a steaming arc, as one car, like a firefly, spun along the road far below.

Emrys sold them more than a hundred sheep. It was always done, he explained. When a farm changed hands some of the sheep would stay behind. You needed a flock that knew the ground, that knew what was what, he informed them. Two thirds of their number were the Welsh Mountain breed; small, hardy, protected from the weather by their thick white fleeces, which would be shorn in the summer and sold. The remaining third were Suffolk Crosses; larger, black-faced animals with thinner coats. They would deliver bigger, more profitable lambs, but they were more likely to die in bad weather. Scattered among the flock were a few Badger Sheep, beautiful creatures which appeared to be wearing black make-up around their eyes and mouths; a few Radnors, which were russet-faced, and a few Speckles, their white faces flecked with grey. 'Welsh, Suffolks, Badgers, Radnors and Speckles,' Robert repeated. Straightforward enough.

'That's right,' Emrys smiled, 'and you've got thirty yearling theaves, and you'll want to buy another tup when Tommy gets too old.'

'Thirty what?'

Emrys was amazed and amused, but he was tactful about it. Ram lambs were tups, ewe lambs were theaves. A one year old was a yearling, and most yearlings would be theaves, as the tup lambs went to market in their first nine months, if possible before the winter, so they would not have to be fed. Yearlings were sold on as 'store' in their second autumn, to larger farms looking to replenish their stock.

'So what's a wether?'

'Castrated yearling tup that didn't go to market or didn't sell. That's a wether.'

'I see.'

Emrys was in no hurry to move out. His wife Thursa wasn't well. She had 'farmer's lung': silicosis caused by the dead brown dust of old hay. The farm up the valley Emrys had bought was not as comfortable as it should be for a baby and mother, and Emrys wondered if they could stay at the farm while he got the new place ready. He would keep an eye on it for them, and the sheep, until they were ready to move down from London.

# 2

# First Lambing

SEVERAL OF HER boyfriends had tried to marry Jenny. She ducked them, postponed them, pleaded uncertainty and waited for a surge of conviction which never came. Relationships fell through, men who had foreseen futures, who had imagined children with her, rubbed their eyes and turned away. Now Robert stood in their place. Robert, with one divorce behind him, the mixed-up child of his own parents' disastrous marriage. Robert, who wanted security, and believed that it was found in marriage. Who wanted to fit into Britain, to be connected to it. Who was charmed by this intelligent, complicated woman, and who charmed her in return. Who saw her indecision, her uncertainty, and felt it feed his determination. The weaker her conviction the stronger his. One day he said, 'Right then, let's get married!' and went across the valley and up over the top to Ebbw Vale to fix it with the registry office.

Jenny wanted a service of blessing in the village church after the civil ceremony. The school for missionaries' daughters had failed to quell her rebelliousness in the face of authority but it had given her a strong sense of the sacred. She needed to bow before authority now; she had vows to make: to do Right and eschew Wrong. But authority would not have it. The rector of the church refused. Jenny fretted.

'I'm not going to feel married, Ursie,' she wailed to her sister, and telephoned the bishop.

'But the man you are going to marry has been divorced,' the bishop intoned. 'You cannot marry in church.'

'But I just want a service of blessing,' Jenny pleaded. 'Lots of people have them, divorcees . . .'

'In England,' the bishop emphasized. 'But this is the Church of Wales.'

But Jenny did not give up, and at last the bishop relented and instructed the vicar to bless the marriage.

Before the wedding they stayed with Ursula and Geoff. Geoff had definite ideas about how these things were done. The night before the wedding he invited Robert to his local pub.

'It's very kind of you, Geoff, but . . .'

'Come on, come on. Get your coat, we're going.'

'Really, I . . .'

'It's your stag night, for God's sake! Ursula, Jenny, don't wait up. Robert, this way please.'

He marched Robert up the hill, installed him at the bar and confronted him with as much alcohol as Robert had ever faced.

'Geoff, I . . . I'm completely . . .'

'Last night of freedom – better make the most of it! This is for you. Here's to Jenny – what a wonderful woman! Cheers!'

'Oh crikey . . .'

Robert's limit was reached, passed and left far behind.

'I don't think I can drink any more beer, Geoff, I'm sorry.'

'No. Quite right. Scotch over here, when you're ready, my dear! This man's getting married. I mentioned it already? We'll have two doubles then. Yes please, doubles. Better do it properly . . .'

When they left the pub Robert was yawing wildly. The few street lights they passed had grown several new heads. The road seemed lined with inviting places to curl up, but Geoff's duty was not yet done.

'Not far, not far, and it's all downhill!'

'Geoff, I think I'm going to . . .'

'I've got you. Steady! There we go again. Left a bit, left a bit . . .'

The morning of the wedding found Robert pallid and Jenny shaky with nerves. Geoff drove Robert, and Ursula drove her sister. Jenny stared sightlessly out of the windows as the little Morris Minor hummed the miles away. She could not settle in her seat; she shuffled around, fiddled with her seat belt, wound the window down, smoked half a cigarette and threw the rest away, shaking her head.

'Are you OK, Jenny?'

Jenny gasped and clutched her stomach, as if gripped by pain. 'Oh Ursie! I don't think I want to get married! I don't know if I want to go through with it. I'm not sure about it at all! Perhaps we'd better stop.'

Ursie looked at her sister. 'Do you really want me to stop?'

'I don't know,' Jenny cried. 'I just don't know. It's too late to change my mind, isn't it?'

'Well, it is pretty late, but it's up to you, luvvie.'

'Oh Lord! I'd better go through with it, hadn't I?'

'Yes, if you love him.'

'I do love him.'

'Well then. It's just nerves. You'll be fine. He's a lovely man.'

'Yes he is. He is. OK, better now. Phew!'

'Hang on, dear girl. Nearly there.'

They married at the registry office, and from there proceeded to the village church. Now it was the rector's turn to suffer an attack of nerves. Seeing the large crowd of friends Jenny had invited, he pulled her aside and said he could not go ahead with so many 'members of the public' in attendance.

'What?' she cried. 'But you promised! The bishop . . .'

'Direct family only,' said the rector. 'I will perform the service for you and your direct families only.' Trying not to feel furious, resentful and ashamed, Jenny explained the situation and asked the crowd to wait for them.

The window behind the altar was divided into diamonds of clear glass. Behind the fishy-eyed rector, Jenny watched the deep green motion of yew trees against the shining sky. Kneeling beside his bride it struck Robert that it was the second time he had been on his knees that day, having spent a good half hour vomiting into Geoff and Ursie's lavatory.

After the service came the celebration. The editor, the boys from the Diary, Max, friends from the BBC, the newspapers, theatre, politics and the Foreign Office had all made the trek. They bumped along the track fearing the worst for their cars. Jenny sat them all on hay bales, dwarfed by the mountain and dazzled by the view, and the party was a success. People walked and drank and gossiped and disappeared up the mountain and reappeared in the yard and everyone had a lovely time.

And that is important, because beyond the doubtful bishop and the flaky rector and the equivocating omens of Jenny's stage fright and Robert's hangover, it was as if the farm and their friends blessed them unreservedly. Robert always noticed bad signs – his eye picked them out for him – but he refused to entertain super-stition. Jenny always noticed good omens, and kept a hopeful look-out for the world unseen. She wished on new moons and evening stars; she kept horseshoes on their sides, in case it was true that they would be used as boats by witches if placed upright, or that the luck would run out of them if left with their mouths tilted down.

They awoke the next morning to a beautiful day and the sound of hooves on a hard surface.

'What's that?' Jenny poked her head out from under the covers.

'The pitter-patter of tiny feet?' Robert exclaimed. 'That was quick!'

He jumped out of bed and went to the window. 'Darling, there are sheep all over the roof of the shed. How have they man-aged that?'

She joined him at the window. 'What are you doing there?' she cried.

They were yearlings, last season's lambs, grown big enough to follow their curiosity and their love of ash leaves over fences and up the little jump at the back of the shed where the roof met the bank behind. They slid and bleated.

'Hang on, we're coming!' Jenny trilled back. And that was the end of the honeymoon.

— * —

Their neighbours were short spoken, would nod uneasy greet-ings as they passed in the lanes. Derwyn Norster was shy of them, and shouted nervously when they met. There were no hard feelings about the sale, he said. Sitting in the tractor cab behind him, Ira stared at Robert with popping eyes. Near the far gate, at the end of the track, stood an empty cottage belonging to someone who never came. Derwyn owned the land and the out-buildings, and made use of the pens and the barns. The yard was a holding and sorting area. Every time they came and went, Robert and Jenny would be faced with a kind of farming which takes place out of sight of the world. Horses with protruding ribs, chained dogs cringing in the muddy corners of sheds, gaunt sheep with hunched backs. When winter came, everything belled its hunger.

'Would you look at those poor benighted sheep,' Jenny would exclaim. 'Look! It's absolutely scandalous they're so thin! What's he trying to do, starve them to death?'

Robert would wince and go quiet.

Emrys became ever more taken up with his new farm, while Robert and Jenny still worked the weeks in London and some-times could not come for a fortnight at a time. One or other would appear, now and then, and Emrys could see they needed a hand, so he introduced them to Jack Meredith.

The ways of the pre-modern world were embroidered into the lives of Jack and his brother Alf. They had been born up the valley in one of two houses by the forge: they were never sure which, having lived in both. Alf was as old as the century, Jack a few years younger, and they had had seven more siblings. As children they walked three miles to school, where they wrote on slates and had any tendency to speak Welsh beaten out of them. Their eldest brother went to France in the Great War, to work with the horses, hauling shells and stretchers. The family had been poor, and some-times hungry, in a land which crawled with game, but their mother would tolerate nothing but exemplary behaviour: when Jack found a nest of duck eggs and bought them triumphantly home she scolded him. The duck was not nesting on their land so those were not their eggs – Jack must take them back.

He noticed all the animals' doings; had Jenny not forbidden him, he would have done well with a snare. One warm day when he was young Jack successfully tickled a trout. It was basking in ice-bright water below the stone on which he lay. Stretched out, his body flush with the rock, Jack inched his arms into the stream and approached the fish with hands of loving, deathly slowness. As if lulling the creature into a common dream with him, he stroked its belly with the tip of a finger, slowly, slowly drifting more fingers under it, as it hovered, hypnotised. Then with an abrupt convulsion he jerked the animal up and out and into the air in an arc of glittering spray, landing it on the bank. When I was told about this it seemed only a short step from sorcery, a miracle of a kind impossible to imagine now, something from a vanished time.

As young men Jack and Alf had signed on as labourers for the construction of a reservoir on the other side of the mountain. Leaving every morning in the dark, they plunged up and up through the bracken, over the ridge, across the moor and down the other side. After a day building the dam they climbed back up over the top and down, walking nearly ten miles, chunks of it straight uphill.

One of Jack's favourite sayings was 'save a match and buy a farm,' and he and Alf had done so: they bought a place higher up the valley and farmed it for decades, until, too old at last, they sold up to Emrys and retired. Now they lived in a cottage in the village. They had a round-shouldered yellow fridge, a kettle with a bakelite handle, enamelled tin mugs and, on the floor, beady mats woven from bright patterned plastic. They did not need to speak much and watched television a lot, travelling, in their retirement, the world they had not seen.

They had pipes in their pockets and sticks with clefts for their thumbs: if they were at home the sticks leant against the wall by their front door. They shaved with cut-throats every morning, and once a week took the bus to collect their pensions. On Friday nights they put on their best clothes, polished their shoes, brushed their white hair and went to the Red Lion. The landlady, Maud, was a fiercely partisan woman who often refused to serve strangers, according to an obscure system of whims. She adored the brothers; their chairs were the nearest to the fire. They were, as everyone said, proper gentlemen.

Jack had a diffident certainty about him; he was not a sage so much as a true witness, one who had seen and understood the century through its gradual encroachment into the valley; who had watched the coming of the tractors and the end of the horses; who had seen certain valley fields become enslaved by nitrogen fertilisers and drenched in pesticides, leaving the grass an unnatural blue-green and the hedges deserted by wildlife. He believed that people who were 'too fond of the world', by which he meant farmers who overstocked their fields in pursuit of profit, came to a bad end. The history of industrialised agriculture, with its despoliation of the environment, diseases and bland, distrusted products, has proved him right.

To reach our farm Jack would walk over the bridge, up past the campsite and on up the lane to the bottom of Pritchard's Wood. Skirting along the edge of the trees, noting any fresh excavations around the badger setts (Jenny would always ask for the latest news there), he would then traverse the steep Lower Meadows before climbing up into the First Meadow and appearing in the yard. It would be a day's labour for most septuagenarians, but it was nothing to Jack.

He was shy around Jenny at first, a bashfulness she assaulted with barrages of questions. 'Come on, Jack,' she would cry, 'what's the gossip? Oh go on, do tell!' Little by little it would come out. This family hates that one, having done so ever since they shared a boundary fence. So-and-so had it away with his sister under a bush – but her husband thinks the child's his. That man's a thief, always has been (or was once, it came to the same thing). This one is a tidy farmer – this was the highest praise. The area's traditions were not much changed since a day towards the

end of the twelfth century when the travelling scholar and cler-
gyman, Giraldus Cambrensis, Gerald of Wales, arrived at the top
of the valley and asked what was to be found further down. He
records his discovery thus:

> The natives of these parts, actuated by continual enmities and
> implacable hatreds, are perpetually engaged in bloody contests.
> But we leave to others to describe the great and enormous
> excesses which in our time have been here committed, with
> regard to marriages, divorces and many other circumstances of
> cruelty and oppression.

Jack and Robert found a quiet friendship which pleased them
both. Jack showed Robert how to put in a fence post. First the
crowbar, four and a half feet of solid iron ending in a dumb point.
It would sink into the turf by itself. You found a place where there
were no rocks, drove the bar in and stirred it, drilling a cone in the
red earth. You did it again and again until most of the bar was
buried and you could hardly stir it more. Then the post went in.
You gave it a couple of taps with the sledgehammer, and then
stepped back, hefted the sledge and swung it round and over in a
great arc, smacking the post a mighty blow and driving it deep into
the soil. Jack did it in four, if the ground was good. Then it was
Robert's turn. He managed the crowbar, got the hole pretty much
straight. The sledge was amazingly heavy, but he was strong, and
delivered a good blow. Jack stood impassively. The second shot
wasn't quite so handy, Robert's shoulders and forearms ached and
the post hardly moved. By the third his muscles were screaming
and the hammerhead glanced its target; a crack appeared in the top
of the post. The next splashed white chips out of it, leaving a long
splinter of wood dangling by the bark. Jack shifted unhappily.

'Want to try not to split the post. Rain'll get in and rot it,
otherwise.'

'Right,' said Robert, breathing hard, 'I see.' He looked at Jack.
'Tricky.'

'Aye,' said Jack.

\*

Now Jenny had her farm on the mountain the journeys to and
fro were quite different. The opening of the M4 reduced the
journey from Hammersmith to the farm to 163 miles, a figure
which burned itself into my father's memory. (In the early years
Jenny could not drive. She made the trip as his passenger, or as
British Rail's.) When they reached the outskirts of London she
thrilled at the rise and glower of the infinite city; Hammersmith
was the gateway to all its light and rumbling complexity, its
talk, turn and change. Newport, hull-down, muddy-kneed and
crooked low under the dark hunch of Wales, marked the beginning of something much older than men and their works;
another kind of time survived there, primitive and silent, amid
the humped shapes of the hills. When she went up by herself she
would take the train as far as Abergavenny and look for Len Cole,
her taxi driver, who did not mind going all that way into the
mountains, then up the pitches, through the wood and along the
track, to see her safe inside. The dark on moonless nights was
sepulchral, and the house would be freezing.

'Thank you, dear Len, you've saved me again. Would you like
something to drink?'

'Oh no thank you, my dear. You'll be all right now?'

'Yes, yes, I'll be fine. Crumbs, it's cold! We really must get a
stove or something . . .'

Exploring the house, she found rags, nests of hay and scraps of
newspaper wedged between boards in the ceilings and floors;
tatty brown clumps stuffed over the lintels and lining the cracks.
She went round with many grimaces, pulling them out, unplugging, scrubbing and scouring. 'Euch! God, how disgusting!
Incredible . . .'

It was only after days of this cleaning, on a windy night, when
draughts emerged everywhere, torrents of small cold devils, that
she realised she had undone generations of careful lagging, that
everything had its purpose, and that dirt was better than chill.
As the wind grew, the house began to sing, whining and moaning at the corners. Things sounded and shifted and she felt scared
and safe at the same time, remembering the great thick walls.

The stand of larches and firs behind the house rushed and gasped. She slept uneasily.

When Robert's car bumped up the track she was excited and delighted and she took him on a tour of her latest discoveries. In the firs behind the house there were goldcrests: fearless, tiny green birds with streaks like gold flames on their heads; they made a minute piping sound. In the little gullies where the mountain folded into the fields there were woodcock; long-beaked, shy and exquisitely camouflaged in black and bracken plumage, they jumped up when you were almost upon them and fled on skirling wings.

Arm in arm they walked along a green lane – their green lane, they reminded each other – where hazel and blackthorn met overhead and the thinned autumn foliage clicked and shifted with the business of birds. Robert pieced together half-remembered songs and hummed them to her and Jenny felt like running and jumping and kicking her legs in the air, and would have done, had she not been wary of scaring the sheep. The flock looked at them, bleated and made off, streaming through gateways and broken fences in panicky haste.

They went as far as the larch wood, a tousled clump on the skyline marking the extent of their land. They fell silent as they walked across its floor of dead needles; trunks like slim silver pillars rose into a dense canopy, thickened here and there by shaggy, chaotic nests big enough to carry a man.

They were watched, then suddenly ambushed.

'Ravens! They're ravens,' Robert exclaimed, as huge birds crashed out of the treetops and flung off into the wind, croaking curses.

Back at the house he unpacked a box he had brought from London. There was food, wine and books – an *English–Welsh Welsh–English Dictionary*, *The South Wales Landscape*, and one other, a special present for Jenny. A huge book, double the height and thickness of a normal hardback but narrower, decorated on the cover with a rich painting of a tawny owl: *The AA Guide to the Birds of Britain*. She was delighted at the beauty of the plates.

Curled up in bed, Robert read to her. He loved reading to her and that night they started a new book, a new collector's edition with a preface by the author, Graham Greene.

'Are you lying comfortably?'

'Yes, Robert.'

'Good. So, *The Heart of the Matter*. Part one . . .'

They arranged to take their holidays in March to coincide with the lambing, but the lambs came before their leave.

Robert arrived a week before Jenny and threw himself at the work of feeding and preparing. He walked the flock, staring at the ewes, and when the first few began to birth he consulted Emrys or Jack. When the lambs came thick and fast, he knew it would be a fight against a tide of unknown foes.

His approach to the unknown is unvarying: identify the problem, talk to anyone who can tell you anything, buy the book, understand the principles, practise and perfect the trick. By this method he taught himself everything from playing the flute to long-distance swimming to winning at chess: could hill farming be so different? Decades later books like *Sheep Farming for Profit* and *Quantitative Genetics in Sheep Breeding* stand dust-covered on my mother's shelves, unopened since the day my father finished them. They appear to be monuments to two utterly different ways of living: hers founded on passion, instinct and experiment; his on logic, realism and method. They approached their first lambing, and their adventure, with contrasting styles but equal determination.

Jenny came to join the struggle, enthusiasm and excitement crackling out of her, and Robert took her around the animals. They set off, slithering on the dead, yellow-green grass, squelching through the red mud at the gateways.

The flock was strung out across the unfenced Hill Fields, sheltering under thorn trees. The new lambs were scraps of uncertainty in wet white coats, unsteady on long legs.

'The ewes are very big,' Jenny observed, as the animals set off in their usual way, lumbering hurriedly, bleating over their shoulders.

The new mothers circled their children anxiously, unable to abandon them. After a thorough search of the fields they concluded that things seemed quiet for now and returned to the house.

'Well, that was a bit dismal. What shall we do now? If only we had a fire,' Jenny chattered, wrestling her boots off. In the corners of the room, beyond the reach of dim light bulbs, the damp seemed to gather in unseen cobwebs. The night outside seemed as large as the hill, and close around the house. 'We could unblock the fireplace,' she said suddenly. 'How about that?'

'Sure . . . Sure?'

'Well, I don't see why not.'

'OK then. I'll equip myself with an implement.' Robert jerked the front door open (it stuck on the flags whenever it rained), strode out and returned after a couple of minutes with the sledgehammer, the crowbar and a small claw hammer. He laid them down with a clatter and stood with his hands on his hips, sizing up the white plaster.

'Right then. Stand back!' He hoisted up the sledgehammer.

'Hold on, darling! I think take the plaster off first.'

'Oh. I was just going to wallop it.'

'Yes, sweetheart, I know. Just take the plaster off and then wallop it. We don't want to do any structural damage, if we can help it.'

Chuckling, Robert swapped hammers and attacked the surface just below waist height with the claw. Plaster came away in flat white cakes; damp slabs fell revealing dirty bricks. He worked upwards swiftly, as high as his midriff, then up to his chest and still there was no sign of anything but brick.

'It must be huge,' he said, ripping and scraping, already spattered with lime flakes and dust.

He reached shoulder height and suddenly there was wood, a horizontal line of wood, scored black where the hammer had scratched off the covering plaster.

'Bingo! There it is.'

'Wow! It really is huge. Pray no one's cut the beam or anything awful.'

Robert worked his way left for over a yard before the brick ran out, and then there was a thick smear of cement. He went back the other way for another yard.

'Have you ever seen anything like it? It must be enormous. And the beam's fine, isn't it? Do you think they've filled in the whole space? Oh, I hope they haven't blocked up the chimney!'

'We'll find out.' Robert tapped the brickwork. The hammer rapped flatly. 'Can't really tell. It feels as though it might be hollow, though.'

He passed Jenny the hammer and she tapped a line across the middle, her head tilted to one side.

'Yes, oh yes. Are you going to wallop it then?'

'Unless you think it'll bring the roof down.'

'Go on then. Just please be careful, darling.' She stood back and Robert measured a practice swing.

The hammer went back, paused, and flipped forward. There was a crash. Plaster cracked, jumped and crumbled. The hammer struck, and again, and on the third blow a chunk of brickwork disappeared, leaving a black space. He swung repeatedly without pause, aiming at the edges of the widening hole. The wall crumbled away. As he worked over to the left a section of brick gave way and they could see a curving stone buttress, a shelf and, in the wall, an iron door.

'It's a bread oven,' Jenny cried. 'And what a great beam! Why would they cover all this?'

When the last bricks had been battered out they were able to survey the whole hearth. It started six inches above the floor, with stone flags four feet deep. It was over two yards wide, high and huge, changing the aspect of the entire room. Robert peered up into the chimney, drew back and smashed the hammer up, dislodging fragments of wet chipboard. He pulled it all out, wincing as soot and twigs tumbled down, and looked again. It was dark and there was no light at the top.

'There's a real draught. It can't be blocked. I reckon they've just stuck a tile or something over the top.' He was filthy and sweating, but smiling broadly.

'There you are, missus. A fireplace. The biggest in Wales.'

'Whoopee!'

They carted all the rubble out the back and dumped it, then got out the tin bath and boiled the kettle a dozen times. Jenny watched Robert wash. She loved his back. There was a war memorial at Hyde Park Corner; a classically muscled young hero standing over massive machine-guns cast in bronze. Jenny thought the figure had Robert's back.

'Do you think we should have had another look at the sheep?' Jenny asked, as they made their way up the stone stairs and ducked through the low door into the bedroom.

'Oh, I don't think so. They seemed quiet. Fingers crossed.'

The horror struck in the dawn, as they were waking. By the time they had made their way across the soft fields, ranging from hedge to hedge, checking, anxious in the quiet, it had taken its prizes and departed on black wings. Robert saw it first: a young ewe on her side in a patch of mud by a fence. He started to run. She had begun to give birth late in the night, perhaps as they were going up to bed. Now she was exhausted, unable to stand. She had kicked as she struggled, on her side, scoring the mud in arcs under each hoof. She looked at them and panted, covered in mud, and around her tail, blood. Jenny moved the tail aside. Hanging out of the ewe was her lamb's head, and one foreleg. Blood covered the small face, and Jenny realised that one of the eyes was missing. She took the leg and pulled, the small damp limb slipping out of her grasp. They changed places, Jenny talking to the ewe softly as Robert tried to free the lamb. He slipped, swore and heaved. The ewe groaned and Jenny cried out in sympathy.

'OK, got it. It's out.'

'Is it alive?'

'I don't think so.'

They passed the little body up to the ewe and she nuzzled it, raising herself a little now. Jenny cleared out the mouth, found more blood.

'Christ, I think the tongue's gone. I think they've taken the tongue.'

'It's dead, isn't it?'

'Yes, I'm afraid it is.'

They stood and moved away from the ewe. She licked the corpse, nudging it. When it did not respond she bleated.

'What a bloody, bloody thing. It must have died of shock, do you think?' Jenny wiped her hands on the grass.

'Maybe, yes.' Robert looked at his feet.

There was nothing to say. They went around the rest. A pair of small twins had been born in the night. They were licked clean white and circled adoringly by their mother as they trembled and peered about, delivered to a huge cold planet. Their umbilical cords were short bright strings. Jenny and Robert watched them for a while.

'We'll deal with the dead one after feeding, shall we?'

'Yes, I'll bury it. We ought to find out about this business. We could have saved it if we'd been up.' Robert looked at her for confirmation. She nodded.

'Yes.'

'So we'll have to go round them more often.'

'Yes. We can take turns.'

'We should talk to Emrys as soon as possible.' Robert's voice was quiet with anger at their ignorance. 'We need to know how you tell when they're going to do it, how you tell when they're doing it, what you do, what goes wrong, how you deal with it, what happens when it's over. We're in the dark.'

'Yes, OK, quite right. We'll go down to the valley and call Angela as soon as we've done the feeding. She's got hundreds of sheep.'

'And we'll call the phone people and get them to put a line in.'

They trudged back to the house, feeling their knees muddy and wet. A spatter of rain came over the hill and three crows rasped angrily at the hurrying couple.

'And we'll have to do something about those buggers, 'Robert said.

\*

The telephone box was on the main road, opposite the garage. Angela ran a huge Herefordshire farm: she was one of the few friends from Jenny's previous life who could help her in this one. Angela's voice was loud and firm down the line.

'Don't panic, Jen, it's just like people. They look broody. Sometimes they split off from the rest and find a place they like. Not always, though. First the water goes, and that's what you look for. The tail will be all wet and there's a bit of blood and stuff. Then you see them nesting. They turn round and round in the same place and they sit heavily and you can see they're trying to get comfortable. Then they start pushing. It takes a few hours, from beginning to end. Just like people.'

'Right, then what?'

'Well, if he hasn't fed them too much . . .'

'I shouldn't think he has, frankly.'

'Good. And if they've done it before, the lamb should just slip out.'

'And what if it doesn't?'

'Well, you want them coming nose first, with the front feet under the chin, they should look like they're diving. If they're having difficulty, getting tired, you can just give them a pull. But what you had this morning was a head.'

'Yes . . . and one leg.'

'Yes, a head is no good, you really want to watch for them. The shoulders are too wide to get out, when the legs are back, so the head just hangs there and the ewe gets exhausted. When you get one don't panic, just push it back in, find the front legs, pull them under the chin and try again.'

'Crumbs.'

'You'll get the hang of it. The trick is to spot them quickly because in the cold the head will swell up and then it's an absolute bugger.'

'Right.'

'And keep an eye out for twins, especially with first-lambers. They can get into trouble with the second one. And make sure you get anything really weak into the shed and out of the weather. And you should get some penicillin and some syringes. And spray – purple terimicin spray from the vet. Give the umbilical a squirt of that, stop infections.'

'Oh Lord, luvvie. This is all absolutely terrifying.'

'Give me a ring soon. I've got to dash, we're having triplets all over the place.'

'Oh, dear Angela, thank you. Go quickly! I'll ring you soon and say for God's sake, help! What do I do with this?'

'Yes, do. Bye now, Jen.'

'Bye.'

Jenny went back to the car and studied the notes she had made while Robert went into the box and called the phone people. Filthy Land Rovers rattled slowly by, heads inside turning to look at her.

Spurred by the disaster they patrolled almost ceaselessly.

'It's a great mistake having them all over the Hill Fields,' Jenny panted. 'Much too much walking!'

It was true, Robert agreed. They were working over thirty acres of sloping ground, quartered by thorn trees, banks and woods. Ruined or incomplete fences left much of it open, haphazard lines of wire enclosed only patches. The land faced the north wind which came straight across the gully from the far gate, hypothermia and death whistling in its teeth. When the sheep sought shelter they would hide behind the mounds of collapsed stone walling, under the thickest thorns, in the sunken heart of a copse: all had to be searched and searched again.

So they walked and watched from first light until after midnight. Sometimes, on dry nights, they would see another torch moving on the other side of the valley, someone else doing the rounds. Births could happen at any time. Ewes would look broody for hours, for days, and do nothing but charge for the hay which they hauled each morning. Or it could be all over in half an hour, the small wet baby appearing between patrols; they would shake their heads at each other and admit they had not noticed anything different about the mother, before or since the

birth. Feeding was brutal work. Without a Land Rover or tractor, they wobbled overloaded wheelbarrows down muddy slopes,
shoulders aching and the barrow pulling to get away.

In between feeding and lambing, there was hauling and
chopping firewood, collecting and carrying water (in ten-gallon
drums which threatened to pull arms out of their sockets),
patrolling and repairing fences: it was exhausting. One night,
having recuperated a little in front of the fire, Jenny found her
legs so stiff she could not get up. Laughing weakly she cried to
Robert to come and help her. Sprawled in the other chair, he
groaned, 'Can't! Can't get up! Too tired . . . too weak . . . better
leave me here with Jack's gun. I'll be all right . . .' They got the
giggles.

They agreed a division of labour: Jenny would do most of the
late rounds, as she did not mind staying up and loved her bed in
the mornings. Robert, whose days naturally began at daybreak
and ended around ten at night, would do the earlies.

Setting out into the night with just the torch for company was
a nervy business for Jenny. Sometimes, depending on the currents
of her imagination, it was terrifying. There were certain places
she never liked much, eerie patches which she hurried past, her
senses prickling. The dark lump of shadow behind the Big Barn
was the worst; a glum, impenetrable contrast with the rest of the
yard, which was illuminated by the yard light on the end of the
barn. At the beginning and end of each round she had to pass this
place, where the ground rose steeply through knotted darkness
up to the mass of the fir trees which guarded the house from the
north wind, and which looked tall and wild, seen out of the
corner of her eye as she hurried by; gloomy presences concealing shapeless fears.

She would try to go quietly down the track, but you cannot
be silent in an anorak and wellingtons, every movement sounds
loud. Once out in the fields you cannot see anything without
giving away your position: you are either blind or completely
exposed. With a flick of your thumb the beam from the lambing

torch leaps forty yards, and picks up the reflections of pairs of eyes well beyond that. You turn very slowly, carefully and deliberately searching out and studying every sheep within range, fighting the urge to whirl and cover your back.

In time she learned to trust the sheep: if they were calm there was nothing to worry about. Only when she heard them calling, or found them jumpy or bunched together, on their feet and alarmed, only then would she admit fear.

There were absurd, darkly funny moments. Emrys told them about one foul morning, when, stumping out into the wind and rain, the first thing he found was a dead lamb, newborn and apparently perfect but dead, lifeless in the muddy bloody grass. He slapped it and pummelled it to no effect and, in a burst of temper, hurled the little body into a tree. He came back an hour later, still angry, 'And the bugger was bleating!'

There were calm periods, phoney war, when the weather would smile and the patrols would yield nothing more than easy singles to attentive mothers; then with a shift of the wind the temperature would fall, ewes would inexplicably abandon their lambs and everything would veer towards disaster. Any March night in the lambing fields could turn into a battle.

One lamb came quietly during the drizzly afternoon. Later, when the sky had lowered and the light was quite gone, they found a ewe in trouble. She lay on her side, pushing, but she jumped up when they came close. After watching her lie down again and struggle, stagger up, lie down and struggle, they decided to catch her. They slipped and slid, and three times she evaded them until finally they cornered her down by the stream and Robert's lunging dive took him within reach of her back leg. He tipped her over and held her while Jenny investigated. Robert moved around the ewe, angling the torch towards her tail.

'What have we got?'

'Only one leg. The other must be back . . . steady!' The ewe struggled. Jenny lowered her voice, forcing herself to sound calmer. 'Steady on, silly old thing, we're not going to hurt you . . . there, there . . . what's this? A foot, yes, I've got a right foot . . . but no left.'

Jenny heaved, pushing the lamb back, then worked her hand inside the hot, contracting channel until she found the left fore-leg. She pulled it forwards, worked it gently, teasing and pulling carefully, fearful of damage, until it was aligned with the right leg. Now she worked at both together, and the ewe groaned, her flanks flinching with contractions, and Jenny pulled and pulled and at last drew the lamb out into the cold night. She cleared yellow amniotic slime from its mouth and suddenly the lamb coughed and shook its head: the miraculous, unbelievable igni-tion of life.

'Wonderful!' Robert smiled, and wiped the rain off his face.

'Hold her,' Jenny panted, pushing her hand in again. 'Yes, there's another one – it's twins.'

'It'll be a while, won't it?'

'Yes. We'll let her get on with this one, shall we?'

They withdrew, leaving the ewe muttering over her lamb, licking it greedily.

'What's that over there? Oh Lord, don't tell me.'

'Another bugger,' Robert said quietly.

'Oh Lord!'

Barely twenty yards away in the rain-flecked beam of the torch lay a black-faced Suffolk ewe, on her side and struggling. She would also have to be caught. Again they separated, circling in quietly from either side, and again the ewe fled; up the fence, down the fence, until they cornered her in the same place they had caught the first, where she and her lamb still were. The Suffolk made a final, hopeless charge. She blundered past the new mother, grunting and plunging in panic. The new lamb was barged mewling into the stream before Robert's hands came down on the runaway's back, his fingers clawing for a grip in her thin, wet wool.

'Christ!' Jenny cried, and Robert half-laughed; a mirthless, tension-breaking sound, as Jenny rescued the bedraggled scrap of life from the freezing water.

'Welcome to Wales,' Robert said, as Jenny rubbed it and pushed it towards its mother, then came back to kneel beside the second capture.

'Oh shit, Rob darling.'

'What is it?' A certain tone comes into his voice when he feels that the fuss is not justified; an edge of annoyance.

'A back leg. One back leg!'

She pushed it back in, groped for the other and began to work amid the slow, hot, tight inches, until she had its other leg. She pulled and rested, pulled and rested, encouraged the ewe and pulled again. She grunted with effort as she gripped the soft wet stubs of the lamb's feet and heaved: the lamb, its amniotic fluid and the placenta emerged in a wallop of heat and liquid – reds, golds and slimy whites bright under the torchlight. This time there was no cough, no bleat, no shudder of life.

'Nothing much happening,' Jenny gasped. 'Come on, lamb.' She cleared its mouth with her finger.

'Give it a shake.'

Jenny picked the body up and swung it from side to side. It was breathing, she thought, but very weakly. Robert jiggled it, rubbed it. 'Oh please come on, lamb,' Jenny implored it. 'Live!'

They backed away, leaving it to its mother, and stood and watched as fingers of rain found ways into their collars. The ewe licked the little body eagerly but it did not respond, so Jenny went down again, and worked on the lamb, rubbing it and talking to it until at last there was movement in the skinny frame. 'It's going to live,' she announced, delighted, as the mother ran off, bleating despairingly.

Robert went after the ewe, driving her back towards her lamb, but she was now so flustered that she did not pause and went trotting on into the next field. He pursued her at a run across the sloping ground, his wellingtons heavy and his balance precarious. He overtook her and turned her, dropping back as she approached the lamb so that the ewe slowed too, but again, calling desperately, she overshot it, ignoring the little white heap in the torchlight. He cursed. Twice more he turned her back, and twice more she overshot.

Farming, when it is like this, is a kind of hell. The sheep frightened out of its few wits; each failed attempt at the problem exacerbating it; the rain relentless; the sense of absurdity and irritation swelling in the stomach as you run back and forth, back and forth, your legs heavier, your strength lessening and spirits sinking until you are almost overcome with the misery and senselessness of the situation in which you find yourself, lumbering along the flank of a mountain in the cold, old dark, for the benefit of a sheep you would now happily see dead. And now she is running towards other sheep, in case her lamb has somehow materialised among them, and you are trying to overtake her because you know what will happen: she will be even harder to catch among her fleeing companions, and chasing heavily pregnant ewes through the rain and darkness is certain recipe for premature births and lambs born dead.

Finally, after almost an hour, Robert caught her and carried, pulled and dragged her out of the fields, up the track, across the yard and into the barn. They penned her in the race with hay bales and presented her with her lamb.

It was warm in the barn, out of the wind. They watched, speechless, as the lamb tottered around under the mother's tail. She encouraged it, nuzzled it, and its head tipped back, its back dipped and its tail shivered. Jenny and Robert grinned tiredly at each other. It was suckling. That moment, a lamb's first drink, was already a benchmark. If it drinks it has a chance, they had learned.

Suddenly they were aware of their wet clothes, runny noses, heavy limbs.

'Very good,' Robert said. 'Forty-eight from thirty-four!'

'It's not standing very well, though. I hope I didn't dislocate its poor legs when I swung it round like that – quite stupid!'

'It'll be fine. We ought to go and see about the twin.'

They trudged back to the field, keeping the torch off until they were near the corner by the stream. Then Robert flicked it on, and there was the ewe, with her first lamb standing and now bleating, and there on the ground was the second twin: tiny, unlicked, abandoned.

'Forty-nine from thirty-four,' Robert said, levelly, 'if it lives.'

They caught the first lamb, which alarmed the ewe, and placed it near the second, which was alive but flopping helplessly in the mud. But the mother was only concerned with her elder child, and kept leading it away from the humans.

The humans shook their heads. 'I know,' Jenny chimed, 'I'll hobble it.'

She caught it again, loosely tied its front legs and placed it beside its twin. It fell over. It bleated. The ewe bleated back and nuzzled it, steadfastly ignoring the feebly struggling sibling. Robert looked sceptical. 'Trampled, soaked and incapacitated, and barely been alive an hour!'

Jenny gave a frayed giggle. 'Oh well! We'll have to get them into the barn then.'

'You heard the lady,' Robert muttered to the sheep.

Jenny carried both lambs, one under each arm, the torch dangling from a string cutting into the crook of one elbow. She paused every few paces to show the mother that she had them, while Robert steered the ewe, which followed her babies, calling lustily. In the barn they built a second pen and confiscated the favourite, leaving the mother with her unwanted second twin. The ewe eyed it. Bleated. The lamb bleated back. She muttered to it, nuzzled it.

'I'll stay, sweetheart, you go to bed.'

'Sure?'

'Yes, yes – you've got to get up in a minute!'

It was after two. Jenny woke him at five, on her way to bed, to say she had called the vet about a prolapsed uterus, a thing like a pink balloon of flesh hanging underneath one of a hundred near-identical dirty white tails.

'It's the phantom,' Robert mumbled, his eyes tightly shut.

'What phantom?'

'I saw it too. A prolapsed uterus. Wasn't there when we went to look for it.'

'Well, I saw it and the vet's coming.'

The vet did come but there was no sign of the phantom uterus.

Gwyn Dinas was a tall young man who farmed cattle and hundreds of sheep at the head of the valley. He had a young wife and a small son, and needed more ground than he owned. Jenny and Robert agreed to rent him a field, and some of his sheep appeared one morning in the Quoiker. Jenny declared they were the tiniest, thinnest, most pathetic animals she had ever seen, with the exception of Derwyn's victims at the far gate. Robert frowned and nodded. Jack Meredith said nothing. Gwyn had little money, he knew. The animals were bound to struggle when the farm had no money. As the days passed and the rain stayed, Gwyn's animals looked worse and worse, standing on mud, bleating and belling at feeding time. Gwyn did not come and did not come and at last Jack was unable to stand it.

'Going to chuck those buggers a bale,' he said, and went down the track to them, lugging the biggest hay bale he could find at high-port across his chest.

'Something in their bellies anyway,' he said, when he returned.

Jenny loathed the sight of the starving masses at the far gate, and returned the dirty looks of Derwyn's sons with glares of her own. But the plight of Gwyn's sheep was almost unbearable, so close to the house and on her land. Jack and Robert impressed on her that she was not to feed them, since Gwyn would probably stop coming altogether, and it would do them no good. Then one of them died, became a pathetic, sodden smear of wool against the fence and she watched out for Gwyn, and when he came, charged down the track to confront him.

He was standing over the body, looking at the rest as they ate furiously, silent, for once, gobbling hay.

'Gwyn!'

He turned.

'Hello there.'

She had thought him a callous bastard, over the days when he had not come, and it was as a callous bastard that she addressed him.

'Look, one of them's died now. Look! It's dead!'

She was almost shouting, and she felt tears rising in her eyes.

'Aye,' Gwyn said. Then he crouched down over the little body and ran a large hand gently over the wet wool. 'Poor little bugger,' he said quietly.

Oh God, thought Jenny, he's upset too. She went back to the house, not quite crying, and resolved to feed Gwyn's sheep whenever they needed it. Gwyn seemed to come more often after that, and no more of them starved to death.

— * —

And then, slowly, came the miracle. At first it seemed too frail for the weather: catkins shivered in late snowfall; buds were tiny green huddles; wind-flung birds barely held the sky. But one day at the end of the third week of April they noticed thicker colours in the air. The pale paintbox of the fields had darkened and the once-tired brown hill had turned a rich, wet mauve. Suddenly a warmer light surrounded them; it was, at last, the bright spring.

# 3

## A Farming Year

THE WEATHER WARMED and west winds tore down trees in Pritchard's Wood. Jenny went walking there one day, marvelling at the great glowing carpets of bluebells. Needing a pee she squatted down among the stalks. She was finishing when she felt with sudden and awful certainty that she was being watched. She jumped up, hauling up her trousers, and looked around for the spy. Nothing. Something drew her gaze upwards, into the canopy, which was bright now, jewelled with many young green leaves and soft yellow buds. And there, not fifteen feet away on a branch, were the watchers. Three tawny owls, hardly more than chicks, huge dark eyes staring, gravely amazed. 'Hello, darlings,' she whispered, and backed slowly away, beaming her delight. The owlets blinked.

After the hell and thrill of the first lambing the mountain year becomes a series of weekend trysts with their other life. The farm's claims are held in check, thanks to Jack and the M4. Robert and Jenny travel up the new motorway for the flag days of the farming calendar: haymaking, putting the flock out on the mountain, the shearing, the sales. The daily tasks and crises are left to themselves and Jack. He keeps an eye on things, but there is work there for three men, and he is only one, and old. He is not expected to bury the dead, gather tons of apples, mend miles of fences and rebuild walls. There is no one to dig channels, throw out stray sheep, repel marauding dogs or repair hedges.

So apples and corpses rot into the ground, pecked over by birds. Bands of ragged strays raid the Hill Fields, coming and going over fences which rust and sag, pushing through rambling hedges in which the badgers have made wide runways. Streams riddle their own courses through the red earth, woods thicken with fallen trees, old walls slip and blush with lichens in gold and silver-green. Birds and animals consolidate their holds on the house and buildings: in the fireplace one morning Jack found an astonished young kestrel, which had dived down the chimney after a mouse. As he approached, the bird threw itself on to its back in the ash, talons out, hissing, ready to die fighting.

'So what did you do, Jack?'

'Put my cap over the bugger!'

The big events of the year find them up to their elbows in farming. Some of these are ghastly, like the day they castrate the tup lambs, with tight rubber rings around the top of their scrotums. Each lamb is caught and lifted up, presented to the vet, who stretches a ring across the jaws of a sinister steel pliers, leans forward and snaps it over the root of the woolly little bag of the lamb's testicles. The lamb kicks desperately, bleats. The grip of the ring will cut the circulation; after a time the scrotum and its contents will drop off. It will not hurt for long, the vet says. It will all just go numb.

'But it's just frightful! It's a horrible thing to do,' Jenny laments, at the end of a long Saturday in the pens. The lambs which have been done look miserable. They sit down, pathetically trying not to move.

'Can you imagine what it must feel like?'

'Barely,' Robert replies, wincing. 'I'd rather not!'

'It's frightful,' Jenny repeats angrily.

'But farming is frightful. You can't deny it,' Robert returns briskly. She shakes her head, but not in dispute. It is a glum fact. The tup lambs are sold to the abattoirs to subsidise their mothers' next year of life. If they are not castrated they will not grow, and the markets will not take them. At least their sisters survive for a few years. They will be sold to other farmers to produce more lambs, until they are deemed too old, when they will be slaughtered too and turned into dog food. Meat is most certainly murder, and not quick, clean murder either.

Jenny can barely reconcile these year-to-year truths with her moment-by-moment love of the animals. She vows they will all have happy lives, swears that nothing will die needlessly, if she can help it, and tries not to think about the abattoir. It is a barmy equation, Robert feels, all his logic affronted by her sentiment. But he does not confront her with it. It is not logic, nor measurement, nor calculation that holds them here.

In May there is drenching. With the coming of the rich, fresh grass, the flock begin to 'scour': glossy green splashes of manure appear under their tails. Drenching means gathering, catching and forcing a squirt of chemicals down every throat. This stops the diarrhoea and reduces the chance that flies will lay their eggs in the soiled wool. Reduces the chance, but does not remove it.

The flies swarm with the warm days. In a calendar rich with stomach-turning horrors 'fly strike', as the treatment bottles call it, is among the worst. They lay their eggs in tails, sores, dirty clees. From each egg comes a maggot, a wriggly little yellow tube with a mouth at one end and an anus at the other. The mouth eats, the anus expels. The excrement stinks, which excites other maggots and draws more flies. Maggots and flies are wonderful things for clearing up corpses, but they are quite terrible when they find a purchase on the living. Undisturbed, maggots will eat a sheep alive. At first their little bites itch, so the sheep scratches, rubbing itself on tree trunks or fence posts. This opens small cuts, widening the maggots' menu. The sheep jumps and twitches and rolls in the grass; it makes no difference. Eventually, the sheep withdraws to some quiet place, and there, silently, the maggots eat it.

The solution is vigilant patrolling. Jenny and Robert go together, in the evening, as the sun catches the golden meadow grasses and draws intricate, gothic shadows out of the tall silhouettes of thistles. They stoop along the field boundaries, looking into the quiet spaces between the clumps of nettles and the dark shadows under the trees where the sheep go to hide when afflicted. When they find one alone, or scraping or lying hunched, they move in with great slowness, soothing the animal with soft words. Then in a dart one of them grabs it, and they examine the problem.

'Yes, look, maggots in her tail! God, how disgusting . . . look, the little bastards.'

The maggots burrow furiously into the wool as Jenny squashes them, rakes them out with her fingernails, kills them in the grass. Robert is not squeamish, but neither is he sorry that she has automatically taken the lead. Like a surgeon's assistant he passes her tools as she asks for them. First, the shears: a single piece of looped steel, moulded into two flat dagger-blades. She snips and clips until the tail is a thin white cord, the pink flesh showing through the shaved wool. Robert looks up through the mosaic of leaves to the dreaming sky, darkening now, over the hill.

'Terimicin please, darling.'

He passes her the aerosol and she sprays the injured area with bright blue anti-bacterial agent. The lamb bucks with pain. 'All right, sweetheart, I know it stings, I know, but it'll save you. Cream, please.'

Robert removes the lid from the small plastic tub and holds it for her. Jenny scoops out a thick wedge of sour-smelling yellow paste and smears it generously over the tail, the rump, and down the back legs. It will kill any eggs and repel flies for a few days. 'We mustn't forget to ask Jack to check her.'

'All done?'

'Yes.'

The lamb scrambles away from them.

Jenny wipes her hands in the grass. 'Very good,' she grins. 'Probably saved his bacon. Supper time soon, do you think?'

Robert makes a face. 'Maybe a drink first, hmm?' They both look down at her hands, streaked with green shit, yellow paste and blue spray. He starts to laugh. She snorts.

— * —

One of their friends had a cine camera, and he filmed Jenny and Jack at work in the pens. There is no sound, but it is, at last, a few minutes of proof, visible evidence of the proper summers I have half heard about, half imagined; the vanished, varnished weather of another time. It is 1973, but were it not for the purple swirls on the dress which covers the bulk of my mother's belly (which contains me), and the coloured film, it could be 1873. Jack is wearing an old fawn mac. He has it on backwards, like a smock, the belt is bowed across his middle. His old tweed cap is brown and he looks thin, a thin old man with his coat on backwards, patiently, gently catching sheep which my mother then injects. There are no concessions to her pregnancy. There is no taking it easy. She is absolutely absorbed.

It looks like June; the sheep are still in their coats, so it is before the shearing and the heat. It has been raining and now it is warm, the nettles are thick and gloomy green, you can sense the ferocious toxin in their dark stalks and tiny spines. The pens are in a dreadful state. The floor is a thick churn of mud and sheep shit, humans and animals stumble wherever they move. The pens are walled in dry stone, but not cleanly. Where the walls meet the ground there are tumbles of rocks, the sheep slip and jump around them.

Then they are inside, having a break in front of the fireplace. There are two high-backed wooden chairs, nothing else. It is not the room I remember, which was carpeted, with pictures on the walls and a sagging sofa on either side of the fire. This has bare stone flags, it is no more than a shelter, a place to rest between bouts. My God, I think, watching it. They had nothing.

My mother is smoking and sipping coffee from the blue and white mug she still drinks from, thirty years later. Jack puffs on his pipe. They are talking about the sheep; she asks him something, watches his face as he replies, then she nods slowly, thinking. He adds something and puffs his pipe. And it hits you, as you watch. This is not downsizing. This is not an image of Londoners trading the rat race for the quiet life, this is not about city people bringing their energy and money and drive to a haven away from the traffic and trivia. This is far simpler and much more frightening than that. It is a leap backwards through centuries of time. It is an attempt to gather in the fraying threads of old ways and plait them into a lifeline. It is one woman and one old man in a bare room, and the essence of their discussion is survival. How he survived, by his flock's survival, and how she can survive by hers.

She drains the last of her coffee, throws her cigarette end into the ashes, and they both go back to the pens.

— * —

Then it is shearing time. It will need more than a weekend; they take a few days off and plan the movements of the flock like generals disposing their troops before battle. They prepare the barn under Jack's instructions: the stone floor in the middle is swept and swept again (the shorn fleeces must be kept clean and free of hay); a great hessian woolsack is tied in place (a stone in each top corner so that the strings will still grip when it bulges full); a door is lifted off its hinges and set up as a table on which Alf will roll the wool. They lay in quantities of bread, cheddar and cider. On the evening before, Gwyn and another neighbour, Jessie Morgan, who will be shearing, come to inspect the facilities. Their approval is a great relief.

Early the next day they are back, roping their shearing machines to the beam, laying out bits of old carpet on the floor, oiling and tightening the blades of their clippers. Jack and Alf arrive. Jenny and Robert gather the first batch, collecting them from the dew-sparked field, pushing them in procession into the yard. Suddenly the sheep are not being gently herded by two amateurs. There are loud whistles, Gwyn's dogs slicing across their lines of escape, men waving their arms, shouts. The sheep pour into the barn in turmoil and the gate is closed smartly behind them. Jessie and Gwyn take off their jackets.

Jack and Robert will be the catchers. The first two ewes are hauled over the low side of the race and balanced on their rumps, straddled between the shearers' legs. By precise placing of their feet the shearers contrive to keep the animals immobile with their hooves in the air, while leaving the shearers' hands free: the left for turning and restraining the sheep, the right for the clippers. They tug on the start cords and the barn fills with the rattle of the shearing machines.

First the clippers draw a line up the breastbone as far as the throat. Then the animal is tilted to one side, the shearer leans forward and begins to draw steady stripes along the length of the body, starting low in the belly, then moving in parallel up the flanks. The underside of the fleece is a creamy gold, it falls away from the blades like a blanket of foam. There is an oily, spicy smell of lanolin, which will cover everything for the next two days. After a minute and a half of careful work, during which the shearer is bent almost double, the complete fleece falls away from the ewe, leaving her smooth, hard to hold and frisky. The shearer skims the last of the wool from her tail, switches off his machine and shouts, 'Pitch!'

Jenny, six months pregnant, darts in with their brand, an iron 'C' on the end of a short shaft, thickly covered in oily black marker. She carefully imprints the initial on the animal's shoulder before it is released. Then the ewe scrambles away, hooves skidding on the stone floor. As she reaches the sunlight the ewe skips, leaping into the fresh air and the bright yard, kicking her heels with pleasure, while her coat is collected by the roller. Alf picks hay and dirt out of the fleece before folding it, rolling the sweet, slightly sticky wool into a fat bun. He twists and teases tufts from the neck, making a thread which he uses to wrap and tie the bundle before pushing it deep into the woolsack. Robert manoeuvres the next ewe into place, Jenny dabs a nicked rump with yellow paste, Gwyn pulls his cord and the machine chatter starts again.

The heat swells. The sunlight lancing in through the slit windows thickens with motes, clouds of hay dust kicked up by the penned and wheeling flock. The shearers never slacken their pace. Bent over, they undo each fleece to the insistent rhythm of the clippers. Sweat slips down their foreheads and drips off their noses on to newly shorn flanks which twitch as if fly-tickled. Each animal is as fresh and as fearful as the first; each must be held, turned, bent this way and that. The practised certainty in the men's movements seems to calm the ewes and only a very few struggle for more than a moment.

By two o'clock the barn is empty, eighty sheep bell and skitter around the yard, fast and delighted in their near-nakedness. Work stops and Jenny serves lunch on top of the low wall in front of the house. The men eat bread and cheese, their thick, delicate fingers thoroughly washed but still reeking with the oily smell of the wool.

'Oh, no thank you, Jenny, no, no,' they demur, refusing top-ups to their small mugs of cider as though the sips they have had are already an indulgence.

Robert and Jack drive the ewes back to the meadow, returning with the yearlings bleating in front of them, a river of bobbing heads, pricked ears and baying tongues.

'They're looking well, Jenny,' Gwyn says. Robert notices her pleasure at the compliment, and they all see how fast it evaporates, moments later, when she feels there is too much aggression in the ring of men and dogs driving the fretful animals towards the great dark door of the barn.

'Quietly,' she demands. 'Steady, please, Jack!' She lowers her voice, without sheathing its harder edge. 'They will go quietly. There you are, good girls . . .' Gwyn and Jessie are careful not to let their smiles show.

Then they are shearing again, stretching the afternoon across the backs of more than forty animals. The mood in the barn follows the rhythm of hard work: optimistic for a while, then turning quiet, as muscles tough out time and minds are consciously averted from the work still to do, then dipping as someone struggles with a particularly resistant animal and swears, then lightening again in an exchange of smiles or a joke. The smell of wool and sweat blends with the sharp reek of fresh droppings and hot urea trampled into the hay floor of the pen. The only breaks come when one of the woolsacks can hold no more and the men pause to heave the bulging, brown belly across the yard to one of the sheds. 'Five bags full,' Jenny sings, unable to help herself.

Tea is taken at four o'clock, but not lingered over. Everyone is slower now.

'Saved these for last, have you, Jenny?' Gwyn grins, as the final batch are driven into the barn. There are only five of them but they are much bigger than the yearlings: three wethers and two rams, the latter stamping their feet and swinging their horns at Gwyn's dogs.

There is a stampede as Robert goes in to catch the largest. He takes him under the chin, straddles him, and half rides, half guides the animal towards Gwyn. They both struggle to turn the ram over as he grunts and pants, fear and adrenalin bulging in his wide eyes and heaving sides. There is something grimly telling about the overpowered ram, the king of the flock, as ridiculous and fragile, in his proud vanity, as any man. His great fleece roils off him in a creamy wave and is borne away like a treasure. Shorn, he looks scrawny and silly, with his too-large head and curling horns, like an old man in white thermals wearing an extravagant hat. While they have him down Jenny inspects his feet, Gwyn peels back his lip to look at his teeth, they spray a dash of anti-septic on his forehead, which he has scraped raw, fighting the other ram, and then they let him go. He stands up, uncertain for a moment, as if experiencing a mighty head-rush, before trotting out of the barn.

The sun has gone by the time the last animal bucks out into the yard and the machines stay silent behind him. The shearers straighten up and wink at each other. Jenny congratulates them, thanks Alf and Jack, briefly rubs her husband's back. He can feel the sweat suddenly, cold between his shoulder blades. Gwyn and Jessie pause, Jessie accepts a cigarette and they let the achievement settle for a moment. Then they pull on their jackets and bend down again, opening tool boxes, unscrewing clippers, cleaning meticulously. Jack goes around the barn with an old feed bag, pick-ing up the dags: lumps of wool from around the animals' hocks and tails, matted with manure. The Wool Board pays a penny or two for a sack of dags, so a farmer collects them.

The shearing machines are taken down from the beams and stowed in the back of Gwyn's Land Rover. The door is put back on its hinges and the last woolsack is lugged across the yard to the shed. Eight bags full, and barely room to close the door. Then everyone gathers around the bailey wall for a glass of cider and settling up. They fix a figure per sheep and Robert writes out two cheques, adding a little to the agreed figures, for luck. After a couple more sips, for luck, the men pile into the Land Rover, with a word to the dogs, which leap in the back, and in a splash of headlights and a spurt of smoke they are gone, rattling down the track. The barn and the yard seem very still after their departure: a satisfied calm pervades them, like the sweet green dew-smell which rises from the meadows. They leave the barn doors open to let the air circulate, and go inside to wash and eat and sleep. The water stings in small cuts and grazes, skin which looked brown becomes white, and no amount of scrubbing can remove all the purple spray from fingers or the dark rims from the ends of nails. The thick kiss of the sheets feels wonderful.

A few weeks later there is dipping, which the Ministry of Agriculture insists upon, which involves dropping every animal they own into a deep concrete trench filled with toxins: organo-phosphates which will one day be banned and blamed for farmers' illnesses, depressions and suicides. Where the dip splashes on skin it burns. Inhaled, it gives headaches which last for days. But it kills every kind of tick, louse and parasite, and brings the sheep a few weeks of relief from the flies.

— * —

Jenny's job took her back to London but Robert stayed on at the farm. The thought of returning to London depressed him. Perhaps he could make Wales work. He contacted the local *Chronicle*. Did they need a reporter? They might do, the editor hedged – did he have any experience?

At the age of twenty, Robert related, he had been covering an area of South Africa the size of Britain for a radical newspaper. After his flight to England he had joined a provincial daily, from where he had gone to a London tabloid, rising rapidly before moving to one of the national broadsheets.

When could he start? the *Chronicle* enquired, and there, suddenly, was the problem. Actually, Robert realised, he could not start. He could not face it. Alone at the farm he rose early every morning and climbed to the top of the mountain, timing himself, doing it quicker and quicker every day. His record stood at eighteen minutes, which meant going like hell up a viciously steep gully, followed by the conquest of a punishing series of ridges as the ground changed from bracken to hummocks of thick whinberry wires, rising at last into the whale-head of the top, and a scramble up its scree of rocking stones. Behind him the view deepened and widened, dominated by the grand mass of the Brecon Beacons. Below their northern flank the hills and fields of Radnorshire undulated softly into mid Wales; to the south was the massed escarpment of the Heads of the Valleys, sunlight flickering on car windscreens as they slalomed down the hillside towards the Usk. Turning around on the top he could see into England as far as the Malvern Hills, and on a clear day, from the far end of the ridge, a pewter sliver of the Severn estuary at the mouth of the Bristol Channel.

He would lie on his back to recover his breath, gulping down cold draughts of the sky. Gazing up into slowly unfurling banners of cloud, he could almost feel the earth turning beneath him.

When he had recovered his breath he would descend, and see what needed doing.

'I'm think I'm going to put a new roof on the stable and the Beast House. What do you reckon, Jack?'

'Get someone who knows how to do it, that'd be the best.'

'Mmm. I thought I'd have a go at it myself actually. Save money.'

'Oh no, I don't know. It's not so easy.'

'Well, I've got this book . . .'

Jack was unconvinced. Robert set about acquiring roof tiles. One tile, he learned, is not the same as another. They are all ranked by size and position; they have names. He stripped the roof down, salvaged tiles which could be reused, replaced beams and battens which had rotted. He bought roofing felt and polythene to protect his progress from the rain. Soon a new stone skin began to grow across the skeleton, and Jack began to smile to see him up there, with his book, patiently measuring, fitting, pegging.

'Tidy job, looks like,' he conceded, at last. Robert could have hugged him.

One afternoon, as he was working quietly in warm May sunlight, Robert heard, coming across the meadows, the high cry of a horse. The cry came again, and again, and it was unnatural – not a whinny but a sort of whickering scream, repeated at irregular intervals. Robert climbed down his ladders and began to jog, then run along the track. As he neared the far gate and Derwyn's sheds he could hear a man's voice shouting, blending into the screams. He vaulted over the gate into the yard. There was a commotion in one of the pens, and there was Derwyn, bright red, a thick stick in his right fist, and there was the horse, terrified, plunging away from him but unable to escape, her back scored by blows which Derwyn continued to deliver, oblivious of Robert's arrival. He was shouting, 'You bloody bugger, you bloody bugger you . . .'

'Derwyn!' Robert jumped into the pen. 'Derwyn! What the hell d'you think you're doing?'

Derwyn ranted and lunged for the horse again. Robert went for him. Seizing the club, he aimed his shoulder into Derwyn's chest and drove him hard against the wall of the pen. Derwyn cried out and sagged, panting, as Robert released him. The fury died out of Derwyn as he saw its match in Robert's eyes. There was a fight there, if he wanted it, and in a moment they both knew that Derwyn did not. He looked confused now, and frightened. He began to say something, a plaintive, whining sound, but Robert cut him off.

'Enough! That's enough.' He picked up the club and hurled it as far as he could. He opened the gate and stood back; the horse saw her chance and ran. He waited for Derwyn to come through, closed the gate behind him and turned away without a word. He walked slowly back to the house, lugging a deep gloom. He was halfway up a mountain, money was short, and his nearest neighbour was bonkers.

He finishes the roof, patrols the sheep and conquers the mountain every morning. Sometimes he walks down to the valley to drink at the Red Lion in the evening, and he climbs back up again later, a bit drunk, very tired and aching for bed. But still he wakes in the dead hours, riddled with suspicion and the fear that they are making a mistake. Outside, the night is a dark and silent maw. The yard light, one bulb high up on the end of the Big Barn, burns like a solitary certainty: there is a farm here, high on the mountain, and there is someone at home.

I can imagine him, at ten to four in the morning, wrapped tight in the covers, staring, with his eyes closed, at the trap he feels he is in. Doing sums and knowing, absolutely knowing, that there is never going to be any money in this. Lining up the tasks to be done, measuring guaranteed expenditure against uncertain income. Reproaching himself for having no job, wondering how he is going to get back into the world, imagining his colleagues and rivals, their London lives, their progress, their families, knowing that everything there is moving, while here nothing moves, nothing has ever moved. The house is sunk in deep oblivious peace, except for the few feet around him, in which the air is unquiet, tense with his frustration. I can imagine his anger, at himself, at Jenny. What on earth are they doing here?

He rides out the anger, waits out the fear. He feels better in the morning, as the view and the mountains greet him, and his spirits rise in answer.

He finds a new job with a reputable, if lowly-paying, Sunday newspaper. The farm is a challenge again, not a life. It is another world in a weekend. It is a privilege and a stewardship for which the price, as he sees it, is farming. Jenny will not countenance any retreat from it.

Robert watches her, one afternoon, talking to the vet. Her intuition is sharpening all the time. She has a gift for seeing, sometimes sensing signs and symptoms, and she is accruing a knowledge of treatments. She is synthesising Jack's ways and sayings with the vet's diagnoses: the latter never concludes a visit to the farm without submitting to a detailed interview. He is in the middle of one now. Jenny listens intently, her head tilted to one side, while he explains something. As they talk, standing quietly in the pens, a ewe approaches Jenny and nudges her leg. Unthinking, Jenny reaches into a pocket and comes out with a couple of nuts, little cakes of beet-pulp which the sheep adore. The ewe guzzles them and stands for a moment while Jenny scratches between her ears, quizzing the vet about the powers of vitamin B12 and when you should administer it. Robert loads his pipe and lights it, watching the exchange as he puffs.

It is not merely that she has found something which interests her, something that she wants to do: she has already left want and interest far behind. Sometimes it is as if everything here – the red earth of the yard, and the dull stones showing through the dirty whitewash of the Big Barn, and the young nettles crowding its corners, and the sky with its arms around the mountain – as if all this speaks to her, requires that she be there, in the pen, with a sheep at her knee. As if the land and the heartbreaking view need her to complete it; as if this ancient place, which is never quite still under the tumbling shadows of the clouds, as if the old house and its small estate of toppling fields and whispering copses, borrowed from the hillside, and falling, all of it, near-motionlessly through time, as if all this loves her, possessively, as much as she loves it.

In early August they wean the lambs: dividing them from their mothers, and splitting ewe-lambs from tups. It is hard, heartless work. The animals are separated by hand into different pens before each group is driven away to new fields at opposite ends of the land. They must be out of each other's sight or they will spend hours trying to break through the fences. Moving them is fraught with frustrations, as animals hurtle back the way they have come in desperate attempts to thwart the flapping, fuming humans. When it is done the groups cannot see each other, but they can hear. They cry to each other for three days and nights. Jenny lies awake, listening to them, guilty. The night rings with the bleats of sheep and lambs, but she hears mothers and children. A month later she will give birth to me.

They take the first batch of lambs to market in the back of Derwyn's van. This seems doubly incongruous now, because at no time in my memory would it have been conceivable to ask any favour of the Norsters beyond the implied plea in the usual line: 'Yours have jumped into ours, again,' and because the idea that there was ever a time when Jenny allowed her beloved animals to go anywhere, even to their deaths, in the back of one of Derwyn's vehicles is quite amazing. But this is the time before my memories begin, when my father was farming, and there was more attention being paid to ends than means.

He kept a diary of sorts, a kind of ledger. His energy and determination are bold in its pages; he may never have meant to be a farmer, but here he is, farming, and he means to win its battles. He writes at speed in a broad, forward-leaning hand, the words often lifting off the pale blue lines. There are no corrections. It is like a ship's log, a record of weather conditions, incidents and figures; only once or twice does he write narrative.

The first lambs to market were a mixture of four Suffolks which, he records, went for £10.70 each, and seven Welsh, which went for £9.55.

'Seemed reasonable to me,' he comments, 'but quite a rebellion by many farmers who had brought big lambs for which they wanted £12 plus but were offered little over £11. They refused in quite large numbers to sell.'

At the end of August the hay is brought in, having been left lying in the field for ten days. The whole process, from cutting to baling and hauling, should take four, as Robert notes. It will have lost its freshness and much of its nutrition. But it has been a lousy summer, and he has not been there to plead with and chivvy his neighbours, who have had their own problems with the harvest. Trying to cheer him up, Jack says the bales are not so bad, considering.

In September a neighbour is killed. Mr Jones was making a turn at the top of a steep field in his tractor when the machine toppled over, crushing him. The field in which it happened runs up alongside our first pitch. Whenever we struggle up it in the future, in various underpowered and overloaded vehicles, I think of Mr Jones on his game little grey machine, with no cab or roll bar, jaunty until the last second, when its wheels became unglued from the earth.

At the market, the prices fall. The best fetch £9.50, the worst £7.20.

'Pitiful,' Robert comments. He tries again in early October but it gets worse. They arrive at market with thirteen lambs in a borrowed trailer to find a huge crowd and thousands of sheep. Sheep in the pig pens, sheep in the cattle pens. Their best go for £7, the worst for £5, 'and wouldn't have made that if one of the auctioneer's relatives hadn't done some illicit bidding on our behalf. Most depressing.'

A week later, 'our yearlings reached £11.90, with a little help from the auctioneer's assistant, which was the top price of the day by a good £3. But I refused to sell then and we loaded them in again and took them home. I'm sure everyone thought I was mad. But we had decided that they should fetch £14 at least, although as Jack says, correctly up to a point, you can't make your market at home.'

There were always rumours that somewhere, in one of the local markets, the prices had suddenly bobbed up the other day – that some dealers whom no one recognised were there, paying good money – but their financial position was weak, and worsening. In an effort to improve lamb weights, and therefore the profit they might make, they decided to buy a larger ram. They had started with two rams purchased from Emrys: Tommy, a big yellow-eyed old man with magnificent horns, and Beacons, so called because his humped back reminded Jenny of the view of the Brecon Beacons. The new animal, Ron Vaughan, was purchased at the market. Jenny wrote an account of his arrival.

I had admired Emrys' Suffolk lambs with their chocolate faces and black-stockinged legs, but I was doubtful about an Othello jumping about on our little white ewes. After much debate, Rob and Jack went to market. I waited with some trepidation for their return. The trailer pulled into the yard, Rob got out, grinned, and then Jack emerged, towing their purchase on a piece of rope. They stood, waiting for the verdict. The ram was young, but large. He had beautiful ears, long and black, adorably tipped up at the ends. His legs were strong and black, his eyes a liquid dark. Jack was looking at him like an immensely proud parent. 'The best ram in the market,' he said. We named him Ron Vaughan, after his previous owner, and waited for October 25th. October 25th was one of Jack's most important dates. (Another was May 18th when all animals should be turned off fields destined for hay.)

'There's nothing to beat a March lamb,' he said, so October 25th was the day selected, ewes' pregnancies lasting five months. The day dawned gloriously, golden sun and a crisp frosty wind. We got up early. 'A perfect day for tupping,' we said, as Jack arrived, keen to see his child perform. Our twitching little ewes were waiting obediently in the pens, and then, panic. Ron Vaughan was *gone*. He was nowhere to be seen. We pounded about – how could he have gone, how could he have disappeared – he had been in the back patch – just outside the kitchen . . . And then Rob spotted him. He'd somehow escaped out on to the hill, no doubt tempted by Derwyn's mountain gypsy flock who had been patrolling beguilingly along the hill fence.

Ron Vaughan was glimpsed surrounded by bracken and two or three gypsies, wasting his talents. As we approached, the gypsies ran away and he panted after them. We started climbing and running, Derwyn's ewes climbed higher and dodged lower and soon Ron Vaughan was collecting more and more amorous females as he waded his way through the bracken, trying to do his best.

Up and down we rushed, 'Bugger it, bugger it,' we gasped. At last Rob caught him. We dragged him back. Jack could only say 'Well well well.' Ron Vaughan looked as if he needed someone to mop his brow.

So they prepare for next year's market, while this year's is glutted with sheep, demand is falling weekly and there is nothing anyone can do about it, beyond the auctioneers' feebly sly attempts to run up the prices. But they have to get rid of the rest of the tup lambs, or they will end up feeding them through the winter, to no purpose, so at the end of October they try once more.

It becomes clear even before they reach the market that it is going to be no better: the streets are full of Land Rovers and trailers. The market is a sea of grey chaos; vehicles manoeuvring in all directions, frustration and tension on every red face, the rain slanting down, thousands of sodden and crying ewes and lambs packed into every pen, jammed into trailers, wet wool bulging through the slatted sides, overflowing the sheep pens, the pig pens, the cattle pens; the gutters run black with their manure. Farmers grip the hurdles which barely divide their animals from all the rest, staring across the churning lake of soaked white backs and wailing tongues at the little knot of wet caps around the auctioneer, whose chants are all too short, and on every glum face is the knowledge that this is all loss. And among them, one of the very few sellers who has another way of making a living, perhaps the only one who does not have farming anywhere in his history or his blood, Robert is trying to get rid of four old ewes and the last dozen tup lambs.

The ewes are up first: two go for £2 each, but nobody wants the other two so he gives them away. It gets him a few looks but it is not unheard of. Then the auctioneer moves on to the lambs. The ring of bidders and watchers, mostly watchers, moves with him. The odd hand reaches into the pen to squeeze a rump: experienced fingers can tell how much meat there is under the wet wool. Heads shake. These have had orf – a blistering gum disease which stopped them eating much for weeks – and are underweight. And they have not been castrated, which meant, as Robert explains in his diary: 'we couldn't keep them on, as we could have done if they were wethers, and for the past few weeks they have been losing weight, instead of putting it on because their minds were on other things.' They fetched £3.80 each, making a total of £49.60 for the day. 'Not too clever, as Jack would say,' Robert writes.

While anyone with any sense would be trying to get out of this doomed, archaic business, Robert, who has a great deal of sense, seems to be doing everything he can to get in. In the months which follow he buys hundreds of stakes for new fencing, hires a builder to re-roof the back of the house, dips and drenches the ewes, digs a drain across the paddock, accumulates a stock of 'cake', nuts and oats for the winter – bag by bag, driving loads up from town each time he comes – and hires and harangues a man he refers to as 'Davis the Drainage' who eventually installs a 1,500-gallon catch tank at the top of the Quoiker, which, coupled with a pipe down to the house, one fine winter day, finally brings running water to the farm.

At first it is only a temporary tap by the back door. 'Wonderful!' Robert writes in his diary, and it must have been, after collecting ten-gallon drums of freezing mountain stream water, in all weathers, and hauling them up a hundred yards of rising ground. It is the first significant improvement to the house in three hundred years, and not the last. Soon afterwards he has the north end dug out of the red embrace of the mountain, and the damp wall which emerges reinforced with breeze-blocks. Then he puts in for planning permission for a bathroom, the beginning of a process which takes months.

He visits more frequently than Jenny does now, and there is a sense that they are managing separate spheres: she is often in London, with their nanny and first child (me), while Robert comes down at the weekends to work on the farm. During the week, the feeding and day-to-day tasks are in Jack's hands. His sayings tend toward the negative, but they are faithfully recorded.

'At least it's not so cold today.'

'Not so bad, no.'

'Apparently it's been the warmest December for a hundred years.'

'Ah – a green Christmas means a full churchyard!'

'Does it really?'

'They do say . . .'

Despite the relatively warm winter they are short of grass: they have too many sheep for the space and much of the hay has gone mouldy. In these circumstances every square foot is valuable, and the great many moles which live under the fields are looked upon as a menace. Their red-mauve hillocks were everywhere, Robert records: 'The moles have made an awful mess of the second meadow. Jack has trapped a few but says there are some educated buggers there. He reckons to trap them in the end so long as the wind doesn't move to the east – for you'll never get them then, he claims.'

Jack campaigned against the moles across the years. Educated they may not have been, wary they certainly were. Long snouts testified to their superb sense of smell. Jack, who smelled of must, pipe tobacco and rain, tried not to handle the traps at all, cocking and placing them with sticks. He approached the chosen ambush point from downwind and carefully positioned the trap astride the mole's tunnel, steel jaws gaping, handles sticking out of the ground. Often he caught nothing and could be seen in the meadows, moodily flattening molehills with a spade. When he was successful the velvet-coated corpse would be brought back to the house in triumph and passed to my brother and me: we marvelled at the incredible softness of its coat and the great shovels of its front feet, like the hands of an ogre, long nailed and long fingered, angled backwards, for breast-stroking through the earth.

# 4

## Two Wishes

HE SWINGS THE car up the yard, stops at the top and switches off the engine. Three hours' solid driving and he aches, yet he hesitates in his seat for a moment. When he opens the door and climbs out into the yard the warmth which has been with him since London will be sucked away into the cold clean air, and another lambing will begin. He taps his fingers once on the steering wheel, smiles ruefully, and goes for the door handle. It will be a week at least until Jenny joins him and there is much to do.

Now, at last, he writes more than notes in the diary.

This passage comes after an extreme night, in the days before Jenny arrives. He has a vivid story and no one to tell it to, so he writes it down. It begins on a snowy night. Earlier on he has noticed a sheep looking odd, broody. At a quarter to ten he goes out to check on her.

The snow was now quite thick on the ground and the moon, though behind the clouds, was full. The torch seemed to flood-light the whole field. She was still in the same place but now a big black head glistened under her tail and she was very wild. As I followed her doggedly, still undecided what to do, across the fields, hide and seek round the hedge, scattering the ewes in every direction, it started to snow again, quite heavily and driven by the wind. She turned back and as she headed for the bottom corner I decided that was the only place I had a chance of catching her. She seemed to have the same thought and rushed wildly from side to side but I finally got her down the bank and then the problem was that she had two exits with a ten-foot stretch of hedge between us. In a flash of inspiration I stuck the torch in the hedge and crept round the other side. She watched me but seemed baffled by the light coming from the other direction and by the time she had decided which way to run I had her. It was just the head and I could feel no hint of a leg so I turned her up, balancing the torch on her bottom, and tried to push the head back but she fought like mad and I nearly lost hold of her. It took about twenty minutes to drag her up to the house and get her in the barn and then I went to get Jack. It was about 10.45 and luckily he and Alf were still watching telly in front of a very hot fire. It had stopped snowing and we managed to get back up the hill without the car skidding too badly. A nightmare performance, but Jack eventually managed to push the head back, the lamb bleeding from the mouth and its tongue hanging out and deep purple. Then we got one leg forward but couldn't get the head back through the hole and though he tried the wire loop he's never used it before and couldn't get it to hold. So I rang the vet, we loaded the ewe into the boot and I got to Abergavenny at midnight to find Mr Jones waiting. He got the loop in very quickly and the second leg, which he said was across the lamb's chest. Still, he had to pull very hard indeed. Miraculously, the lamb, which was an enormous Suffolk, was still alive. And then Mr Jones pulled out a second. I had all three back in the barn by 12.45 and after another quick round went to bed.

The reporter's accuracy in no way diminishes the drama, which is loud between the lines. His struggle through the snow; the heart-lurching drive down the hill; bursting in on two old men, their faces fire-orange and television-blue (they did not like to have the lights on at night for fear of the electricity bill). Driving back up, rigid silence in the car as he hauls it around the vicious corner at the top of the first pitch and sets off along the icy ribbon of road above the drop into the black and white wood. The desperate, medieval scenes in the barn, and the last resort, the call to the vet. The victory, and unmistakable pride in the throwaway last phrase. Not the sort of thing everyone does, or could do, before going to bed.

He is vulnerable without Jenny, up there alone, in the same way she will be without him. And she will be more frightened, more exposed to the merciless weather and the limits of the strength in her arms. But the elation of it, the thrill of it, the sense of vivid existence, of triumph made all the sweeter by the fact that you did not really know what you were doing, which he relishes here, as he recalls it the next day, she will feel also, and more so.

It is striking how like her he sounds, how he sees and says things in the same way. 'A big black head glistened under her tail and she was very wild.' It could be her speaking; moreover, the charged tone precisely recalls the farm as I knew it, as I and my brother lived it. We experienced it as an adventure and not just because all childhood is an adventure: Jenny taught us that ours was unusual, that living in the way we did, so close to nature, was an intense and dramatic life, and to be taken as such. The fact that it made exactly the same impression, on occasion anyway, on our father, the most logical and laconic of men, is somehow reassuring. It really was like that.

When Jenny arrives they use Robert's diary to pass news and messages. When I first opened it, thirty years later, their exchanges struck me like the confirmation of a rumour I had long wished to believe, evidence of something I had half willed and half imagined: a time when they were happy together, committed to their great adventure. His writing:

> Beautiful badger girl born overnight, #58 from 45. Jack drew a single before lunch. Derwyn came up with a lamb with a torn throat to show what the fox had done. Can't think why.

Here her smaller, vertical script interrupts:

> Jenny thinks him absolutely mad to rush around displaying a dying lamb when he should be caring for it for heaven's sake. 10 p.m. SNOW. Saw fox again in the Horse Fields – lying flat to the ground with bright red eyes then streaked off. Saw fat rabbit under the holly by the road. Young ewe doing it under top hollies. Sheep v. nervous of me – migrate when I get close. Wish I could wear my waterproof trousers but would probably cause a stampede.

She has a busy night, delivering lambs, moving newborn twins and their mother to a less exposed part of the field and going back to the house for a milk bottle. (They have learned a lot in their first years: lambs can be jump-started with a suck of milk drawn from another ewe and stored in the fridge. The first pints a ewe makes are thick and golden colostrum, rich with protein and antibodies: a few gulps stands anything on its feet. The word 'colostrum' in its yellow syringe had the ring of manna about it.) She concludes the entry:

> Ewe below hollies by the gate delivered one. Have no idea whether it's the first of twins – too cold to stay and find out. Confused by ewe and lamb of Derwyn's whose wretched bull is non-stop belling plus a bereaved ewe. It's bloody cold. Everything b. cold me bloody cold and FED UP! Finish 2 a.m. (2 broody.)

The next morning Robert begins, dryly:

> Jenny must have really stirred them up. Overnight: three sets of twins and two singles, one v small. #68 from 52.

There are almost no records of them doing a job together, the division of labour keeps them to different halves of the clock, but by their tones they are happy; Jenny's protests about being fed up are designed to provoke his smile. Another life is taking place around the edges of the lambing. Their relationship is as invisible as I am (I appear occasionally, as my initials, normally around 1.30 a.m. when I demand attention between Jenny's late rounds of the sheep) but it seems a good partnership and close: Jenny was now carrying their second child.

The weather yaws from snow to sun and back again; Jack was right, a freezing, killing spring followed the green Christmas. But in the diary the even, flowing lines of Robert's strong script record an orderly progress. The team is functioning beautifully.

*5 April*
Snow and snowing. 88 from 68. Thaw at lunchtime. Four weak-ening sets of twins inside, also two other sets, cripple in one,

rejected twin in the other. Suffolk single in the bottom of the Badger Wood. 89 from 69. Lovely evening.

The fringe work at lambing is just as draining as what goes on in the fields, the main theatre. Those weakening sets of twins and the cripple will need feeding, as will the weeping rejected twin. When a surrogate mother can be found, it will need hours of being pushed to her udder.

He is still up at midnight, helping another birth halfway down the Badger Wood, which is perilously steep, dark-crowded with the shapes of hunching trees and slippery in the thaw.

More snow comes the next day. Jenny and Jack spend the afternoon 'unplugging' and marking lambs. The remains of the colostrum, fuel of life, squitters out of the lambs as a thick yellow paste, a waxy cream which hardens and crusts, causing life-threatening constipation. Unplugging it requires unsqueamish fingers and a brave nose: the smell comes from a vile region somewhere between faeces and rancid butter.

'Heavy snow, blizzards, drifts,' Robert reports the next day. 'The crippled Suffolk twin died (its mother mercifully lay on it) bringing the number of lamb deaths to five.'

Considering the conditions, it is an excellent score. The day after that they have a lamb born dead, and the story of the rejected twin ends happily. An old ewe has a single in the night 'which she licked and left to die. Jack skinned the lamb and put the skin on the reject for whom it was some sizes too small, but the ewe didn't seem to mind.'

It is a common trick among sheep farmers: the corpse is skinned, yielding a perfect little jacket, with holes for the head and legs of the orphan you want to foster. You dress it and pen it in with the bereaved mother, nice and tight, so they cannot get away from each other. The ewe, smelling her own lamb, her beloved, though she knows something is not right, will, in the end, stand for a suckling. After a day or so they bond, and the adoption is complete. You throw the shrunken little skin away, somewhere out of the reach of dogs and foxes.

A week later the end is in sight, Robert scores 144 from 115 and allows himself to calculate the distance to the finishing line (44 to go). They share a page only once more, when a tame lamb called Rudi, which they are feeding, disappears. At the same time an abandoned lamb is discovered, in Robert's words, 'twitching in the rain in the middle of the Quoiker. Jenny administered whisky and milk and the lamb recovered – revealing himself to be Rudi.' Jenny continues:

> Who is now (11.55 p.m.) fully recovered from what must have been a monumental hangover from whisky and penicillin and is avid for more. Failing that he has curled himself up in his mother's bowl much to her obvious irritation. A warm night! Worms out and would you believe it zipping in and out of their holes. All seemed quiet in our fields but as for the cacophony issuing from wretched Derwyn's wretched animals . . . last time it was miserable cows. This time it's horses screaming and what sounds like an expiring ewe and two lost lambs on the hill. Wind from the west. Cloudy.
>
> 12.30. Have fed Rudi and Reluctant Drinker again – I think he has sucked but please check him first thing because he's very hungry.

The last pages in Robert's diary record a small outbreak of orf, which they treat and contain; a successful operation by Jenny to induce the birth of twins by opening their mother's cervix, and a trouble-free end to the lambing. They go back to London on 19 April, return the following weekend to drench 75 yearlings and calculate that they have had 175 lambs from 144 ewes, with 15 still to go. That week, on 21 April 1975, in the basement of their London flat, Robert writes a letter to his wife.

The dedication, 'Dear Jenny', and the sign off, 'Yours, as ever, Robert', are handwritten. The rest is typed.

The letter is all about money, the gravity of their 'plight', as he describes it. He begins by saying that because his recent attempts to make her understand or even engage with their financial situation have failed, and caused 'tension and ill-feeling' between them, he has decided to write down the facts as dispassionately as he can.

There follow lists of expenditure and earnings. First, his personal costs and earnings, then the farm's, then hers. Everything is included, from feeding the cats (£3 a week) to tobacco (his pipe and her cigarettes) to capital expenditure on the farm. He takes account of inflation, notes the absence from their budget of things like presents, pensions, life insurance and entertainment; lists all the different costs and incomes of the sheep in the last year – from £200 from the Wool Marketing Board to £3 per ewe for the sale of ten old ewes – and uses this year's figures to forecast the sums they can expect to make next year.

It is clear that they are in trouble. He is spending more than he is earning. The car, which has done 32,000 miles in the last twenty months, is the largest contributor to his debt, which is increasing by £30 a week. The farm is £1,247 in debt, and losing, with the cost of travelling to and from it included, another £40 a week. The rosiest projection he can make for the following year, if they have a good lambing and sell 200 lambs, leads him to forecast a further loss of £1,200 when the cost of the car is included. And they are expecting another child, which means, he thinks, that they will have to move out of their small, cheap London flat, into somewhere bigger and more expensive.

He notes that she has £2,000 in an account which she insists is her own, and outside their marriage, and that she is proposing to borrow another £3,000 to install a bathroom at the farm. Even if they could find a loan provider, how can they go further into debt to cover living expenses, he demands, when they have no way of paying off any interest, never mind the loan itself?

He thinks the situation not merely unsustainable, but mad. Her reaction to his worries, he says, has been a grand 'Oh, we shall just have to go further into debt,' which he finds 'baffling and infuriating'.

He notes, in an amazed tone, that her solution to all this is that she should take the children and go to live at the farm.

He has three objections. First, he works in London from Tuesday morning to Saturday night: he does not want her and their children to live 160 miles away. He does not want to live alone at the flat or share it with a lodger who would help pay its rent; he wants to live with her and the children in London, where he works. Secondly, he says, he cannot afford the farm, and thirdly, he does not believe she could cope alone with the farm and two small children.

He says she has proposed three alternative solutions: first, that they should keep the farm and buy a bigger flat, so that she and the children might divide their time between Wales and London. Fine, he says, except that he cannot afford the farm or a bigger flat. Alternatively, they should get divorced, he should sign over farm, flat and child to her, and pay maintenance. But he does not want to get divorced, he says. She has no grounds for seeking it, except that he cannot afford what she wants. 'I love you and the child. I want us to stay married,' he writes. And he cannot see why he should sign over flat or farm. Her third solution is that he should earn more money. He points out that his paper is not a wealthy one, but that he likes the job, and has recently been given a pay-rise: hardly grounds for divorce.

His solution, he says, is simple. They should sell the farm, pay their debts, sell the flat and use the proceeds to buy a 'respectable' house in London. She has already rejected this, but now he begs her to see that it is 'the only possible' course. He says he will sell their car – a Volvo – and use the money to make repairs to their decrepit Volkswagen beetle, in which he will make the necessary trips to Wales to do whatever needs to be done to prepare the farm and the stock for sale. From next weekend, he says, he will not be responsible for any more bills incurred by the farm, other than those relating to preparation for its sale, which would certainly not include any further building. Unless he has her agreement, he says, he will have to take steps to give the disclaimer legal validity.

He finishes with an apology:

I am truly sorry that you will undoubtedly have found this letter rough, unloving, offensive and pompous. But I am deeply disturbed about the possible legal consequences of the mess we are in, and there must be no misunderstandings.

Yours, as ever, Robert

At first reading, this letter confirmed my childhood impression of their relationship and its fate: an idea that my mother the mad romantic and my father the icy rationalist were pulled apart by her recalcitrance and his caution; a mutual refusal to compromise or defer. But now I am not so sure. Nowhere else, in no letter, diary or exchange of notes is love ever mentioned. But here, in a letter purporting to be unloving and rough, is something like love, and love's desperation. And, depicted only in the echo of its plea, but clear nevertheless, is an image of a woman prepared to ditch a man who loves her because he cannot afford to keep up with her, a woman with an airy ruthlessness in her romanticism, who seems to have already chosen, or at least threatened to choose, the mountain over the man.

Before her reply, three weeks later, Jenny Williams writes a feature for the Friday 9 May edition of the *Evening Standard* – 'on being a midwife to a flock of sheep'. In places she quotes Robert's diary, and reports him using a torch to dazzle another sheep before catching her. She quotes Jack on infection: 'the worst enemy of a sheep is another sheep,' and signs off:

> The cuckoo came on 22 April and we now have 179 lambs with ten ewes still to go. We have lost weight. I need a new pair of wellingtons and the feed bill is enormous.
>
> But the ewes, however elderly, have done us proud and their lambs run races, as they should.

On the following Wednesday 14 May 1975, on *Evening Standard* notepaper, she types a letter to her brother-in-law, and legal consultant, Geoff.

She has four questions. Is it legal for Robert to refuse to pay all farm bills? He is joint-owner, they arrive in the main addressed to him. Secondly, would the legal disclaimer he threatens be granted? Thirdly, can she, as his wife, be forced to live where he decrees? Finally, even if she lived at the farm against his wishes, married or not, is he not obliged to support his children?

She notes, 'Since his BLAST of the Trumpet Rob has been incredibly nice, and much relieved.' And she concludes:

> I have absolutely no doubt AT ALL that were I to sell now – when the prices are bad, when the house is still not right, and without trying to give the children a country childhood, the resentment and boredom and frustration I would feel in suburbia would ruin our marriage in any case. If my effort – if I decide to do it – does not work, THEN I will consider selling; and that is still the safety net.

— * —

With the end of that exchange, we enter a stranger time, a time which I find harder to picture than these scenes which I have described but did not see. We are approaching the time when my brother was born, and now my own memories begin.

Everything I have written hitherto has strong foundations in imaginative truth: either Jenny or Robert, or a diary, or an instinct has vividly described to me what I have described here, and though it is true to my sense of what happened, it is also a story, a conjuring. I do not – could not – remember it, and this has added a storyteller's certainty to my handling of it.

But from now on I feel I know less: memory is much less reliable than invention. I recall incidents from before my brother's birth, and I remember the night he was born clearly, but the string of pictures I have of the next few years is like my father's diary: portraits of a small corner, concealing the rest of the world.

The life of 'Pim' at this time was, I think, happy; my lovely young nanny, Lindsey, would tickle me to make me behave; my mother came home after work; I remember the farm when the bathroom went in (Jenny borrowed £3,000 from her mother) and I can hardly have been two then. My ability to recall scenes from that life has been commented on by both parents; I remember Lindsey and our trips to Notting Hill and a shop called Serendipity. She bought me a magnificent red wheelbarrow at another shop, telling my mother, when she returned to find me wheeling it about the flat, 'I had to, he just loved it so much,' and I see the expressions of the shopkeeper, Lindsey and my mother now as I did then, with great pleasure. The wheelbarrow, I think, we still have. I knew there were tensions between my parents, but I also knew and shared their contentment and collaboration.

I remember their happiness and excitement the night Alexander was born. I was uncertain about the whole business and spent the hospital visit stuffing myself with hula-hoops from a bowl beside another mother's bed. When they asked me, in that traditional consolation for the put-out eldest, what I would like to call him, I replied, heavily, entering rather grudgingly into the spirit of greeting and celebration, 'Twinkle. Twinkle twinkle little star.' (I had already been saddled with the pet-name Pim, because I was a fussy and tearful child – 'nimsy-pimsy', in my mother's rather horrible phrase. So it was thanks to my pedestrian taste in nursery rhymes and tremulous response to the world that Jenny's heroic children, Horatio and Alexander, became known as Pim and Twinks.)


1976. I remember Alexander and me being bathed together, and read to. The four of us went to the park, the seaside and the zoo. There are photographs of the famously hot summer; everyone wears floppy white sunhats, sits around on burnt yellow grass and smiles redly at the camera. My father has long fair hair. In the photos he looks straight into the lens, evenly. The camera never seems to catch him unawares. My mother sits around, feeds children, plays with us, watches Robert. She is often talking when the shutter clicks, he is quieter. There were long drives down the motorway, Jenny told the tale of the Pobble Who Had No Toes as we crossed the Severn Bridge, and her family listened; on one night-time journey I remember my father laughing as I bestowed magical powers on my mother and she cast a spell: 'Abracadabra, turn this tatty Volkswagen into . . . a magnificent chariot!'

There was a Christmas dinner at the farm, when Robert cooked the goose with its neck and head still on (the beak looked like crackling). I can still hear Jenny's horrified squawks and his peals of laughter.

I watched Alexander closely. I vaguely remember the incident which my mother described to my aunt involving a hammer I had found. I was hefting it. My mother had just finished feeding my brother. 'Oh well done, darling, you've found Robert's hammer. Better be careful . . .'

Aunt Ursie's reaction, 'Watch out, Jenny, it only takes a moment,' seems an uncharitable assessment of what was going on in my mind, but like all elder brothers, I certainly considered my sibling's demise in the years to come, though never with such apparent coolness. He was quick to start crawling, then walking. He did not say much.

The fireplace at the farm was our first adventure. Left one afternoon in front of the cold hearth, I contrived, by a series of mimes, to persuade Alexander to join me among the ashes and cinders. He did not look too happy with their taste, but he joined in readily with the daubing and delving. When my mother discovered us she screeched in impotent vexation. She marched us to the bathroom, stripped and scolded us. I am not sure if I was given a slap, but I certainly would have been without Alexander's involvement. I remember the reproach in his eyes as she scrubbed him over the basin. I like to think we were allies from then on. It was obviously fortunate that with his developing speech Alexander became able to give his side of the story, and say who started what.

I do not remember Robert and Jenny arguing, they concealed their disputes, but they were quietly pulling apart. Robert built a shed in the garden of the London flat which he furnished as a study and retreated into: it seems utterly reasonable now, but then it was Robert's Shed, a symbol of separateness.

Then there was the way they referred to each other by name when talking to us, a habit which my brother and I adopted: it was not until we reached double figures that we dropped Jenny and Robert and started calling them Mum and Dad.

They read to us a great deal. We were relentless in requesting the same favourites, night after night. My father found himself reading the same stories in exactly the same way, turning the pages, using almost the same intonations, like a travelling player, methodically recreating a narrative brio. His core repertoire included at least ten books, but we normally chose from the same two or three. The canon included *Cannonball Simp*, about a small black dog whose owner abandons her (she becomes a cannonball at a circus); *Shady Glade* (the machines tear up the animals' forest, so they ride a boxcar through mysterious cities to another, safer Shady Glade); and I went through a craze for the books of Richard Scarry, which was certainly partly visual. I was very keen on the adventures of Lowly Worm, who had an apple-shaped car which he drove fast and sometimes badly. 'Where did you learn to drive?' someone shouts at him.

'Where did you learn to drive?' I echoed.

'Cape Town!' my father answered.

'Why?'

'Because we lived there.'

'Why . . .?'

'Well, we lived abroad. I was born in Shanghai . . .'

I learned to read with Peter and Jane and their dog, Pat. We read the lot, every evening after my bath, as far as the adventure which features a large yellow helicopter, and a quite mature Peter and Jane. They lived in an eternal summer, as did most of the human characters of our children's books: it was left to animals and pink monsters to experience fear, shame and confusion. I was given a toy which made a great impression on me: a small plastic R2D2 from the film *Star Wars*. I loved it, from the miraculous moment it appeared at the head of my bed.

My mother left me notes in the same place, folded pieces of paper with the message written in tiny script. They were stories, fragments of fairy tale and role-play. I dictated replies to her, which she wrote out in the same way. I clearly remember one of them referring to a 'him', obviously my father, and the feelings I recall, as one of the notes was written, read or delivered, are all of conspiracy. It is such a clear and strong sensation, as vivid as remembered love or guilt, and I think that moment became part of a secret subconscious album, like a collection of dark documents, assembled to explain their divorce. Part of my guilt. For the child of divorce is guilty, or feels himself to be, of a kind of original sin, the deeds of which I have always felt I could almost remember, even when I was very young.

Soon outings were conducted by one or the other and there was a growing sense of their individual existences: they ceased to share the same frame. Robert went running in the evenings after work. There were long silences when they were together, their division became the norm. Now working night shifts at the BBC, Robert was fatigued and depressed at home. Jenny took it personally: he switched to nights so that he didn't have to see me, she said.

They still hummed up the motorway at weekends. They still lambed together, in 1976 and 1977. At Christmas and during beach holidays with Ursie and Geoff and their three children they appeared together, like a husband and wife, but they faced different ways. Robert looked to his work and London; Jenny to the farm and the children. Now his logic seemed cold, her passion selfish; with the evaporation of love and excitement it became hard to remember how their contradictions had ever been submerged. And as he sank into that mystery, bitterly embracing his own miseries, Jenny proclaimed herself and her certainties ever more loudly and more desperately. Her heart was no mystery at all. It beat for her children and her farm.

Farming had nothing more to offer Robert and he was an outstanding journalist. He was making his name, destined for awards, promotions, plum jobs, Baftas and Sony awards – successes and satisfactions he would never find at home. For all his wife's domination and determination (and hadn't he deferred to her over Wales, over the farm, over the sheep?) she could not change that fact. He did not abandon his family, but he never looked like coming back. His career and his future were in London.

Jenny took stock on 17 December 1977. Her diary is also a kind of ship's log, but she is a very different kind of captain.

We have decided that while Robert makes good at work during the next year the children and I should come and live at the farm. It makes sense. I can help Jack feed, Pim will go to the village school – a dear little place where he will be one of only 27, in a class of 12. I shall have to leap up in the mornings for a change, which will be good for me. I am anxious about two aspects:

a) That we'll only see Rob at weekends, and b) that the evenings will seem long and scary. Ever since that wretched burglar broke in I've lost confidence at night. We seem such a long way away from the neighbours. I don't know which is more scary. A quiet night, when I can hear the cat swallowing, and the embers clink-clinking, or a wild one when the barn door bangs and the wind rushes through the attics. I am taking three precautionary measures. A telephone extension in the bedroom, a dog from the RSPCA in Newport or somewhere and a television set so that I can watch the reassuring puffy features of Richard Baker reading the 9 o'clock news! And without a daily paper I won't feel so cut off. We will be here for at least 9 months. It will all depend on Pim's progress at the village school. Jack will be 75 on January 25th.

The life she has left behind sounds miserable. Staying in bed as long as possible while Robert goes off to work and 'makes good'. The London papers – sections of them written by friends and familiar names – sharpening her sense of being out of the loop. Wishing she had not given up work: she had a nanny for her first child and stayed on at the *Standard*, should she have done the same with her second? It makes no difference now. Now she is sitting with her back to the fat embers of the great wood fire, her pen steadily crossing the pages.

Robert, the children and I came in convoy to the farm. Two cars were necessary. He took the children and 2 TV sets (one for Jack), and I followed after with everything else including the kettle. Toys, teddies, books, Christmas presents, pictures, sponge, clothes clothes clothes. It was a yellow dank cold day, with a wind. Grey and bleak it looked from Hammersmith flyover, but if someone had suggested we wait another day or so I would have felt almost relieved. We stopped once or twice. The bonnet on the Morris is tied down with string because the catch is broken. But it doesn't feel very efficient. I watched it bouncing up and down.

We eventually came up the track to the farm. It always looks so bleak and unwelcoming. The whitewash looks flaky, the stones dripping, and to get out of a warm car to open up a cold house and to be brisk and cheerful and pleased to be here is always an effort. I keep my coat on, try to see the children keep theirs on too, and make for the kettle in the kitchen which is an ice house. Then upstairs, make the beds and put in electric blankets. After tea we all feel better. Pim and Twinkle rediscover their toys, the cats appear to be fed and I light the fire Jack has laid. It is dark, we are warmer, the children are in bed after cold washes, Rob lights the cooker and after London the wind outside and the smell of fresh air and the feel of the hills around us in the dark make me wonderfully peaceful. We go to bed. After a while the mattress grows warm.

*Sunday 18 December*
Spent the day organising, unpacking, discussing sheep and feeding with Jack. Rob left at 7.30 for his last stint in London before his fortnight's holiday. Twinky cried when he left, and Pim was miserable. We watched his car lights bobbing and retreating down the track. They felt bereft. I felt, because I'm not settled in yet I suppose, apprehensive. The children had a bath, we talked in low voices. I was listening to the sounds in the yard and wishing I'd asked Jack to stay the night just to tide us over.

'Are you absolutely sure, Jenny,' said Pim as I kissed him goodnight, 'that there is nothing here to harm us?'

'Absolutely sure,' I said. And came down to check the bolt on the front door and sit with my back to the fire imagining prowlers and peeping toms in the yard. Later I turned on the wireless and painted the wall behind the shelves in the kitchen a pinky brown colour which looked, I thought, quite horrid. Went to bed quite happily nevertheless.

*Monday night*
Still painting. I was sure someone was outside watching me through the kitchen window!

She kept no record of that Christmas, beyond going to buy a huge tree for £1, but they were adept conjurors, and with the firelight, the shining baubles, snow, carols on the gramophone and the certainty of reindeer galloping across the stars and a man coming down the chimney, which was wide enough for the fattest Laplander, our Christmases glowed with delights. There was no television, then or ever. I remember Robert plugging one in, and fiddling with it, while it snowed and fuzzed, and eventually giving up. It was hauled upstairs and abandoned in the Beast House bedroom. 'We don't have television,' ran our standard line, 'because there's a mountain in the way of the signal.'

Instead they both read to us: *The Tailor of Gloucester*, *Papa Panov's Christmas*, *The Lion, the Witch and the Wardrobe*. All the myths and traditions of the season made perfect sense at the farm. The lanes were full of dark holly, which we hauled in by the feed-bagful; there was mistletoe in the hedges, the fire roared with great Yule logs, and on Christmas night it seemed perfectly obvious that all the animals would talk. And it snowed. One extraordinary night, after the snow clouds had cleared, we went tobogganing under the moon. It was an unearthly scene; the valley a twinkling masterpiece, as if the starlight had thickened and fallen on the world, covering everything in soft, cold perfection, leaving only the outlines of hedges and woods, dark-etched shadows against the glowing snow. The world tilted as we slid and sped, the sledge hissed and we exulted, speeding down the field under the bright canopy of the heavens.

Alexander and I loved the whole season and over the years we gorged on it. There would be school Christmas, and the farm Christmas, and Christmas with our cousins, and then – in the years when he no longer came to the farm – for a week after Boxing Day, Christmas in London with Robert. We made the most of everything: when the decorations came down it was winter followed by lambing, and no one has cause to dread this pair like hill farmers and their families.

— * —

I began my time at the village school. The 'dear little place' appeared to me a frowning presence by the main road; its moody stones and high windows might have been designed to shut out the view, the valley and the world. The shadowy schoolroom seemed to remember and yearn for ranks of Victorian children, scribbling on slates, chanting in time, kept in order by the teacher's bark and the cane. Now there were two dozen of us, more likely to be drawing pictures than learning anything by heart, all itching for break time and the chance to charge up and down the field outside playing British Bulldogs. My mother said that if we yelled loud enough and she was feeding in our lowest field she could sometimes hear us, which was a comfort.

The other children were all neighbours in the village; I was a peculiar oddball, articulate with adults, uneasy with other children. I longed for the weekends and for really bad weather, for anything that would keep me at home. I was lucky: in January the quarter-pint milk bottles which waited outside the school door sprouted columns of glistening golden ice, and the temperature continued to drop. February in particular, in Jack's phrase, was a little bugger of a month. With Robert gone, the weather closing in and nothing ahead but months of feeding and lambing, we were suddenly embarked, as if in an old stone ship, on the adventure Jenny had both dreaded and longed for. It is the winter of 1978.

*13 February*
For the last week we have been in the grip of icy winter. Everything looks dead – the fields, hills and sky have lost their colour. Hard, pale, deadly cold. The hardest frost for nine years they say – snow half-hearted, but small flakes and vicious. Northeasterlies drive it in bitter puffs. My old sheep with their thin coats must feel it over their backbones. The fields are harder than London pavements, crossed by dusty tracks where the animals walk at feeding time. Their hooves drum on it and several fall over. Walking as sheep do on tip-toe, with ruts and molehills hard – it is no weather for high heels. The cauldron has grown a wide crystal rim, the trough in the Quoiker is embalmed and

curtained in icicles. Pim and Twinky stood on the ice in the yard trough without making a single crack and even the bucket of water I left in the Beast House for two of Gwyn's sick lambs had frozen by the morning. It is a worry to me. Taps are frozen. The children are running out of clean dry clothes because of the lack of hot water – I make dashes to town for food whenever I can but the pitches are either covered with a skin of ice or snow and I frightened myself three days ago when the car barely made it.

Jack is in a bitter mood also. He caught our bug – diarrhoea and vomiting. Like ours it was short lived and he looked better today. And having wrestled with the bales in separate fields and guilty silence I told him so when we met briefly at the meadow gate. 'You look better, Jack.'

'Think so? I don't feel it. Feel bloody weakened.' A pause. 'How are you then?'

Me, retaliating with immense irony and a bright smile. 'Thank you so much for asking, Jack. Not really so bad. Our water has all frozen since yesterday. I'm carrying it from the stream.'

'Aw.' With that he marched off, once again abandoning his stick. Never asked about the children and at any other time he would have offered to help me carry the wretchedly heavy oil drums in which I lug the water. But I expect he reckons we're plague-ridden. Pim has a terrible cough but otherwise we're better now, and although it worries me how to keep fed, warm, clean and mobile, this sudden winter is strangely exciting. The evenings are eerily still now that the wind has dropped. The evening sky is an angry orange with growling clouds and the distant hills are bleached. The veins of the Beacons are black against the thin snow. Even the buds and the tight catkins on the alders which were a purplish pink ten days ago have blackened and shrunk. You can almost hear the frost cracking its fingers. I use the car to carry bales to the meadows jolting over the frozen mud, rattling and jarring the undercarriage. Every time I bring it back I wrap up the bonnet with an old mack and a sack, put stones under its wheels and release the hand brake. I wonder if there is ice banging in its water tank. Then before we come in we stand and listen, looking over our view. The sheep yellow, one or two bleats from distant lambs, cars changing gear in the valley, the roar of the stream heavy with snow, the evening wide. We saw a new

moon three nights ago. I bowed three times, Jack showed it 10p
and lent it to Pim and me to do the same. Even Twinky waved it
aloft. So sharp and clear was that little moon it looked as if it could
cut. I made two wishes sliding them into one.

Two wishes sliding them into one! How characteristic that is.
Greedy and selfless; pointless and urgent, romantic and fearless
too: as if she has never heard of the danger of wishes, of the possibility that they might come cunningly and cruelly true. Perhaps
there is some essence here, encapsulated in this moon-dreamt
moment. My father fixing on someone beautiful, wilful and
unusual, whom he also hoped would be conventionally sub-
servient and devoted. My mother taking a man with brains, looks
and cutting ambition, who stood outside all the clubs she aspired
to, who stood, in fact, outside himself. The purchase of a
mountainside, the application of passion and curiosity to the
dispassionate and primitive business of hill farming; the disre-
garding, by her, of its flaws and ills, by him, finally, of its wonder
and blessings – underneath everything there was this impulse:
two wishes, sliding them into one.

### 14 February

Sunny but cold. Jack arrived. He looked sour, and was. Seems
unable to make one cheerful or pleasant remark. Complaining
now of cold and sore throat. At least we can't be blamed for that.
I took him home as soon as possible and joy oh joy, at 1.30 there
was a clanking in the pipes and the loo filled up with water, the
taps spouted. Did a great wash of clothes before it freezes again
and gave the children hair-washes in a really hot bath for once.
Watched an oil tanker attempt to reach us across the Far Meadow,
but having circled the fields once or twice sliding on a skin of
thawed earth it retreated. In the evening we went to look at
Gwyn's puppies. They are ten days old and the remaining three
are fat as toads. The little girl we have chosen has a white tip to
her tail and growled a tiny growl when I picked her up. Children
very excited about the idea of having a dog. Thinking of names.
I have thought of Floss or Tess. 'What do you think of Tess as a
name, Jack?'

'Doesn't matter what its bloody name is, so long as the bugger comes when it's called.'

### 15 February

I had a bath! And was getting dressed in the bathroom when noticed the oil tanker had reappeared and its dauntless driver, Mr Ferguson, was preparing to unwind its fat pipe and discharge some 300 gallons into our tank. Fantastic Mr Ferguson. He is a man among men. He drives that tanker like a knight charging into battle and there it was sliding and skidding all over the yard as he backed it, only just missing my car and almost flattening the pen wall. He lost the air in his brakes, waited a few minutes, said 'I'm crossing my fingers now,' and then, taking one hand off the wheel to wave his arm out of the cab window, he drove like a man possessed and thundered off down the track.

'He would have routed the German panzer divisions!' I shouted to Pim and we waved and waved as he crashed away.

Jack reappeared later. Less said, as they say, soonest forgotten. I told him to stay at home until he felt better.

Bitterly cold. The winter now upon us is a malevolent yellow. Robert was coming then didn't.

In the absence of the husband, father, man-of-the-house, we were often at the mercy of men, many of whom were coming then didn't. Jenny spent hours, days, on the telephone and in neighbours' farmyards, trying to persuade them to come up the mountain with their cargoes of oil, sheep feed, hay-making machinery, snow ploughs, trailers, tools. She flirted with them, cajoled them, pleaded and demanded, swore when she failed, cursed when they let her down or ripped her off.

'They'd never dare if I was a man,' she stormed regularly. 'They always say they'll come and then they just bloody don't! They'd never try it on like that with Robert . . .'

They knew there would be good money in it: a single woman, apparently desperate for whatever they had, would be charged the top price. Even so, many preferred excuses to the fearsome drive up the mountain, the dizzy pitches and the chassis-gutting track. That winding drive up into isolation, and the lone woman at the end of it, revealed many characters.

Among them were 'good men and true', in Jenny's phrase, without whose kindness life would have become untenable. Foremost among them was Jack, of course, though they gave each other hell when they lost their tempers.

'You're like Mrs Thatcher!' he shouted at her once, and she could be, too – hectoring, relentless, utterly uncompromising. The comparison really got her, though.

'Jack! No! You can't mean it!'

But there were men like Dai the Garage and Gwyn and Pat, who gave their time and strength and skill again and again, because she asked it of them, and never vented any frustration.

Dai became accustomed to the early morning call, 'Dai, I'm so sorry, the bloody car won't start, I'm so sorry, could you possibly . . .?' and to the mysterious 'pinking' sound in the engine, and the snapped fan belts and expired starter motors: our succession of little vehicles performed as tractors, taxis and Land Rovers. Lined with hay, dog hair, mud and sheep shit, they hauled bales, children, animals and feedbags up and down the pitches until they collapsed in heaps of stinking scrap. Dai was their nurse. His smile of greeting, as we pulled on to his forecourt, held a mixture of incredulity and amusement.

'Hello, Mrs Clare, all right?' he always opened, hopefully.

'Hello, dear Dai, well, the thing is the wretched dog has chewed through the seat belt again . . .'

'Oh, right,' he nodded, eyeing the moss growing around the rim of the back window, a rapid grin flitting across his features as he added it to a mental inventory which included the mushrooms which appeared in the boot, and the pair of sheep's ears now poking up over the back seat.

He was patient, forever dashing back into the office to produce VAT receipts for petrol, and generous, charging the bare minimum for maintenance and commiserating with Jenny when the price of a new part caused her to cry out in pain.

'A hundred! It can't be! It can't be!'

'Oh they are, they are. Terrible, I know. I'm sorry . . .'

There followed a moment of silence while she stared at him, forlorn, then he laughed helplessly, and she threw up her hands and grabbed her head in dramatic distress. 'Oh well! That's that then!'

Gwyn, with his expertise, his Land Rover and trailer, his shearing machines, his strong sons and intelligence network of friends and associates, was Jenny's link to the market, and her best hope at shearing, and a prized consultant on all kinds of questions: where to sell, when to sell, which rams to keep back for breeding, how to keep foxes away from the lambing fields.

'I've seen him twice, Gwyn, he's a big dog fox – I don't mind him eating the afterbirth, but I'm worried he might take a lamb, if it's in trouble . . .'

'You know where he's coming and going, do you, Jenny?'

'Oh yes, I've seen his run, there's a gap in the wire, and you can smell him.'

'Get some pitch or some spray, if I were you, and dab it all around there. Something strong – chemical. He won't like it. That'll be the best, since you won't shoot him . . .'

When she missed the bank, or there was a cash flow question, Jenny relied on Pat in town. Pat's grocery shop was on the corner near the ruined walls of the castle, a position which allowed Pat, who spent most of his time on the pavement, a view up and down the High Street. He was a large, sandy-haired man with a red face behind glinting glasses. His voice was very loud; his shop seemed to me the centre of the little town, and Pat its embodiment. He hailed everyone by name. 'Mrs Clare and the boys!' he shouted, as you approached, and, apparently without prying, knew everyone's business.

'Oh Lord, I've run out of money. Perhaps Pat will help,' she muttered, through her smile, as she brought the car to a stop.

'Don't stop it here, Jenny,' Pat boomed. He often directed the traffic.

'Dear Pat, I've stupidly missed the bank . . . could you possibly cash a cheque?'

He regarded her for a short moment, and smiled. With the cash came two oranges, posted through the window into our hands. 'There you are, boys!' he bellowed.

An excellent actress, Jenny did an affecting damsel in distress, but for men like these she did not have to perform. And when the car broke down and she had to get us to school, or the oil burned low in the middle of winter, or when the sheep simply had to go to market, she was as needy as she appeared to be, and 'good men and true' responded. When they had done, and accepted her huge, grateful thanks and small cheques, how many different men must have driven away down the hill, shaking their heads at her strangeness, her prettiness, pig-headedness and determination to survive without one of them at her side.

From the house we watched and waited for them to come, over the brow of the top pitch, along the lane, up the track; and later, watched them go, in their tractors, Land Rovers, vans and cars.

Tankers were particularly prized: in the happy expectation that North Sea oil would fuel a warm, cheap future, Robert and Jenny had installed a Raeburn – a poor man's Aga – at the heart of the house, in the kitchen. As well as rendering that room habitable during the winter, it heated the water. The arrival of Mr Ferguson's bright red face, large voice and small Shell tanker was always as exciting as she describes. For his part, Mr Ferguson, though he delivered to many hill farms, must have dreaded his missions to ours. He was brave and became more cautious. He often aborted attempts and never encountered the disaster he feared. In later years, when tankers were bigger, he stopped coming. Jenny lamented it bitterly and worked the phone again. His successor, Mr White, nearly died trying to reach us.

It was a low, wet winter evening, tipping towards a dirty night, when the bright headlights of the oil tanker appeared suddenly over the top of the pitch. Mr White had never been before, and as he steered through the twisting wood he hoped the worst was over: surely there could not be anything as bad or as steep as the horrible turn at the top of that first pitch. He gunned up the second pitch and felt great relief as the road levelled out gently at the top. Across the fields he caught sight of the yard light and a small farm with its back to the looming mountain. The woman on the phone had instructed him not to try the track at the top of the lane but to go across the meadows. He climbed out and opened the gate, noticing how cold it was up here. The valley was a way below. The grass was dark with rain, but he could make out a faint double line which led diagonally across the fields towards the house. He hauled himself back into the cab and set out.

'Oil tanker!' we cried, and from the window on the landing outside the bathroom, which had the best view, we watched him come.

He crossed the Far Meadow without difficulty. The tracks took him through a gap in a hedge then turned gently uphill, to his left, towards the gate in the top corner of the Middle Meadow. From there an easy track led to the farm. Halfway across the meadow Mr White felt the wheels lose their grip. The tanker paused, lost forward speed, and stopped. He revved the engine and re-engaged the gears for another go, but the wheels spun impotently. Then, slowly at first, the tanker began to slip sideways. As it slid down the gentle slope it leaned, the oil tilted to the downhill side and the slide gathered speed. Peering out, Mr White could see the field ended in a rusty fence, beyond which there was nothing but space and dark treetops. That fence ran along the top of a ten-foot bank above an extremely steep field, one of the Lower Meadows: ripping through the wire, falling, toppling over and over, the tanker's bounding roll down the Lower Meadows would end far below, in the stream and a spectacular explosion. Thirty yards, twenty, fifteen, the tanker turned a slow balletic semicircle as it slid towards its destruction.

It was a shaken man who eventually settled in front of the fire with a cigarette. He had telephoned his firm and his wife to explain what had happened. He was grateful for supper – some cauliflower, a lot of cheese sauce and a rasher of bacon – and refused Mrs Clare's offers to top it up with bread and more cheese. He tried to refuse to join her in a whisky but she was insistent, and poured him a bigger measure than he would have asked for. Her two fair-haired children had extravagant names, posh English accents and identical bowl haircuts. They watched him carefully. At their mother's suggestion they produced a pack of cards: he showed them the basics of poker, explained his nick-name, Chalky, which came from his time in the Merchant Navy, and told them a few stories about that.

He went to bed, after telephoning his wife again and wishing her goodnight, in the Beast House bedroom (named after the shed below it, they said) in a pair of Mrs Clare's husband's old pyjamas. The Beast House was cold under its pitched roof, and accommodated guests, like the princess of the pea fame, atop three double mattresses piled on an old iron bed frame. The room smelled of wool. Burrowing into clammy covers and lying very still, Chalky White listened to the wind skimming over the ridge of the roof, and felt a draught, like a cold finger, brushing his cheek. He dreamed strange dreams.

We were sorry to see him go the next day, after they'd pumped his oil into another tanker and Derwyn's tractor had towed his vehicle back to the road. The field was scored and churned to within yards of the fence, everyone had shaken their head over the near disaster, there was a small slick in the middle of the meadow (which would kill a patch of grass for years) and we would be lucky to get another tanker, ever, but our oil was resup-plied and we had all enjoyed putting Chalky up: the more we waved at departing men the more we wished they would stay, particularly back in 1978.

*16 February*
Feeding almost impossible. Snow and ice. Rob came at tea. Snow after dark.

*17 February*
Very cold but sun blazing by 10.30. Snow thin and very crisp – a bitter east wind but Rob and the children tobogganed in the first meadow. Methuselah is in the Beast House with her lamb. It has a small black patch above one eye – Long John Silver. She is just managing to give it a sip now and again I think. Fed all day it seemed. No help. Robert had a sleep during the day and went to

bed at 9.00. He doesn't want to talk to me. I have been trying but am giving up because I sound banal even to my ears. It was a lovely day though – warm in the sun and then ice crystals clinked in the snow as we walked over it. A woodcock rose from the stream by the cauldron. Marsh tit by Ty Newydd and fox and badger tracks crossing the lane on the pitch and rashly heading for Derwyn's fields.

*18 February*

The worst day of this winter – from every point of view. I have walked around all day with a heart which really does feel as heavy as lead – with dread and apprehension and responsibility so heavy that I found myself turning to Jack of all people for comfort. 'The spring will come?'

'Oh ay,' he said. 'It will.' I long for just one kind word. But ashes. And I'm smoking too much again. A terrible east wind. Almost gale force. The children are frightened by the noise of it in the attic. Dire warnings of 'considerable snow and drifting in S. Wales'. I thought desperately today of shifting us all out of here – perhaps sending the children back to Rob to somewhere where you can be sure of heating and food. Thinking again about selling the sheep. Must do what's best for the children, no matter what. As for my personal happiness it truly doesn't matter. The poor sheep with their thin wool are crouching round the yard and in the woodshed. Methuselah's water bucket in the Beast House has frozen twice. We'll lose our water tomorrow I expect. The ground is rock hard. How do moles fare? And rare birds hop around the kitchen door despite the cats – a yellowhammer, nuthatches, field-fares, redwings. No sun, anywhere, at all.

*Sunday 19 February*
Blizzard.

*Monday 20 February*
Worse. Deadly wind. No water. Dwindling hay.

*Tuesday 21 February*
Ice on snow. Couldn't use wheelbarrow. Flat tyre on car.

*Wednesday 22 February*
Very tired. Wind dropped. Worst weather in South Wales for thirty years.

*Thursday 23 February*
Dug out. Back to normal. Pim back to school – shopping.

*Friday 24 February*
Car tyre mended.

*Saturday 25 February*
Rain rain rain. I feel tired – the week spent surviving. No time
to write this.

This desperate record seems to contain the final fracture: the
day she spends feeding while he toboggans with us is the first of
all the rest. Henceforth he regards the sheep as her business.
When he comes to stay he sleeps in the Beast House bedroom.
He goes to bed in the middle of the day, burying his head under
the pillow. Now I know what it was: wretched depression. But
then it was a mystery. 'What's wrong with Daddy?' we asked.

'He's just very tired,' Jenny said, thinking she was lying.

'What have I done?' Jenny pleaded with him, missing the
point. This was about him, not her. He will not allow any illu-
sions: he is out of it, she is on her own.

'What will happen to us?' she asked him once.

'You'll manage,' he said.

She repeated that story bitterly, but in its cold way it was a
compliment.

His resignation from their adventure crushed them both: his
depression dried his tongue; through guilt or anger or self-
disgust, he could not talk to her. It drove her wild – there was a
pale splash on one of the sitting room walls where she missed him
with a coffee cup – and she made my brother and me promise
that whatever we felt, however angry or upset we were, we would
never 'go silent': she made it taboo. We kept our promises,
throughout our childhoods, teens and twenties; shouting, wailing, swearing and ranting with abandon, but never going silent.

I failed to keep this going and now today is March 20th, Monday.
I thought the weather would never allow us to drench and inject,
with the storms and the rain and Jack's horror of wet trousers and
'messing' with sheep in wet weather. But Spring did come, most

wonderfully, for six warm balmy days and with Rob here at the weekend to look after the children Jack and I drenched and injected and took our time in the warm sun and enjoyed it. We – Pim Twinks Rob and I – were out and about without our coats and I even persuaded Jack to take off his jacket though he insisted on piling another old mac on to protect himself from possible dampness in the fleeces. I tried not to talk to the sheep too much which I know Jack finds soppy. 'Come on, darling,' I say if I'm not careful – 'stand easy.' Jack confines himself to 'Stand still, you bugger' and hisses a lot like an angry snake, or perhaps an old ostler with a troublesome horse. If things are really bad – if the animal is wildly frightened or finding being held unbearable and rears and struggles Jack's ultimate anger and impatience becomes 'Well. Well. Well.' It is wisest then for both sheep and me to keep absolutely quiet. I like handling sheep. I like the opportunity to look at them closely and stroke their heads. Their eyelashes are long – their wool comes in many textures – short and tough like Elizabeth's – hempy and long like the old ewe with shadows under her eyes – wavy and silky which looks like it's been to the hair-dresser. I am better at injecting than I was, though to get these short fat needles under the skin and not between the skin layers nor into the ribs is tricky. And sometimes in pinching the skin up you go in and out the other side and only notice when the stuff drips down the wool to the ground. Now and again we paused for Jack to rest, for me to have a cigarette and open another 200 mls of the drench. It protects them against horrible ills and hopefully their lambs. From across the valley we heard foxhounds in full cry and through the warm afternoon saw the pin figures of the horses and riders as they rode along the tops. 'Got an earth in that spin-ney there,' said Jack pointing to a dim cluster of trees. The voices of the hounds had stopped. 'The vixen will be in cub by now,' I said, and hoped they would leave her alone.

We were pleased with ourselves when we'd done. Jack said his legs ached, so I did too. He said he felt buggered up, so I – not to be outdone – said I was too. I have become allergic to his endless complaints and to forestall them I'd been saying things like 'Catching them here isn't hard is it, Jack, just awkward.' But it *is* hard, no matter how tamely they stand, and Jack had caught and held, with only two upsets, over 200 sheep. A grinding task done with marvellous patience and stoicism. His touch is quite wonderful – we could so easily have miscarriages after crowding them and bumping them, but moving between them as we do nothing is rough so we didn't get miscarriages.

What we did get was a shock. The sheep were all released and there they were grazing away in the evening sun when one by one they all sat down. This seemed odd because we took them some more hay which they should have been famished for, but what was odder were their ears. They were all hanging like dishcloths. 'Look at their ears, Jack, for heaven's sake, look at their ears! What on earth's happened to them?' He didn't say anything for a moment, just gazed. The flock looked like rabbits in the rain, with their ears dangling straight down. Some had one ear still standing up, though on the way down, and the effect was appalling, rakish. In the eyes of the animals was a resignation and gloom. They looked ill. And very funny. 'I've poisoned them. That's it. Poisoned them. That drench was recommended by the vet but just *wait* till I telephone him.'

'Never seen the like of that in my life,' said Jack. We wagged our heads, I vowed vengeance on the vet, we prophesied dead ewes, dead lambs and all the time they just looked at us with their tea-towel ears and reproach. It was a golden evening, still and warm, birds busy in the hedges. Tired and rather giggly I drove Jack home. Next morning most of the ears were up again.

We went up the valley to Gwyn's farm and collected our new pup. The little dog was eventually named Lark. She was bouncy and intelligent and she loved men. She was very fond of Jack, who showed her more tolerance than affection, and she adored Robert. Her favourite thing was walking up the mountain with him, or any of the male students who came to stay with us and work during the lambing – the 'lambers' – or, when we grew older, despite our shouts and sticks, which scared her – my brother and me. But we were five and three, years from our first unaccompanied climb to the top of the mountain. Lark could have been a good little sheepdog, but she was lazy and poorly trained – Jack was not expert in teaching and handling dogs, nor was Jenny. To get Lark to work well took a lot of coaxing and shouting and some luck; if anything went wrong, or anyone lost their temper, she would look at her feet, lick her lips in a pained way and skulk into the nearest hedge, out of reach of retribution, withdrawing from the game. Neither furious shouts nor pleading through gritted teeth would coax her back then, and her two cocked ears and light brown, slightly raised eyebrows could be a very galling sight, as you ran to and fro, chasing bloody sheep, while she watched. Squirrels and moles drove her wild with hunt lust. She would chase anything from a bee to a car, and spent hours and hours sitting neatly at the feet of trees, like a black question mark, her head tilted back, eyes fixed on a squirrel. Even for a young dog she had superb hearing and would give you advance notice of any interesting sound. When she came and sat on your feet it would be a few minutes before you heard the first grumble of thunder, which terrified her. I think she would have liked a more various life than the farm offered her. The approach of walkers would be signalled with great excitement, and you had to watch her then or, when the little figures appeared on the sky-line, Lark would be off to join them. If she gave us the slip she would have to be recovered, hours later, in the best case, from the campsite in the village, where, having befriended everybody, charming them with her prettiness and self-possession, she would be in the process of relieving them of bacon and any other titbits she could get. Recovery missions could be entertaining.

She had been missing all day, having disappeared, deliberately, exactly when she was needed for work, and finally we piled into the car and went down the hill to look for her. Sure enough, at the bottom of the campsite, chained to a post, there she was. A young German woman was feeding and petting her.

'There she is, the creep! They've chained her up. Christ! She's feeding her bacon. Would you please get her!'

We were in a hurry, anxious not to encounter the owners of the campsite, who were as sick of this as we were. As Lark saw the car she flinched. I leapt out, charged over and unclipped the chain. From the car, Jenny and Alexander scolded over my shoulder.

'Wretched animal! Come here!'

'Bad dog! Bad dog!'

The young camper was distressed, and protested on Lark's behalf in poor English and, incomprehensible to us, German.

'She's very – (cuff!) – very – (cuff!) – naughty!' I huffed at the woman, cuffing and dragging the cringing, reluctant hound towards our beaten up and filthy car.

'Get in the back, you bloody thing!' shouted my mother.

'Bad!' yelled my brother and I, and we rattled off in a flurry of foul looks and curses, which changed as we went into hysterical laughter at the camper's expression.

Lark was a funny, lovely dog, a welcome fourth resident of the farm. But perhaps her greatest contribution to my life, and certainly to that of my brother, was her son, Toss, a dog who once saved our lives and also almost killed us, and himself, laughing. Before Toss, though, was the first spring of Lark's life, that of 1978.

Celandines, crisp leaves of the Lords and Ladies (Wild Arum), warm blue skies, two blackbirds nesting in the garden hedge, a pair of nuthatches in the ash tree – a frog and frogspawn in the pond, ravens flying high with large twigs in their beaks, heading for the larch wood. In the warm sun the ewes weren't so hungry for bales.

Since then the lion element of March has ousted the spring. Snow again, a thick wet blanket deep and soft and not even useful for tobogganing. Bitter northwest winds and southwest gales. Jack and I feed feed feed – a dreadful chore I have almost come to dread. He is so slow, and the sheep so ravenous for the nuts it is well nigh impossible to keep one's feet as they descend like stormtroopers to attack the buckets. I have vanished under their trampling hooves half a dozen times but even eyeball to eyeball with Tommy, buried among sheep, he never used his horns.

Rob arrived on Thursday evening in the sun. So we were prepared, waiting, excited. Huge are the ewes; one or two quite alarming. I pray I haven't overfed them to bring gigantic lambs they can't get out.

But like watched pots they do not boil. The old green biddy brought a tiny, perfectly dead premature lamb yesterday (Friday) and today (Easter Saturday) two lovely Suffolk twins and a small Welsh tup, but that's all. They boil and boil but do not come. I'm glad in a way because the weather is dreadful today. Hail pinging down the chimney, northwest wind slicing through the meadows and rain with drops as large as peas thudding on the roofs. Not a good day to be born. Later, dark curtains of snow and sleet swept across the meadows with a rushing sound. You could hear it coming. The wind veered in the evening – went warmer to the west. The sky was wild and lemon, black snow clouds herding over our mountain to the east – large stars in islands of duck egg blue. Just before dark – to confirm my worst fears – I drew a truly enormous lamb from one of our calmest yellow tickets. She had tried and tried and lay with her head on the ground watching me – almost asking for help. Since then, to Marigold, a stocky little tup whiter than snow, on Easter Sunday at dawn.

Easter Monday – The lambs came.

Easter Tuesday – Pat crossing the street to say, quietly, 'They found my father, yesterday, drowned in the river.'

# 5

# Battles

O UR VALLEY'S RECORDED history begins in violent conflict. One of its earliest stories concerns the Trwch Trwyth, a herd of Irish swine, one of which had between his ears a comb, a pair of shears and a razor. King Arthur, so the story goes, learned that these objects were vital to the fortunes of his kingdom, and sent word to the Trwch, a band of cursed knights who had been turned into swine. The Trwch responded, hotly, that their lot was already as terrible as it could be and that nothing would persuade them to surrender their implements. Arthur's messenger replied that Arthur was resolved to have the kit, and would not be deterred. Hearing this, the herd put the people of Ireland to the slaughter, swept eastwards, crossed the Irish Sea and landed in Wales, goring, tusking, raging, rampaging after Arthur and his people. So began a dozen wild scraps through west and mid Wales. Many people died, but the pigs took casualties too. One boar, Llwydawc, became separated from his kin and was pursued to the Ystrad Yw, in the county which is now Breconshire. These boar were so terrible that a brush with their razor-sharp and septic hair was enough to kill a man. The men of the Ystrad Yw were farmers in peacetime, who cooked meat and drank milk (but ate little bread, as was common in Wales). They passed their time in the hills and brakes, wore their hair short so that it did not catch in thorns and brambles, and were not strangers to the arts of war. Chroniclers record that the people of this part of South Wales, their flatter lands being vulnerable to invasion from across the Severn, and the hills their refuge and playground, devoted enthusiastic thought and practice to fighting, exercising and tactics.

They shot short, immensely powerful bows made from young elm. The effect of their arrows, at close range, was compared to the arquebus: a large matchlock musket on a stand.

The boar made his stand somewhere in our valley, almost certainly near a stream, and I would guess high up, where he would have had the mountain at his back. *The Red Book of Hengest* (*c.* 1350), recording events which would have taken place hundreds of years before, says that Llwydawc killed a great many men and animals in the fight. I imagine it took place at dusk, under a flying sky, the thorns all laden with cold rain and the grass slippery as ice. Fat streams babbled over their red banks. I have often charged through the bracken and scrub in similar conditions, but never with a real spear, or a sharp sword. I have chased animals along the hill fence, and cornered them, and I can imagine what it must be like to try to kill one then. But not a great boar, the size of a small car, though both heavier and quicker over this terrain, on his trotters, their split nails sharper than razors, the rotting flesh of his previous kills lacing their edges with poison. You are close to him now, your brothers beside you, panting, and he's watching you, looking specifically at you. He squeals, something like a scream, and comes. Imagine the speed of his charge, as your vision narrows, shutting out the open mouths and raised hands of your friends as he comes, head down, tusks like great bloody teeth and his red eyes steady on your groin and lower belly. It is awful to think of running for your life over the stones and slanting stumps of the gloomy hillside, so perhaps you would fight. Or perhaps, at that instant, you heard your brother's bow loose, and his perfect, killing shaft, exploding through its heart or brain, dropped the monster at your feet.

The men of the Ystrad Yw killed the boar Llwydawc, after losing scores of their own. What they did with the body is not recorded. They would have dragged it away from the stream, but I cannot imagine they ate it. Perhaps they torched it on the mountain. Nothing but the myth remains.

Human invaders left permanent marks on the valley. The remains of Roman forts and roads are still here: there was a squadron of Spanish cavalry based on a small tump where three valleys meet, and perhaps their genes linger in the population, many of whom are small, dark-haired and bright-eyed. Centuries after their withdrawal, the Normans arrived, sweeping into the mountains from the northeast. They built fortifications and churches, and their descendants formed a nobility whose allegiances lay with the kings beyond the border. Centuries of struggle between natives and invaders were fought out in the fields around their castles; Jack used to say that certain of the flat valley meadows were rich and fertile thanks to gallons of intermingled, battle-spilled Welsh and English blood.

My brother and I began fighting as soon as he was able to challenge me, and we continued, occasionally in anger, but overwhelmingly in play, for years. I was bigger and stronger, with more reach, but he was brave and passionate, and crafty. He could throw and kick better than I could; though he took a while to speak he walked early, and when he could run he was very quick. I'm pretty fast over short distances, and if I have to I can run for a while, but Alexander could keep out of reach. He was capable of ripping my jacket, kicking out, socking me in the head with a well-flung stone and then sprinting off.

When he did exactly this, once, I returned to the house in tears. Jenny was unsympathetic – I had punched him. 'You didn't have to slug him, Pim,' she said. Another fight in the wood led me to deal him another, this time clearly unjust blow. He was outraged, and I admitted he owed me one.

'You can do what you like, I won't hit back,' I said. I turned and began walking away. Alexander came up behind me and smashed me one over the ear and the back of my neck. It really hurt, I spun round, fists bunched, to see him regarding me with suspicion and reproach. I hissed and unclenched my fists.

'Well done,' he said, with feeling.

The battle remained one of the principal metaphors of our life. Conflict against the elements; the lurking presence of death; the confrontations with horror, day-to-day victories and the under-lying fear of final forced retreat were often with us. As the first snows, pale outriders of winter, occupied the crests of the high-est hills, Jenny pulled on her tattered lambing coat, her boots and her hat with a blend of resignation and anticipation, the very image of a seasoned soldier going out once more, and when the weather finally relented, months later, she took them off with the tired relief of one whose bloodiest work was done.

*23 May 1978*
After a long cold spring, the first day I could cast my clouts. Yesterday, amid trauma and swearing from Jack we drenched the lambs in humid sun. We also sawed off the tip of Tommy's horns again. The most beautiful morning – wonderful to be alive and here – sparkling dew, the air cold and clear – the sun jumping up over the hill behind us, the hedges, the young green leaves, the swallows' backs, Lark's new coat, glowing in the sun.

Lazy afternoon. The children ran home across the meadows and were hot in their jerseys. Then they played in the water trough and tipped buckets of water into the yard making a stream down to the pens. Jack, *fanatical* about waste, told them to stop. I lay in the hedge underneath his garden and pretended to be asleep until Lark came and told me she loved me by walking over my face. I listened to the sounds in the hot afternoon – the hiss of the water in the trough as the ballcock bobbed – the children talking and chasing Lark – a flock of rooks on the mountain, on the sky-line tumbling, lambs bleating now and again – northwest wind sighing through the firs behind Jack's garden, and absolute silence from him planting leek seeds one by one.

The first day of summer. I thought back to the winter as I looked back into the yard; the children at the trough, Lark, the swallows.

The snow and blizzards, ice and the struggle to get the bales across the yard in wheelbarrow and toboggan – the *bitter* wind – and now young leaves uncurling on the sycamore, starlings, great tits, nuthatches, stonechats and redstarts, wagtails nesting around the house and the cuckoo calling furiously for its mate and with its greedy marigold eye spying out nests of smaller birds and deciding which to disrupt. A thief in daylight but bringing a dangerous gift.

I found Pim a strange flower and saved it to show him. A Wild Arum with its single sinister green petal, and when we opened it to examine the pistil and the stamens and the premature seeds which grow into fruity scarlet berries in the autumn, he was delighted.

Jack's garden was an almost secret place, mysterious and abundant. Out of bounds unless Jack was there, it was both alluring and forbidding; enticing in the same way that Mr McGregor's garden drew in Peter Rabbit of Beatrix Potter's tale. The garden was on a crown of ground overlooking the yard gate, screened from the track by tall hedge trees. The garden gate was at the top of a tottering path of stones cut into the steep bank behind the Big Barn; beyond it the garden was a castle keep of growth and life. Among the bean poles, with their bright red flowers, like scraps of a pirate's kerchief, were butterflies; skippers and cabbage whites, kissing and shimmering between the stalks. In the far corner was a rhubarb like a vast sea anemone; around the edges were more butterflies, meadow browns and red admirals, stumbling about above the thick perimeter of nettles. In the middle was the earth, the rich, dark red earth, a deep cake of colour and worms. Jack cut it and turned it with endless slow care, and miraculously, it seemed to me, it gave him bright startling carrots, twisted like witches' noses; parsnips and potatoes; onions and cabbages, peas sweeter than sugar. While he worked we scrambled up and down the bank below the gate, plucking at the pennywort which grew between the stones. The waxy little dishes of the plant's leaves intrigued me; I reduced them to a sticky paste. 'It's an antiseptic,' Jenny said. 'Ask Jack. When he nearly sliced his sister's leg off with his scythe his mother filled the wound with pennywort, and it healed. Poor Beat! Imagine! She came too close when you were hay-making, didn't she, Jack?'

Jack nodded, and I looked at his strong, thick-veined hands on the smooth shaft of the spade. I had seen him swing his scythe.

I looked at Alexander's legs and imagined it, imagined being the perpetrator of something like that. Jack smiled.

*Thursday*

Another glorious day – cold to start with N.E. wind but by lunchtime HOT – T-shirt only weather. Sorted the Patch out after drenching, tailing and marking the lambs. Spot does seem to be cured. Her udder is soft again. She and Arabella and Loppy (who worries me a little because I love her so much and she so small these days) have gone back to the flock. Spot's lamb – Arabella – is quite beautiful. The pride and joy of this year's flock. She always trots up for a talk and nibbles the tops of wellies to get attention. Jack said, 'I will miss her – she do always come to me.' I went to collect Pim and then on to town to buy dog meal (Lark must now be vegetarian I've decided) and cold cream and 2 pairs of plimsolls.

Children got out at Far Meadow gate. They set off across the field to talk to Jack who was 'tidying up the meadow' in preparation for the hay. Pim and Twinky stopped halfway and took down their trousers. Watching each other in a wide field of daisies with the view below them they weed. The level of lead in the air in cities has become alarmingly high according to some expert on the *World at One* today. Moved ewes into the L-Shape. Children, Lark and Jack and I watched Snowdrop and Simon this evening by the old machine. They were playing as it got dark. Hot weather forecast. We need rain *soon* for the grass. Owls carolling tonight.

*26 May – 3 June*

To Pembrokeshire with Ursie and the children [our three cousins] for eight days of hot hot sun. Pimmy got sunburnt. I *sat* most of the time and watched the green surf and the silhouettes of the family running and playing across the sand, and did *nothing*. It was lovely.

Despite a screeching aversion to cold water, Jenny loves the seaside, and she loved taking us to it. Once a year, normally towards the beginning of September, we went to the west coast, sometimes with family and friends. They were magical weeks, in one of the most quietly wild and beautiful regions of Wales.

There is one near-endless beach with tiny stones glinting like gems in its rock pools; there is the red beach, which has a stack of boulders like a dinosaur which you can swim through, and where once after a great storm we watched the largest waves I had ever seen lining up to swallow the rocks and torment the cliffs in sets of seven. In the infinite splashes of blue and white above the coast there were choughs and ravens, peregrines, kestrels and squadrons and squadrons of gulls, still-winged on perpetual patrol, line astern across the updraughts.

We always stayed in the same cottage in the same village, rented to my mother for a nominal fee by her old headmistress. It is the only place where I have been able to wake up at exactly the end of the night, and it became a tradition with me to dress and go down through the quiet to the front, then up to the point, and out along the cliffs, wide-eyed and suddenly awake, watching the sky gently extracting itself from the dark arms of the sea. Oystercatchers in their dinner jackets pipe the reveille, jackdaws chatter, boasting about their dreams, and out beyond the islands the gulf sky to the far southwest is a particular pale white-blue, the tone of pure air, washed, rinsed and scoured by last night's squalls, catching the sunrays now, as the swells of cloud billow with light and the first warmth of the morning reaches for the cliff tops, where the thick and sodden turf rolls over, like God's green shoulder, down to the gasp and grasp of the sea.

These weeks awakened and fuelled my fascination for birds. I do not know which I learned to identify first, probably one of our very own carrion crows (always referred to as 'the bloody crows', 'those buggers' or 'those bastards'), but I remember the thrills of my first close encounters with buzzards, like magnificent little Welsh eagles, and ravens, kings of the crow family; fast, manoeuvrable and powerful as hell, with their beards and great knife bills. I looked them all up in books, poring over their stats and pictures – I preferred paintings to photographs of birds; within a love of birds, as in a love of fungi or flowers, is a love of art and art-rich books, where most of us get our best views of the rarest species.

I liked the jackdaws which hung around the playground at school, clearing up after break times, but on a dawn walk along the cliffs, though I adored their chatter, from a distance they had the drawback of behaving, looking and almost sounding like choughs.

Choughs are the Spitfires of the bird world. They fly better, look better, sound better, and in fact behave better than all their crow cousins. Their plumage is blue-black, with the same iridescence as the handsome rook. Their legs are bright, wax red; their matching scarlet beaks are both elegant and businesslike: down-curved, sharp. They fly like stunt pilots, hurling themselves into the swirling currents below the cliff edge with casual élan before rocketing up above you, flaps down while they take a look around and make sure you're watching when they break, peeling around, gathering speed for a quick climb and a near-stall into a dramatic stoop, a wings-closed, vertical plummet towards the sea. 'Chow!' they shout, and 'Chaw!'

They pull out whenever they feel like it, broad black wings, long fingerlike primary feathers extended, catching all their velocity and turning it to pure control; horizontal, diagonal or vertical speed, whichever the bird fancies. You lose him for a second and the next instant he's sitting on a rock, looking at you, and keeping an eye out for ants. Choughs would make excellent pirates – they have it all, even the battle-cries – but they have not developed tastes for robbery or murder. They prefer to catch their own ants. Piracy they leave to skuas.

The wonder of birds lay partly in their liberation from the land, and partly, paradoxically, in their miraculous conformity. It always amazed and delighted me to find birds where the books said I would find them, looking just like their pictures, and behaving as their descriptions said they would. So the bird book says of the redstart 'widespread summer visitor, found in old woodlands', and sure enough, in the succulent sunlight of May, there in the ancient wood on the way up to the house, flitting between the hedges and lower branches of the oak, there would be the beautiful bird, with its handsome black mask and flashing scarlet tail.

Birds in their freedoms, in their wills and ways, define a relationship with the land and sky that I crave, hopelessly, in the same way I used to wish for wings. A man in a field is an intruder, a visitor, at best a custodian. A bird in the same field is a focal point, a finishing touch, a vivid, living, acting detail, a flourish of pure existence. I woke up once at the farm, pulled back the curtains, looked out at a sunlit morning, limpid mountain light blessing everything, and saw, forty feet beyond my window, making its way slowly up the grassy bank, a big and utterly beautiful red grouse, his plumage a mottle of russets and chestnuts, his little wattles like scarlet exclamations. He was delicious, in his pride and beauty, as he picked his way up the bank, looking for shoots; he bewitched me. I wanted to touch him, to eat him, to be him; I wanted to watch him all day. I can see him still. His power was that of Wallace Stevens' jar — as the poet says:

> I placed a jar in Tennessee,
> And round it was, upon a hill,
> It made the slovenly wilderness surround that hill.

In exactly the same way, like the moment of creation, the foundation of a point in space, that grouse made the morning surround him.

A component of this powerful attraction to birds is the hunting instinct. A man with a gun in a field is a hunter. When the beasts and birds flee him then, they do not do so, as normal, because he is other, weird, and dangerous by nature, but because, like the fox and the falcon, he is a predator looking for prey. And like the fox and the falcon, he can only succeed in his hunt if he enters the landscape, learns the rhythms and habits of its inhabitants, shakes off his 'civilisation' and returns to the world his species has been abandoning for centuries. I never hunted for food or sport; my outings were more like sallies of war. Much as I love choughs, ravens and rooks, I would happily gun down squawking ranks of their crow and magpie cousins; indeed, I have spent weeks attempting to engineer their slaughter. Daily I looked out of the window and scanned the trees in case one had turned up in the orchard. I regard them as ministers of the devil, and, thanks to their infernal cleverness, and no doubt promiscuity, the entire valley is overrun with them.

Jack and my father went after them with the shotgun, using the old blue Morris as a hide – it eventually broke down near the Middle Meadow gate, and they would huddle in it, the cold double barrel at the ready – but they killed, as I remember, no crows. Crows know when you are carrying, and they understand the approximate range of a gun. I reckon they can accurately assess the different threat presented by air rifles, and they are infinitely suspicious. Their taste for a sheep's eyes and tongue is shared by magpies, which also go for the udders and anus of the victim, and we have known both species drill directly into the flank of a stricken, but still living sheep, plucking out a ribbon of bloody guts like so much pasta.

I have shot at dozens of crows, mostly from extreme range and with little success, except once. One leafy early summer day in the wood I surprised a raucous family, two inky parents and a flock of kaarking kids, and they could not see me as I crouched directly below them, peering through the foliage. I shot one, trembling like an alcoholic in a flood of adrenalin, and they all yelled and swore and jumped around in the canopy, but they still could not see me, and an airgun is very quiet, no louder than clapped hands. My victim lay cooling in the leaf litter while his brothers and sisters shouted and squawked and I inched silently forward. Then, there, unbelievably, twenty-five yards above me and dead ahead, was one of the crows, high in a tree, beak wide open, mid squawk. I shot him too, and took the brace home in my game bag. It is an unforgettable feeling, triumphant, vindicated, but also humbled by the dealing of death; grateful for the chances, guilty for taking them.

*Sunday 4 June*
The rain came at noon. The earth, baked hard, and the house, warmed all through – but particularly the bedrooms, being under the hot stone tiles – seemed hardly to feel it. Two days later after

cooler wind and further showers the fields still need more rain. Yet the grass does grow – not much in the butt – but it *looks* fresh and the 'bents' are high in the Horse Fields, the buttercups and daisies high in the meadows. The cuckoo loud in the ash tree. Hope she's not thinking of invading the nuthatch's snug little hole which is halfway up it. (A perfect residence with delightful prospect over the valley one might say!) – but probably cuckoo too large to push her egg into the hole.

Sheep farmers look at grass with expertise equivalent to an Inuit regarding snow. 'Bents' are long-stemmed grasses with a sheaf of seeds at the head. 'Feg' and 'sheep's feskew' are the best kinds of growth, the thick stuff you get on high moorland, the diet of those lively mountain sheep you see if you drive across the Brecon Beacons or any high pasture. At the other end of the scale there is 'bare', which is self-explanatory, no grazing, and short of this there is 'a bit to pick' – a city dweller looking at a field of this will see acres of short greenish grass, but a farmer will frown and say there's a bit to pick, but the animals will have to be moved soon. There is generally grass under the bracken, but it must be bitter and short of goodness, because sheep are not fond of it. 'Ronk', Jack called it – a corruption of 'rank'. They would rather not eat the growth under the hedges either, though if left long enough on a bare field they will. 'The butt' is the very lowest level of grass against the ground, and thus a measure of its potential crop – a field of short grass which is 'thick in the butt' will sustain a flock for a while. Hay fields, with their many grasses, clovers, daisies and buttercups, are the zenith of the farmer's achievement with his (or her) grass. By being careful with the amount of time the sheep spent in the meadows we gained a luxurious, diverse growth every year, ready for harvesting in late summer. One year, in an effort to improve the yield, Jenny invested in bags of organic fertiliser: sacks of dried seaweeds, sands and tiny little shells. The three of us trudged up and down the fields for days, scattering the stuff by hand. It felt slightly absurd. Then Jenny released a few sheep on to it.

'Oh look, they like the fertiliser . . . crumbs, they really go a bundle on it, it must be the salt . . . Oh, really! Look! They're guzzling it all up, the pigs!' And that was the end of the fertiliser.

*7 June*
My 40th birthday! And I remember so well thinking 13 was old. A dull drizzle on and off all day. Spent the morning walking the flock with Jack and maggoting. We found three with grubs – he got soaked and when I went on alone I found Timmy Tiptoes also twitching. Managed to trim her easily – shears sharper and she very quiet. I talked to her while I did it and when I found the nest in her tail and they began their frenzied wriggling she ground her teeth and seemed almost grateful and cooperative as I got them out. Later I fetched Betty from her farm who came to tea bearing a birthday cake – not the most tactful of coffee sponges, having '40' emblazoned across it in small red balls! – but absolutely delicious and so very kind of her and I haven't had a birthday cake since I was 25. Jack and I and Betty drank Fine Fare Champagne and we lit a fire and it was very pleasant. My husband sent a card but did not telephone. At 10.15 dogs were hunting in the L-Shape and the Rough Field and the sheep over there stampeded to the race at the bottom of the Patch, very distressed and baying to their lambs. Got to bed late and suddenly realised I hadn't seen Annie for days. Worried about her for about an hour – seems so odd she hadn't trotted up for nuts – before being joined by Pim who warmed me up and we went to sleep at last. The end of my birthday.

Betty was a white-haired widow, and the only other woman farming in the valley. She often spoke of her husband, 'my dear Bryn', she said tenderly, seeming to recall a life of complete happiness which death had stolen from her; 'my Bryn', she repeated, refusing to let him go. She lived in a mournful, shadowed farmhouse, with a wild tribe of cats, dozens of them, and a sheep dog, with whom she shared beautifully cooked dinners, served on china. Her eyes were as quick as a bird's. She was like a grandmother and she dealt straight with us. 'How many sheep in there?' she asked shrewdly, after I had crossed her orchard. 'You don't know? A farmer's son should *always* count.' She was an inspiration to Jenny.

'How Betty manages I will never know,' she would pant, struggling with one of the heavy mineral feedblocks. 'But she does . . . she can even bang in posts!'

On another occasion, when she was babysitting us, we discussed one of our neighbours, Idris, who I said 'should be in the loony bin'.

'The what?' Betty demanded.

'The loony bin in Talgarth.'

'You mean the mental hospital, do you? Who calls it that?'

'Mum does!'

'Will she call it that when she's in there?'

I did not have to think long. 'Yes!'

'Well, it's very disrespectful. While you're here, you'll call it the mental hospital.'

— * —

Around this time, in the first hot yawns of full summer, we went badger watching. The conditions had to be just right: a warm, still evening after a sunny day, with no wind to carry our scent.

'Would you like to go badger watching, boys?' my mother asked, knowing the answer.

'Oh yeah!' we chorused.

'Don't say yeah, say "yes". We'll need to be camouflaged. Go and put on something dark green or brown, nothing pale, and meet me in the yard.'

We assembled and set off down the track, remarking on the wild roses which later in the season would carry vermilion berries, like clusters of balloons, each stuffed, as my brother and I well knew, with feathered seeds which made the most vicious itching powder. We stuck to the track and ignored the sheep, Jenny ducking their greetings like a film star trying to go incognito. Down the lanes, under the hazels we went, watching our step, avoiding prematurely fallen nuts. At the bottom of the first pitch we paused by the gate to the Horse Fields.

'From now on no talking,' Jenny whispered. 'Tread where

I tread, and go very slowly. When we get close, do what I do. We'll crouch down and keep very still, like statues. We'll have to wait, but it'll be worth it if they come out. The cubs will be big enough to ramble about, but they'll start off playing around the setts, I should think. We might be lucky. Are you ready?'

We nodded.

One after another we followed her, cautiously climbing the gate at the hinge end and holding it steady for each other. Jenny stuck to the line of the fence, pointing out fallen ash twigs to be avoided. The sun had turned well over the skyline and the black-birds were pink-pinking in the hedges, confirming their claims on the world. The cooling land sent up the first twinges of breeze to nudge the treetops, but Jenny had anticipated it and correctly guessed its currents; we were downwind of the badger setts.

The wood was a dimming, brooding thing. The different heights of the trees formed spires and aerial alleyways above the narrow gully which divided the land. The drop was so steep that we were level with the crown of the canopy; the curly whisper-ing of the stream was barely audible, two hundred feet below.

As we drew nearer the setts Jenny bent double, trying to keep her silhouette below a badger's horizon, and we went slowly after her, copying every move. We inched up a swell in the ground, then crept down, just over the lip of the bank.

Twenty yards from the setts we stopped. Our mother placed us just in front of her and we all sat, settled, and tried to keep com-pletely still. There were more than a dozen holes ahead of us, each with its raised stoop where grass had covered mounds of excavated earth, but Jenny pointed wordlessly to two where the earth was fresh and scattered with the dried grass of badger bedding. We fixed our eyes on these.

As all our human motion drained away we became as still as stumps, and sank slowly into a kind of trance. Our ears brought us every tiny rustle and scuff of the world in its lengthening moments; the distant exchanges of a mountain ewe and lamb; the buzz of a motorcycle from the valley; the pillow talk of wood pigeons. As the light lowered to nocturne blues and lacquering greens all our senses stretched; we felt the dusk's harmony like concert-goers – its mystery, melancholy and promise seemed to spread outwards from the wood. It was as though we were almost invisible, our bodies forgotten, leaving nothing but a set of senses, like a family of ghosts, until a sudden flurry of loud chiming cries burst out of a bush nearby, as brash and outraged as a burglar alarm.

'Blackbird,' Jenny mouthed in our ears. 'He'll leave us alone, don't turn a hair.'

We willed him away, defying him with our stillness. After a series of ringing accusations, during which I sent him a stream of psychic abuse, he relented, and dived away to investigate something else. The first rabbit appeared, conjuring himself from a patch of nettles, motionless at first, as if engaging us in a keep-still competition. A minute passed before he lopped forward and sniffed the grass, whereupon the rest of his tribe began appearing, bobbing and hopping, their white scuts amazingly bright against the shadow-gathering field.

And then, materialising as suddenly as the rabbit, a large grey shape appeared at the mouth of one of the setts. A long face, with a beautiful silky black nose, black eye mask and white cheeks contemplated us with what seemed like great solemnity.

We barely breathed. The badger's snout lifted as she tested the air. She seemed to gather more than scent; she seemed to sniff the atmosphere of the quiet evening, the spirit of it, as though she knew there was something about, but could not detect threat in it. After a few moments of peering at us she emerged, followed by first one, then another, then a third snuffling cub. She nuzzled and sniffed them, grunting softly as if reminding them of dos and don'ts. They were adorable, like fat little bears, full of play and trepidation. Soon they were tumbling around, venturing out and dashing back in, pratfalling and beetling about. I knew my own expression was reflected in the faces of my mother and brother; we watched with disbelieving, delighted smiles. The cubs squeaked and wrestled and rolled, until their mother marshalled them, and for one moment paused, looked straight at us, as if cautioning us not to move. For a few seconds two families regarded one another, then the badger turned, her cubs went with her, and they vanished into the wood.

We gave them a couple of minutes, then stood, stiffly, and backed away as quietly as we had come. We joined hands as we went back up the pitch, and tried to keep our thrill to whispers.

'Magical!'

'Amazing!'

'Did you see them! Did you see those cubs!'

It was a shared epiphany. Having approached so reverently, in the hope of merely seeing our wild neighbours without alarming them, we had, for a few moments, experienced the world as they did. We sped back to the farm, vigorous with happiness. The dew-smell rose in the meadows and we were as light as if we had all been blessed. We had known the edge of an evening wood as a badger knows it. For that twilight time we had slipped the separa-tion between us and the world. We were of the mountain, and of the wood, and it was as though the animals, the wild creatures, had allowed it. It was bewitching.

Our mother impressed on us that we were custodians, privileged and responsible, not so much owners as tenants, like the badgers, of a tiny portion of this crumpled, timeless land. By the Horse Field gate was an oak, older than anything but the mountain itself, a mighty tree, hollowed and bowed, sprung from an acorn, I imagined, when the only lights in the valley at night were the campfires of Owain Glyndwr's armies.

'Do you think it saw the Romans?' we asked Jenny.

'Probably its grandfather did,' she said. 'How I do love this tree!'

We stopped beneath it often. In its monumental age, in the generations of living things which had passed by it, was the assur-ance of our place in a sequence which had no imaginable begin-ning or end. To pause under the prodigious sinews of its hunched shoulders and stare at the valley was to stand for a moment with the great parade of its witnessed history, to sense the vast proces-sion which had passed and which was still passing, from spiders and bluetits to kings on their chargers, and to feel time bending in the face of so much life.

Inside the Big Barn, stamped on the door with the brands each used to mark his sheep, were the initials of the two previous tenants, Emrys and Derwyn. We added our own, and looking at them gave us a feeling of great pride. It was the right place to make your mark, the Big Barn; it seemed to be the last thing about the farm that would ever change, the place where all its businesses of life and death were transacted.

*Friday 23 June*
While the children slept Jack and I worked to make the Big Barn fit for shearing. Moved all the old hay to top bay – swept, and laid bracken over two thirds of the barn floor to protect the fleeces from hay. He worried about the shearing and the weather – also 'very doubtful' about my abilities as lifter and catcher. I am too. Later (9.30) Mervyn drove up bringing his bedroom carpet.
   'They will lie easier if they've something under them,' he said. The carpet – black and quite lushly piled – had been damaged when the roof blew off his house in the winter. Nevertheless a thoughtful and generous gesture I thought. 'Who's the catcher?' said he.
   'I am.'
   'Oh. I see.'
   'You don't think I'll manage it then?'
   'No,' he said, straight and quietly. Then, 'But we'll do the best we can.'
   I like him. Competent, contained, authoritative.

*Saturday*
The shearing of 90 yearlings.

Catching sheep is exhausting, even for a strong man. The animals are quick on their feet; yearlings particularly are lithe and strong. They can turn faster than a human, and they feint this way and that. When they are packed tightly and cannot escape it is merely a backbreaking question of stooping, grabbing and heaving, but as you get through them the remainder have room to duck and space to get up speed. As you tire and your concentration flags your first grab is often in vain; you follow up, but the animal you have missed once is now panicking, hurling itself over its fellows to avoid you. Doing it herself saves Jenny the cost of another helper, and allows her to catch as she prefers to, as gently as possible, with her arms around the animals, rather than digging her fingers into their wool. She hates to see sheep held like that, imagining it must be like being dragged by the hair. She tries to swallow her distress, but sometimes it blurts out. 'Under the chin, arms around her,' she cries. 'Careful – you'll hurt her!' And the men muzzle their frustration, and try to do as she asks. She works all day in the narrow race, talking to the beasts, trying to soothe them, straddling them, guiding them towards the shearers. She sticks at it, and as her strength wanes the shearers take pity, reaching over into the race as she presents each captive, and hauling them up and over the barrier. The first day is tiring but the next is a marathon: 193 ewes caught, lifted and shorn, as well as the rams, Tommy and Ron Vaughan.

*Tuesday*
Earwig walking across my nightie. Cold and dull. Rain is coming.

*Wednesday*
Jack nettling in the afternoon. Visited Derwyn to ask him to cut our hay. Cow parsley and poppies in the hedges. Tonight thick warm mist – total silence. Not even an owl or an aeroplane. Very spooky. Druid weather.

*Sunday 2 July*
Northwest wind dropped at last – warm, wet wind from the west – very strange: cobwebs and raindrops, hanging motionless on the gate – raindrops transforming the wire fences into rectangles of diamonds. Sheep bleating now and again but they must feel as if they walk through a warm bath so soft is the rain. Wraiths of fog rising from the valley floor – white plumes of it against the dark woods. We went to the Iron-Age Fort. Windy up there though – cloud hurling along the tops: Twinky and Pim soaking and cold. Came back to hot baths, beans, sausages and bacon. Tommy and Ron in the yard. Let Piggy and her lamb into the Patch. Picked some spinach and served it up, complete with caterpillar. Must be

more careful next time. Slugs invading kitchen – bloated disgusting leathery black one on mat outside the kitchen door. What *use*
are slugs anyway? Silent, muffled night. Cloud in the yard.

*5 July*
David Hughes came and we found unseasonable mushrooms in
the Horse Fields, and gathered elderflowers for wine and elder-
flower fritters! He went too quickly everyone thought.

David Hughes was a friend of my mother's. An Anglo-
Welshman with slow, kind eyes, an author of novels and non-
fiction, a critic and journalist, divorced from a Swedish film star,
he was a decade older than Jenny and one of her treasured friends.
He seemed to me to have lived several lives. He had a laugh like
someone rolling down a hill, and he hugged wonderfully. He was
looking for somewhere quiet and cheap to live while he wrote
his next book, *The Imperial German Dinner Service*. Whenever
David came it meant good food, a dinner, candles on the kitchen
table, strong cheeses, hard biscuits and bottles of dark red wine.
The adults would sit around at ease, and my brother and I would
play with corks and swords of uncooked pasta, dab the wax and
maul the dog. If he decided to lodge at the farm, Jenny knew, his
presence and strength would transform the prospects for the
winter, and partially answer Robert's arguments: you cannot
afford it, you cannot keep it going, you cannot live half in Wales,
half in London.

*Saturday/Sunday 9 July*
Another cross-roads. For *ever* in green pastures do I ask our ways
to be: the countryside seems to be the only true and right place
to bring up children. But I have condemned them to the city
again. Decided to return to London in September: but I must
hold my tongue.

My brother had joined me at the village school, but our
progress was not sufficient. Jenny, a former teacher, reckoned we
were two years behind our age group in London. Robert main-
tained that the farm was detrimental to our education and fatal
to their marriage, yet Jenny agonised. Would moving to London

save the marriage? She does not seem to have thought it likely: did either of them have any hope for it, really? Would her children's lives be better served by London's teachers, pavements and traffic, or by fields, hills and village schools? Could she stand a return to the office, after the freedom of the farm? Her despair at her decision, and the prospect of leaving, seems of that doubled, underlined kind, underscored by a feeling of futility which in itself will undo an enterprise, but is not strong enough to prevent its attempt. We would return to London, she decided, but the farm would be her safety net; she would not relinquish it.

*Monday evening*

Walked the Hill Fields to talk to the ewes. Thistle and Barty came too. It was evening – heavy and still and thick. Dark under the leaves. The ewes came to me and I stroked their shorn coats, and they gazed up: their faces and eyes the more gentle and fine for being free of all their wool. The two swallows sat on the wire together looking quite forlorn. Why aren't they hatching babies? Are they both males?

*Tuesday*

Our last lamb born under hot sun, among nettles. Betty and Jack came to dinner – a beautiful gleaming sunset: Turner – gold flash through dark clouds – a warm night: loud rain falling on the barn roof. How I do love this place.

Derwyn refused to make our hay. Everyone else making hay during the week of July 16th – 23rd.

*Sunday*

Went to see Mrs Williams re Billy and the hay.

*Wednesday*

The weather breaking. Billy Williams says he can now cut the hay.

*Thursday*

Peter Evans to cut the hay – but starting to rain. I take children to Pembrokeshire for ten days.

*Saturday 29 July*

Return after days of lovely sun. Still hay not cut. Lark ran away again. Jack not well.

*Monday 31 July*
Telephoned Peter. Standing by.

Long range forecast: unsettled, sunny intervals. Drenching driving rain all day. Very noisy tonight. Whisper of autumn? (Leaves – hazels turning olive and nuts growing – hawthorn berries turning brown – driving winds scudding the rain.) Like the seaside. Met Pat. 'Don't wish for money,' he said. 'Just health and happiness, and you *so* happy with your farm and work and lovely children far from the crowds and the rat race. Don't wish for money.'

I haven't told him that I am soon to give it all up, and my heart so aches. Extraordinary. Back from holiday having taken them miles away by myself in the car to furthest Pembrokeshire and no telephone call or any money yet this week or sign of interest from their father. I wonder if it's too late to change my mind. Jack is not well but bought him three oranges. A wild night, curtains of mist and rain hurtling down on us from the northeast and sweeping away over the larch trees.

*Tuesday 1 August*
Pim drew the curtains and said it would be a lovely day. Was too in spells, and very warm: rain turning to mist in the sun and rising. There seem so many mouths to fill at breakfast time – after the children the animals line up. Lark – the cats on the wall, the three lambs wailing for their bottles. Milk, tins and milk again! That's satisfying and I love it; but getting us three dressed, into our shoes/wellies and macs and finding my purse and shopping bag and shopping list is a nightMARE. Called on Jack. He came to his gate in a thundery shower. Looking grey and 'sunk'. I am very apprehensive about this winter and how he will cope. Hope and pray David *will* come. Went to see Betty with the children in the evening. Sunlight at last and a thunderhead in the south. We walked across her meadows to look at a field of uncut hay and sucked clover flowers in an attempt to take the nectar. Twinky brought 'tea' to me – handfuls of dock seeds now ripening on their tall stems. It was a lovely evening. Pim ordered his birthday cake – chocolate, with a Mickey Mouse on top. Got back late. Thunderstorm.

*Wednesday 2 August*

Dull and drizzly. Took the children to the swimming baths in Brecon. Lunched in the Wellington Hotel – thought of the day we bought the farm – August 18th *1971*. (Was it *really*?!) – and I bought the children orange juices in the cocktail bar where Emrys bought us celebratory beers. Everything seemed so bright then.

We had a lovely lunch for £2.50 each. Twinky slept on the floor throughout. The carpets are quite thick. Came home and they had a rain bath under the water butt. Then another hot one upstairs. They went to bed early as the sun came out. I walked down to the Horse Fields and came back via our Quoiker where I saw nothing amiss. Collected a few mushrooms for a feast with bacon. A glorious evening. Then Noel came with two hitchhikers. Germans.

Noel was a young doctor, with thick dark hair, a beard and a bewitching motorcycle. He was the first of the 'lambers' – medical or agricultural students, recruited by notices placed in college newspapers, who were given pocket money, board and lodging (the Beast House bedroom) in return for their help with the lambing. Noel was kind, clever and patient, and could turn his hand to anything, from lambing and roofing to mechanics. Perhaps because of his beard, and our relief and delight at his arrivals, I secretly associated him with Jesus. I think it came from a blend of my tousled image of John the Baptist and the parable of the Good Samaritan, stopping to help when others passed by. Noel's girlfriend Lesley was a dark-haired beauty, moody, funny and fun, whom I once saw naked through a chink in the bathroom door. I treasured this mysterious and gorgeous image, a first innocent encounter with the erotic. Noel and Lesley went through difficult patches, exacerbated by the isolation and non-existent social life of the farm. They separated once, and Noel was in despair, but then Lesley came back and it was all all right again. It confirmed my impression that love was tentative and episodic, like a kind of pain.

As in the diary entry above, the lambers sometimes brought their friends and acquaintances to see the view and enjoy the bohemian atmosphere. We all watched Noel's successor, Tim, christened Tree-Tree by a very young Alexander (Tim was very tall and had bright red hair, so it seemed to fit), as he fell in love with Jill, a nurse. They lay about in the long grass out the back, Tim's considerable length outstretched, his head propped on his hand, visibly, to Jenny anyway, in love.

When lambers left, unless they wanted to return the following year, Jenny asked them to find their replacements. She trusted them to conduct interviews and select the next year's helper. In this way, we met Nicola, who single-handedly convinced my mother that Northerners are very good news; Kevin, who was studying Old Norse at Durham, and introduced me to the band Frankie Goes to Hollywood, and Richard, a former soldier, a Green Jacket, who had the manner of a man who could command troops in action, and who put a Herculean effort into sustaining the life of a pathetic lamb called Dishcloth. There was a hippyish fellow called Martin who was known to his friends as Marty Marty Shitman Hallworth R.O., U.S. Chaplain – a phrase which my brother and I adored. They explained it came from a book called *Catch 22*. Martin was hilarious. He had one particular look, a sidelong, critically appraising pout, which made us scream. Alexander and I relished the presence of lambers, the house always felt more complete with someone in the Beast House bedroom, but we were not always a joy to them. I got a clout around the head from another Tim for repeatedly ambushing Richard and him as they tried to feed the lambs: Alexander and I popped up at their every turn, flinging handfuls of nuts and cackling.

They arranged a neat revenge – one spring Saturday, my brother and I were woken at eight and informed that our teacher had telephoned, requesting that we attend a special spelling lesson. We moaned, mourning the destruction of our beloved lie-in, dressed stoically, and went downstairs to find the lambers laughing. April Fools!

They would arrive at the railway station, where we would meet them, craning to get a first look at the new arrival. One was told, by his predecessor, to look for 'an eccentric-looking woman in muddy wellingtons with two small boys'. Some did not last much longer than the first encounter – including one young man who had been institutionalised, and whose father came to collect him after twenty-four hours, during which time he had masturbated into the pages of several of our children's books. (We were not told about it, of course. Only now do I understand all those stains and glued pages.)

Another was sent away when he fretted overmuch about a cut on his hand. He was, quite reasonably it seems now, reluctant to cook the lunch with blood coming out of his finger, but when a plaster failed to persuade him, he was told to pack his bags. Too wet, we snorted.

For those who made the grade, there was a fierce learning curve, with some unexpected challenges.

'It's like bloody Tom and Jerry,' puffed Tree-Tree, on the first afternoon of his third stay, as he skidded backwards down a muddy slope, clutching a sledgehammer, as Lark jumped up his legs, and we watched closely, and the post he was trying to bang in swayed precariously on the top of the bank above him.

When the old cat Barty died, Noel was asked to perform an autopsy and establish a cause of death. Noel laid Barty on the floor of the barn and undid his corpse with a scalpel. I watched as he carefully extracted Barty's parts.

'These are his guts – as long as a football pitch, if you stretched them out.'

I was impressed.

'This is the liver, these are the kidneys, this is a lung . . . and . . . this . . . is his . . . heart!'

It was a bluish lozenge.

'It's not red!'

'No . . . And nor is it heart shaped. All those love hearts you've seen are wrong.'

Whenever I think of a heart, I think of Barty's.

As he had for my mother and father, Jack provided the lambers with example and instruction. He personified the expression 'a tidy farmer'. Though he worked slowly, when he did a job it was a labour of love and skill. When Jack put in a gatepost, for example, he began by felling a tree. We still have the axe he used, a fearsome instrument he swung as lightly as a golf club, and the stump of at least one tree he used is still there. The top is deeply scored; after they had chopped it down, Jack, a lamber called Chris and Tim-not-Tree-Tree held a coin-splitting competition.

They placed two-pence pieces on the stump and took turns swinging at them, mighty blows, the axe heaved up and over their heads. At first the boys could both hit the coins, but when they moved on to five-pence pieces only Jack was striking the middle, and only he could split pennies. I hoarded the debris, particularly pleased by the twos, their dark copper slashed to a winking edge.

Jack would next strip the branches off the trunk, then dig a deep pit. Sinking half the log into it, he left five and a half feet protruding, on which would be hung the gate. These gateposts are all still there, and good for another twenty years.

*Thursday 3 August*
Noel and Pim went to town to buy rafters and nails and flooring for the attic. Showers and sunny intervals all day. Coming back from town (in the sun) with Twinky the road was clouded with flights and flights of white butterflies. Everywhere we looked! Must have simultaneously hatched in the bracken above the road. Twinky and I both enchanted. In the afternoon I walked the sheep. Saw a hare in the distance. Saw a stray dog running over the Far Quoiker and nosing about in ours. Since it wasn't actually chasing the sheep did nothing. Shots heard in the evening.

*Friday 4 August*
Dull and dreary. Mervyn drove his tractor across our uncut hayfield bringing scaffolding. As he and Noel were sticking it up and I was doing three weeks' washing and also getting lunch at the same time, two friends of Noel's turned up – Di and Ruth. Chaos. Not enough food. I *spun* out some fish. In the afternoon, in the sun, Jack and I and Pim set off to walk the sheep. I went with Lark to the top of the Quoiker, and felt very happy in the wind with the view and Lark behaving herself for once. Then, under the ash trees, was the gutted fleece, skull and backbone of

a tup sheep. Looked almost too big to be a lamb, but it was – all that was left of him was a brown hind leg, a bit of rusty forehead and a horn. He must have died/been killed in the night. Curious and worrying. No ewe bleats for him. She would know already. Lambs never bleat when their mothers die.

*Sunday 6 August*
Rain again. Called by to see Gwyn who says the market's good again – so I suppose I must send some little Welsh tups this time, God forgive me . . .

A wonderful angry sunset. Wind from the N.W.

11.30. Screams tonight – strange and eerie. Is a dog killing another lamb?

*Friday 11 August*
Wonderful morning – sun jumping over the hill. Took 17 lambs – 5 Suffolk Crosses – to market. Orf on one Welsh – another blown up by a sting. His life saved by a wasp. Too many people staying. Whitewashing. Took children on picnic up through the bracken. Shafts of gold through rain clouds from the west – sun and cold wind. The bracken smelt warm though. Green apples. Green plums. Greenish white hazelnuts. One or two fronds of bracken are gold among the leafy green. The council ditcher came to saw down the verges and layer the hedgerows. He seemed surprised anyone lived up here.

*Sunday 13 August*
Wonderful morning. The first of the lakes of mist in the valley. Dew on cobwebs. Wind rattling through the gold of the witch tree. Rams curled in hollows in the early sun. Where are the swallows? Have they left so early? Must ask Jack if he's seen them. The garden giving forth potatoes, carrots with white worms in them, lettuce, and soon peas. Town for newspaper and swings. Dug up the remains of spinach. Sheep still crying for their lambs, under the dark hedge in the Hill Fields I saw two ewes sitting alone as it got dark (9.30) – they looked utterly lonely and their voices are thin and cracked. Soon they'll forget – it's just at night when there are no lambs to snuggle up to. I watch Catkin and her lamb sometimes. Their love for each other would seem quite ridiculous to people who don't watch sheep.

The lake of mist in the valley was one of our touchstones. Following Jenny out through the front door we saw her take a pace into the yard, stop, and gasp: 'Look, children!'

The tops of the browning hills rode like islands above feathered creeks of cloud. The sunlight was dazzling, beating out of the blue above, thrown back by the white below; it was like being in an aeroplane, and like descending in one as we dropped down the lane to school. But it was in ascent that I came closest to the miracle of the mist. It was a closed, muffled day when I began to climb the mountain, a moody shroud hugged the ground. The bracken was a red-mauve tangle, every stem loaded with water, and the grass was a silvered green slick. It was a hands and feet scramble up to the first ridge and a long trudge to the second, as the damp wriggled into my boots and clamped cold hands around my trouser bottoms. As I climbed the second ridge I noticed the air above was brightening, the grey thinning to a pearly smoke. Now there were cobwebs of light in it, a fretwork of gleams. With every foot climbed the translucence changed, now paling, now suddenly staining, and now the cloud all around me was blue. Blue mist! It was enchanting, and strange. Near the crest of this second ridge there was clear sky directly above me, but every other way was azure and opaque. Up two more feet and the top of the mountain appeared, a bright momentary vision, reclining in the sun. I turned around and exclaimed in amazement: I was staring across a great sheet of mist, like a deep sea diver breaking through the surface of a glass-flat bay. And there, miles away but intimate in their revelation, were the peaks of the Brecon Beacons, red volcanoes rising out of a vast white sea. For the next half hour I sat on the shore of the air as waves of light washed the ridge, sometimes ivory, sometimes blue, with the Beacons vanishing and reappearing, like spells, and I marvelled at a cloud of bright luminous sparks, specks of light which swam before me, as if I was seeing stars. They danced in the air: had I not stopped believing in such things I would have said I had met the fairies, on that edge between the earth and sky.

(I saw them again in the winter, coming down the mountain as the sun set. The rays struck a patch of lingering snow, turning its icy crust pink, and there were the sparks, points of white fire on the drift. They looked like a host of tiny butterflies, resting for a moment; it would have taken the merest imagining to say I had seen their wings.)

Though I feel I have crossed every foot of it, it is never the same mountain twice. In another mist, a dark, blind, pre-dawn blanket, I climbed it, after a day and a night of rain. Everything slipped and wept and trickled; under feet and fingers the slopes gurgled and squeezed, like the flanks of a dormant slug. Blind, I felt my way across it, a mite traversing a mammoth, and could hardly believe it, when the sullen dawn came up, and I found myself at the entrance to one of the old sheep folds, exactly where I had aimed to be. I felt vindicated, as if I truly understood one thing, this mountain, as if it was truly known to me.

*Monday 14 August*
Fair. Jack and I drenched 83 or so *beautiful* yearlings. The days are shorter and going TOO QUICKLY.

*Wednesday 16 August*
Day of the clouds. Noel and Lesley and I all of us talked about them to Pim and Twinky individually. This has been the summer of the redstarts and the summer of the clouds. 'Don't forget it's the summer of the earwigs too,' said Pim. I thought I had lice when I woke up this morning. Had a bath and the shampoo top rushed away down the plug hole thus upsetting the works again. A wonderful dramatic day. Noel on the roof – now some rafters off also – kept stopping to watch the light changing over the Beacons – and the showers rushing towards us through shafts of sun. Cold at night. Enormous moon.

*Thursday 17 August*
A sparkling morning. Not one single cloud. Hard china blue sky, sharp light sun vaulting over the hill. Some dew. 'Haymaking,' I thought, 'this minute.' Phoned Peter Evans at 8.30. He came and as the clouds appeared in the west, cut our meadows. Rowan and the first red berries of autumn – Lords and Ladies. Twinky

and I stood in the yard under a duck egg sky and the evening star, listening to owls and watching our bat. We whispered to each other. A glorious day. Every time it looked like rain we sang our anti-rain song. Jack harvested the shallots. Walked by the river, and saw dippers and water wagtails. River red from above – dark and golden brown beside it.

*Friday 18 August*
Peter arrived early to finish cutting and began 'woofling' the Far Meadow. Watched the clouds all day but bright sun and fair wind from the south. In the evening went with the boys to the old castle. Harebells are growing in its walls, violet blue against the pinkish stone. Pim and Twinky ran up and down the gallery and then we piled off to the Tower, stopping to play Pooh Sticks on Robin Hood's bridge – much kissing at the kissing gate, and then round the tower we ran in a bright cool wind, and watched young Friesian bullocks trotting over the grass as the farmer sent his dog to call them in. Pimmy said: 'I'm doing something daring and dangerous and mischievous' as he climbed over the wall and into the meadow. He stood by the weir and then came running back before the bullocks and we watched the swallows dipping their wings as they skimmed the water. Came home and I trimmed the boys' hair and tidied the house just in case Rob should come for his birthday.

I remember this incident clearly and it was striking to re-encounter it in my mother's blotched red diary, which I had not read until I started this work. Among the many reasons I had for beginning was the hope that I would uncover clues to my own predicament, not only emotionally and psychologically, but in relation to authority and conformity, which have been problems for me. And this is a delightful one. Climbing over a low wall and running away from some bullocks may not sound particularly daring or dangerous now; unfortunately, I was in this, as in every-thing, only just starting. My career choices at this point were fire-man (daring), policeman (dangerous) or clown – I adored Charlie Chaplin, and the idea of getting into trouble to make people laugh appealed more than anything else.

*Saturday 19 August*
The hay making.


The great highlight of the summer, the climax of the year, hay making could take days, ideally in a week of sunshine. In the period running up to it Jenny's forecast worship escalated to a peak of devotion, like a monk in Holy Week or a Greek with twice-daily access to an Oracle, the tweed-toned, gnomic pronouncements of which threatened to drive us all mad.

'Unsettled! *That's* no good . . .' or 'Did you hear that? "Another fine day" – and look at it – look outside! Are we supposed to believe him when he says the outlook's good? The poor little man's mad or he's just making it all up . . .'

She ran in and out, staring at the sky, listening to the forecast, calling the premium-rate weather line, and the harvester, and tried to make it all match.

After the crucial decision to cut, the grass was first turned and then woofled: the tractor towed a machine like two spiked spinning lobster pots which whirled the hay, drying it and shaking out seeds for next year's crop. Woofling leaves the herbage in thick shaggy lines, which at last the baler scoops up, its elbowed steel arm pumping up and down, chung-bung, chung-bung, chung-bung, up and down, while bales drop out of the back. The rhythm of the machine and the chug of the tractor are accompanied by the buzz of insects and the thump of new bales on the sward, and a heavenly smell hangs over the meadows. Freshly baled hay is a plaited harmony of scents, reeking of clover, old suns and cut grasses, rain and earth and dew.

In the afternoon we drag the bales into clusters, ready for collection later, and laze about in the shade of the hedge, dizzy with sunlight. Alexander and I chew grasses like proper farmers and watch the haymaker steering his tractor like a horse, looping around at the end of each pass, sometimes raising his eyebrows or grinning at us in greeting. The day draws on to teatime and the last evening, when we all follow the tractor and trailer around the field, and everyone who can throws bales up on to it. This is called hauling the hay and I like it best when it goes on into nightfall, with the last load bumping and swaying slowly up the track to the Big Barn, where the stack now reaches up towards the swallows' nests, the light bulb and the spiders, dangling on their dusty threads.

Coming up towards the Middle Meadow gate that Saturday night, the beams from the tractor's headlights groping towards the house, and with the rising scents and dimming shapes of a blue summer night all around us, the trailer gave a lurch and the load slipped, collapsing in a cascade of hay and cries of alarm. Jack, who had been sitting on the very top, came tumbling down, landing on and in the fallen bales.

'Jack!' someone shouted.

'Jack!' Jenny cried, as she scrambled towards him, towards the silence and stillness in the jumble of lumps below the trailer. There was a pause, then, slowly, Jack stood up. His cap had come off. He put it back on, looking as shaken by the fuss as by the fall.

Then Alexander stepped backwards off the track and fell into a thick clump of nettles hard by the Middle Meadow gate. He screamed. As we know, nettles can hurt – if you have not fallen into a lot of them, you cannot know how much. He was rescued and comforted and hustled home for a bath: nothing really helps, not even dock leaves, as much as the fact of being treated.

Meanwhile the bales were reloaded, lashed, and the work carried on until the last was hauled off the trailer, lugged across the floor and heaved to the top of the stack. There were tired cheers and then a nervy consultation about leaving the barn doors open: hot, damp haystacks have set themselves ablaze, and we all imagined waking to smears of smoke, then gouts of flame, bursting out through the roof and slit windows.

'Do you think it will be all right, Pete?' Jenny asked anxiously, as we surveyed the sweetly reeking heap. It was as though the hay was a God, so much worried over, so much debated, installed now in its shrine, but perhaps not yet appeased.

The adults stuck their hands in between the bales, felt around, sniffed samples, looked at each other. I copied them.

'Aye, should be,' was the verdict, and the haymaking was done. We went inside and began trying to clean up, sluicing hayseeds out of our ears and noses.

The next day I went down the track with a good whippy stick and the promise of righteous destruction speeding my steps. Slashing down nettles with sticks, scythes, boots, anything, was smiled upon. I reduced the clump which had hurt my brother to a tangle of bleeding black stalks and wormy yellow roots. Nettles follow human and animal doings; around gates and pens, at the doors to barns and sheds, at the edges of streams, around feed racks, wherever sheep or men had been, nettles were, poised to strike at the merest contact. A really good sting can burn all night and still be there when you wake. Alexander and I became familiar with all the various levels of venom different plants contained (the little dark autumnal clumps were the worst), and connoisseurs of the lumpy rashes they inflicted. Amazing to us, Jenny seemed able to ignore them; sometimes she pulled them out with her bare hands. 'Ouch! Doesn't it hurt?' we cried. 'Ow, Mummy! Stop it!'

'Oh, I'm used to it,' she said wearily. We were deeply, unreservedly, impressed.

We did a great deal of nettling over the years, and it was very satisfying, particularly with a sharp scythe. Nettles were bracketed with crows, maggots, flies, magpies, thorns, thistles, barbed wire, rain, the Tory party and the east wind: to be loathed and feared.

*Friday 25 August*
Another wonderful day. To the river in the evening. The tops of the beech trees are turning yellow in the woods above the Estate. The corn harvest is nearly done and the squirrel in the wood is making premature raids on the hazelnuts and leaving the shells all over the lane.

Walked round the flock to check the poor castrated lambs. A disgusting and shameful business. Annie rushed up followed by her daughter (now called Ella) and I was amazed to note how jealous she is if I stroke other ewes. Twice she elbowed them out of the way. The rowan trees are burning bushes, flaming berries bright as jewels. The badgers have been excavating too, and at the entrance to one bury, heaped with a frantic pile of new-turned earth, there were bones, two sheep shoulder blades (one of them lamb size) and some chicken bones. This industrious badger has probably dug his tunnel into the back of a fox's den which lies adjacent. I watched the ravens croaking spirals to each other as one climbed and climbed in circles to join its mate soaring miles above us. And almost invisible because so high was a flock of birds flying south. Could they have been the swallows? I have missed them in the yard these last two nights.

### Saturday 26 August

Dull again, rain in the morning. No water. Made rowan jelly – after much desperate boiling potted it like mad and fear, having examined one 4 hours later, it may not be jelly but juice. Walked the ewes. The Quoiker yearlings are quite beautiful. Elegant, long legged, confident, in the pride of their youth. Lovely animals – they gaze with heads high, standing still as you walk by, and some-times wicker a greeting. In them I place my monetary hopes. They have grown so fast this summer. Autumn has definitely come – golden and promising many apples – Jack has harvested his precious onions. They are 'dying back' on the sheep trough.

### Thursday 31 August

A week of sun – mists in the mornings but bright later. Lesley and Noel worked like mad on the roof. Tiles still off. Polythene cover at night – plaster and wood dust in the bedrooms and in the beds if I am slow to make them. Still no water – dust and dirt horribly depressing. Children need a bath. As do I. Today dull and actu-ally quite cold. Drizzle and low cloud. Jack and I gathered Hill Fields and weaned their lambs. Annie knew she was losing Ella. For the first time I watched her come and bleat for her lamb at the gate dividing them, and then she looked at me with anxious reproach. And another thing. Passing the Patch I said, 'That lamb looks miserable – perhaps it needs a drench.' But I'm sure now that it was grieving for its mother (the young ewe with gid) who has been dying at the bottom of the Patch and whom at LAST Jack consented to kill. Lesley and Noel to London leaving plastic flapping. Hope we don't get a strong wind . . . The swallows haven't left quite yet! Saw them flying into the stable this evening. Not quite the end of the summer of Earwigs and Clouds.

### Friday 1 September
Drenched our beautiful yearlings. Had planned to do it in the morning but Mervyn delayed and in the event the afternoon was better. Sunny and warm – jerseys off. Sheep very hot when they arrived at the dip. Waited a good half hour. They gasped as they swam just as bathers when the first wave breaks. Pim found some small blackberries and then Twinky wanted some but there weren't any, only wizened green beginnings. So he ate groundsel instead.

The weaned lambs have scared but they look quite happy in the meadows though jumpy – bunching and running at the slightest excuse. Pim and I watched Jack walking home in the cool golden sun – walking steadily, surely, exactly at his own pace across the meadows, flat fields of canary yellow. We sat on a hay bale in the yard and a single swallow flew by. The green woodpecker has been laughing these last days. Lark has gone. The apples grow larger, tipped with red. September will be luscious with fruits. My instincts are to harvest and preserve everything these days. Memories, pictures, not only berries. The rowan jelly hasn't set but at least I've caught its taste and colour.

### Saturday 2 September
Went early to town to look for Lark. She was seen by the bowling green, upsetting the players and chased away by an off-duty policeman who complained that she 'wouldn't go away'. The sun so bright rolling along the top of the mountain, the distances and edges of hills and trees so clear. Pim remarked on the darkness and length of our shadows. We all wandered around outside and sat in the sun. I could hardly bear to go inside to make breakfast. No sign of Lark.

### Monday 4 September
Constable Clayton telephoned – Lark found near Forest Coal Pit. In town overheard conversation in the butcher's shop –
Butcher: 'Whose funeral is it today then?'
Woman: 'The neighbour's two pork chops please.'

*Tuesday 5 September*

Pim's 5th birthday – and all day we are in a cloud. Warm dank mountain mist. I had so hoped for another bright picnic. Time flies. Only a few days now before I must leave. Every moment so precious.

*Wednesday 6 September*

Vet at 9.30. Went to collect Jack – the swallows are *still* here after all – and we chased lambs up and down the First Meadow. Horrid castrating. Lark ran away again. After rain, mackerel skies of great height and speedwell blue. Squirrels nutting more busily than ever – plums still green but larger. Jack picked last of the peas. The corn is in now. Valley seems quiet – we have finished with tractors for the moment it seems and wait now for ploughing and chain saws. Twinky and I walked in the First Meadow in the evening to stir up the poor stiff wethers. The bracken is just turning on the mountain, the heavy bottle green tinged with brown. More rain tonight. Tomorrow perhaps we can have baths. Noel woken at 1.00 a.m. by 'torch flashes' in the yard.

*Thursday 7 September*

Went to town in the morning with Noel, Pim and Twinks. Noel in the newspaper shop actually heard someone say, 'How much is that dog in the window?' There was also a hot gospeller who misguidedly placed his soapbox near Pat's shop. An unfortunate choice of venue, giving rise to much ribaldry and scorn. Pim thanked dear Pat for his present – a racing car transporter.

Twinky and I chose fish in the market. He stroked the smoked cod because he liked its brilliant orange colour. I chose white cod. Shopped and met Betty for coffee. Met Mrs Thomas who said, 'I thought you'd already left.'

Came back for fishy lunch and afterwards as the skies cleared and blue appeared Jack and I set off to shift sheep. Tremendously involved arrangements and miles of walking until, in the end after MUCH sweat (Jack so afraid of catching cold because he'd sweated so) we achieved 125/127 ewes up on the mountain, lambs and old ewes in the Horse Fields and Lower Meadows in two groups awaiting dipping on Saturday. Walking the ewes up the mountain, pushed by Lark through forests of bracken, was hot – the lights and shades, the iron black clouds against turquoise bands of blue and plumes and mare's tails of silver overhead and the incredible golds and bottle greens of the valleys beneath us made me breathless also. The grass up there has blades thin as needles, but there are whinberry leaves and if they forage they should find enough to live on. How well and creamy they look now, almost inappropriate beside the mountain ewes with their dark wool and spindly, sticky legs. But a month of hard living will reduce that no doubt. Twinky and I watched the evening and the sunset in the yard. Pim and I made wishes to the new moon. He wished for peace in the world, and for wings, to fly. In the distance the rams were fighting – we heard the clack clack of their horns as they clashed, we watched the rooks fly home down to the valley from the mountain, we heard the thin 'tinking' of a blackbird and the twittering of high-flying pipits – the sky cleared and grew palest blue – a wind got up and it grew colder as dusk fell. The swallows have left now. Not a bat to be seen. So very quiet and still tonight. Summer all but gone, and so am I, and how desolate the farm will be – Jack and Thistle all alone again after almost ten months of living here. Jack is very morose these days.

And with that, and an entry for Friday the 8th about selling 26 yearlings for £37.50 each, taking the ewes up the mountain a last time and packing a suitcase, and noting that a ewe called Crosslegs had been bitten – by a snake? – Jenny took us back to London, for one more try at a life which her contemporaries and friends would have understood, and approved.

Now we went to school in Kensington. My father would walk me there, across the park. He and Jenny never argued aloud; any conflict between them was conducted either in silence, or formality. They were polite to each other, and apparently kind and considerate, yet they were utterly separate: two individuals, sharing only us and the basement flat.

At school I learned to recite my times tables, to hate spelling tests and to love and fear girls. I shared my desk with one, who detested me, and I fell in love with another, Catriona, who was three years older than me and used to tuck her dark hair behind her ears in a gesture I adored. We walked in a blue-capped crocodile to the park at lunchtimes, each senior girl holding the hands of two smaller children. I remember one such procession, my right hand in Catriona's left, walking along Kensington High Street, talking to myself in my head about sheep and mountains as she chatted obliviously to one of her friends. I do not think I impressed her much, but she was gentle and kind.

Friday afternoon meant squatting on the school steps, looking out for the car. When our mother appeared, often slightly breathless (she came late to her driving licence), we piled in and set off. Down Kensington High Street, across to Holland Park, and down into the jams at Shepherd's Bush. Via Hammersmith fly-over and Chiswick roundabout, soon we were on the motorway and passing Heathrow. I lectured my mother on the extraordinary size of the jumbo jets flying over us – as long as the Eiffel Tower is high, I claimed – and then we all eyed the first flock of sheep outside London: black-faced things on the side of a reservoir south of the carriageways. In the same direction were the turrets of Windsor Castle, squeezed incongruously between the streams of jets and cars.

Once she had settled into the drive, my mother would begin to tell us stories. Shakespeare's plays told as tales and historical adventures were favourites: Drake and the Armada; great battles of the Royalists and Roundheads; Charles hiding in his oak tree; the exploits of Bonnie Prince Charlie; the story of the Scarlet Pimpernel. The heroics and tragedy of Owain Glyndwr and his great dog Gelert held us in breathless attention. One of the most gripping stories was Hamlet, told on a dark night somewhere in Wiltshire as we rolled past roadworks in a thickly coned slow lane. 'It's a black and eerie night on the battlements of Elsinore, and the sentries are jumpy. They think they've seen something in the dark . . . they're scared. They think they've seen a ghost.'

Sometimes it did not register with me when these were not true stories, and occasionally I lost the connection between a familiar story and its author; years later, I would be seized with déjà vus in English lessons.

When the stories ended my brother and I would start waving to other drivers and punching each other. A tall radio mast at one of the service stations was traditionally hailed as 'half way', though halfway between what and what I was never sure. We would glance over Mum's shoulder, not quite accepting judgements like 'you're doing very well' and 'not long now', and start punching one another again. The Dead Arm and the Dead Leg were a large part of our childhood. A good solid blow, trapping the muscle against the femur or upper arm, causes sharp pain, followed by an amusing numbness. Pile in another blow on top of the first, or add a dead arm to a dead leg, and your opponent can be reduced to a sort of giggling agony. The game could be played either free style, taking shots at each other at random, or more coldly, like Russian roulette, each taking a shot and giving one in turn. This could make us scream as we refined it, drawing gentle circles with our fingers on each other's thigh or arm: 'It's going to go right there, into the middle of this circle . . .' one would inform the other, as the victim convulsed with anticipated pain and near-hysterical mirth.

The approach of the Severn Bridge filled us all with relief; we wound the windows down for a blast of dark sea air, a tradition Robert started, and gazed at the great channel, its vast and smoky waters, and the light buoys balancing their little lanterns on the coursing tides. We were 'weekenders' again, until the next lambing. Jenny made only one entry for that period at the farm:

> The lambing, in the bitter Spring of 1979, was terrible: a battle half lost. Appalling weather. Indifferent/disastrous 'help' – mistakes – incompetence – exhaustion – starving ewes and lambs – pneumonia. Lambing sickness, one case of Black's disease, scrapie. Marigold dead. Lambs with eyes taken – lost/frozen twins. I dread the next lambing already.

The diary begins again in the summer holidays, at the end of July. I remember almost all of it, now. The summer was good, then poor, then good again. Monday 27 August 1979 was, my mother said:

> The Most Glorious Day of the Whole Summer. It's come back – the summer I mean. Pim and Twinky and I woke to see the blue sky reflected in the Big Barn roof. We leapt up and stepped out of the kitchen door into a brilliant sunlit morning – the sky cloudless clear blue, translucent as the sea. Quiet and still, dew on the grass, ravens rowing across the sky to the larch wood – a kestrel hanging above the mountain, and the sheep sitting in hot sun just outside the hill gate. The boys and I had breakfast, then took them up, high this time, on to the mountain. The thin grass up there was gold in the sun; the whinberry wires shiny green cushions. The sheep bleated disconsolately.

Before they found the farm my parents were looking for a weekend place. Many of my mother's friends had such an arrangement – though, as my father pointed out, most of them were rich. My friend Adam's family had houses in Kensington and Florence, as well as mid Wales. Going to see Adam and his mother Clarissa at their farmhouse meant friends, wonderful food, vast supplies of Lego and Star Wars and Smurfs, a trampoline, and a glimpse of recognition, a taste of the good life, one which I assumed to be normal, something inaccessible but not entirely out of reach.

*Wednesday 29 August*
> To Clarissa. Helped to haul her hay. Twinky slept in the grass. Jack and I raked haycocks. I asked him – as we rowed up the hay with our wooden rakes, as the shadows darkened as the slanting late summer sun turned the grass golden and the hills around us glowed – whether this reminded him of his childhood. He said it did. He said too he couldn't bear to see wasted swathes left behind the baler, 'It's like fire on my back, you understand.' He picked up a handful of grass and clover – 'On a frosty morning, for a sheep, this would be wonderful.' I raked less desultorily after that – but it was hot as we loaded the bales and rumbled to and

fro to the barn on the trailer. The boys loved it. Everything. The people, the food, the weather made a lovely generous day. Twinky 'found' a white pony named Taffy. 'Oh Mummy,' he said, 'I do wish I could ride it. Adam does, without a helmet.' He had serious doubts when the animal stood over him, haltered and ready. In the end, I got on and held him in front of me. His first ride. He was most nonchalant about it afterwards. Jack 'really enjoyed' himself also.

At the end of the school holidays we went back to London again. Love and desire were barely memories in the relationship now, but it seems as though Jenny wanted to make a gesture of concession: perhaps she meant to offer the possibility of some sort of partnership based on children and proximity. It was much too late. Along the shelves in the hall were long white spaces where my father's books had been. He was there to welcome us, but he was quiet and subdued. I resolved that I would get up early the next morning so that he might walk me to school. They did not share the same bed; Mum slept next to me in mine. The next morning I leapt up and ran next door to the double bed, and found it empty. The covers were arranged as if it had not been slept in. I knew then that something definitive had happened, but I checked anyway, and he was not in his shed, nor in the kitchen, nor the bathroom.

I came back, crying, and Jenny sat up in bed, and looked at me with such sorrow and sympathy.

'Where is he?' I wailed. 'He's gone! Where is he?'

'Oh dearest,' she said, shaking her head, her face despairing. 'He's left us. He's left me. I'm so sorry. I'm terribly, terribly sorry.'

And she told me that he still loved us, and that of course we would see him again soon, and that she and he were friends, of course they were: it was all going to be all right.

I imagine many six-year-olds are unconsciously and closely attuned to the states of their parents' relationship, their happiness or their misery. In those terrible moments, as I stared at my mother, we confronted a flat and simple truth which we had both been avoiding. My father's disappearance was wrenching and desperate but it was not an ambush: it was a confirmation. My mother must have known some sort of end was coming, and perhaps I had been waiting for it too, as I emulated her, carrying on, child and parent acting, for each other's sakes, as if things would improve. And she must have known that her sentence, 'He's left us,' was not the whole truth, or not the only truth, and though I think I sensed the concealment and simplification of the words, I went along with her. At that moment it was entirely his fault. It was a crude solution, like giving up a hopeless struggle with some intricate knot and pulling the longest string, reducing everything to a small, mean bead.

Now that the big bed was finally empty and my father gone, I wailed in shock, but not in great surprise. I can still see the dim bedroom – the light coming down awkwardly from the pavement level – and recall an apprehension of the emptiness and uselessness beyond my grief, the sensation that there was nothing below it, no hope that it would alter anything. So my crying was agonised, but there was something else in it, too: wrapped in the vivid unreality of the disaster there was a consciousness of it: I was not swept away in unreasoning sorrow. Beneath the tears there was a feeling of conclusion. The fracture had started long before that moment and ran on long afterwards, but in its revelation, in the way it split open, in an instant, the world of the basement flat, it exposed the worst of itself, and left my mother, my brother and me standing more or less where we already were. It was the worst thing imaginable, but we had already imagined it. Uncertainty was crushed, vain hopes extinguished; the days of quiet tension and loud silence were over.

And we did see him soon, and they did seem to get on better now, putting on a cheerful front for the children on the Wednesdays and Saturdays when he came to us. I have vivid memories of that autumn, of them sitting together in the garden with Alexander, as I ran around. Of going to the swimming pool, the parks and the museums with him, of the miraculously clean white handkerchief he always carried, of his smell on it as he wiped our ice-creamy mouths or running noses. Best of all, I remember a conversation we had, sitting on a bench in one of the playgrounds in Holland Park, as we watched my brother exploring a large climbing frame, which was made of hollow green plastic cubes. Alexander's expression was grim, as was mine, and sitting on that bench under a mulberry tree, my father decided the time had come to talk about it.

'Look,' he said, 'I know this is very hard for you, but do you understand why I'm not living at the flat any more?'

'Yes,' I said. 'Why?'

'Well, I just think it will be better for all of us if Jenny and I don't live under the same roof. I'm not going to disappear, I just think it will be better like this. You can understand that, can't you?'

'Yes,' I said. And of course I did not. I understood that he was taking responsibility for the fact of what had happened, for the decision, but there was no sense of why he had made it, except in the overtones. 'Better for all of us if Jenny and I don't live under the same roof.' The implication was that somewhere there was an inexplicable, insurmountable fault. But where was it? What was it?

We all remember the day we finally left the city. Mum took Alexander and me on the Thames on a boat. It was an uncertain London afternoon: glimpses of clear sky between chapped clouds, the river sulking somewhere between brown and grey. When we returned to the basement flat we found the front door broken in.

'Wretched man! Whoever he is, he knew what he was doing,' Jenny lamented, having established that almost nothing had been touched. 'Grandpa Joe's duelling pistols have gone . . . probably the most valuable things we owned . . . It's pretty well the final straw . . .'

The police dusted my tin toy-box for fingerprints, admitting as they did so that it was pointless, and we climbed into the car once again, bound for Hammersmith, the motorway and the farm, this time for good. Jenny wriggled, settling herself into the driving seat, then turned and looked at us.

'Well, good riddance to London, I say – Wales, here we come!' she cheered, and we rallied smiles, hoisting hopes in answer to her grin. Wales! Windy skies blew through the word, wild seas chopped its edges. 'Wales, here we come!' we echoed, and away we went.

# 6

## The Mountain for Good

WE ARRIVED WELL after nightfall. And the approach to the farm was utterly dark, the wood like a Gothic fairy tale, its pale fingers steepled above a goblin legion of knotted trunks and boles; civilisation reduced to the glints of the village lights below, then extinguished, as the road turned upward again, towards the mountain.

The rushing, empty cold of the wind made me shiver as I opened the far gate. The rough turf of the track undulated in front of the car, rocks and ruts shook the steering wheel in Jenny's grip, as if to repel all but the most foolhardy arrival. The walls of the barn and house were ghostly white, a silent answer at the very end of the questing road.

Standing in the yard for a moment, in the dark, before the yard light was turned on, with the smell of the wet fields in my nostrils and a cold touch of the night on my face, I stared to the south, over the mountains, at an orange-indigo glow in the sky. It came from the lights of Merthyr and the Valleys, and looked ominous.

Seen from space, on one of those maps of the lights of the earth at night, South Wales blazes as brightly as anywhere in Europe. We were just beyond the rim of it, in the dark, but only just. The wash from street lights and headlights has banished darkness from the sky above the Valleys and the coastal plain, but what you see now is merely the latest term of that banishment which began during the Industrial Revolution. The last time the lights went out down there was during the Second World War, but the curves of the coast make the Bristol Channel simple to navigate from the air; Hitler's bombers had no trouble finding the great shipping termini of Cardiff, Newport and Barry Dock. From his lookout on the old hill fort at the top of the valley, where he curled up with his shotgun and some cider, doing his bit, keeping watch for German paratroopers, Jack saw the conflagrations in the sky, and the colours of the flames playing above the horizon like a fiendish Aurora. It was not the first time hell had come to the world beyond our hills. During the Industrial Revolution, when the mineral wealth of the South Wales valleys was bled and sweated out of the ground to fuel the changing of the world, chroniclers record that the density of the workings and their ferocious industry made dark the day and lit the night sky with fires.

The front door scraped over stones swollen by rain and damp, opening to the dank smell of mould which lingered around the door, where we left our coats and boots. In the kitchen the cooker needed lighting; as soon as we had unloaded the car Jenny went down on her knees and began half an hour of cursing and prodding the oily old machine as the wicks refused to hold the flame. Upstairs, the main bedroom gave on to two smaller ones; the room overlooking the yard was my mother's, and the one at the back, with a view of the mountain, was mine. In the early years, and when it was particularly cold, we all shared the big double bed in the first room. Now it belonged to Alexander who filled it with a variety of toy animals, two a night, according to an idiosyncratic rota.

The bedrooms were divided by thin wooden partitions which were papered, inexpertly, with jolly flowers. The ceilings were wooden planks lagged with old newspaper: above Alexander's bed you could see between the boards a little picture of a bull and lists of stock prices at some market of long ago. The cracks always made me think of snakes, ever since Jenny told us a story about a night in Thailand when she had been advised that there were snakes in the rafters: 'They said sleep with your mouth closed and you'll be fine! Sleep with your mouths closed, children,' she teased.

She tucked us in and answered the question I always asked her: 'What are you going to do before you come to bed?'

'Well, I'm going to have a cup of coffee, and listen to the radio downstairs. Then I might sit by the cooker for a bit, and then I'll come up, I should think.'

I asked her to leave the light on, and turn it off when she came up, so that in the unlikely event of my falling asleep before she came, if I woke I would know that she was in bed. When I woke and the light was still on I would start up, my heart pounding. Leaping out of bed I would zip through my brother's room, down the stairs, through the sitting room, running over the sofa rather than round it, and arrest my flight only at the kitchen door; opening it very carefully, I would sidle in, dreading that she would not be there.

'Hello darling, everything OK?' my mother smiled, reassuringly.

'Yes,' I would puff, while the world settled back into its right course, and the tempest of my secret fears subsided. 'Are you coming up soon?'

'Yes, I am. I'll see you in a while.'

If she went out without telling me, or stayed in the fields with the sheep after nightfall, I suffered agonies of paranoia and worry. Suppose she broke her leg and couldn't get back? Suppose she met badger baiters and they attacked her? Suppose Something Happened. It was not just that I loved her, and worried about her: she was all there was between my brother and me and the wild, indifferent world, and without her I knew I would have to take charge, and I feared that responsibility.

Jenny tried to calm me with loving, sometimes agonised assurances. 'Don't worry, don't worry, I'll always come back – don't I always come back? Have I ever not come back? No. Well then . . . I'll never leave you, I promise I won't. You're my boys . . .'

When this did not work she tried being deliberately breezy and offhand, airily dismissing my fears. 'Oh stop fretting. It's quite ridiculous! Nothing will happen, and if it does just call Ursie, she'll come and sort it out.' By the telephone there was a bent and yellowing postcard bearing a list of emergency numbers, an ominous precaution. I had a strong relationship with it, formed the evening Jenny came in from the fields with a clutch of different mushrooms. She loved mushrooms but was inexpert in their identification. She held up various specimens, comparing them with a wall chart of edible fungi.

'Hmm, not sure, not sure. That one's definitely all right, and this one might be a blewit . . . but what about these? I must say the drawings aren't very good. Where's that book?'

'I wouldn't touch them if I were you,' I huffed. 'They're probably poisonous.'

'No, I don't think this one is, or these – they might be delicious.'

'But you don't know!'

'I'm pretty sure. I'm going to eat these three anyway.'

'But what happens if you're wrong?'

'Well, I'll be a bit sick or something.'

'Don't eat them!'

'Look, if you're worried, here are the numbers – if I start foaming at the mouth just pick up the phone and say my stupid mother's eaten a toadstool!'

It was funny and terrifying. She fried the beastly things and ate them defiantly as I sat, my eyes travelling between the numbers and her face, waiting for the first sign of disaster. It did not come, and the incident seemed further confirmation of her bravery, which I knew we all needed, and her mercurial foolishness, which I both loved and feared. Hence the nightly attempt to tie her into some sort of schedule.

There was curiosity in the repeated question, too. Adult life was a mystery to me. What did they get up to, by themselves? What was she thinking about, sitting by the cooker? It was as though she was on watch. What was she watching for? Nothing, there was nothing to be scared of. She was careful to maintain that line, and waited years before telling us some of the things which happened when we were at school, or after we had gone to bed.

*

One rainy equinoctial night, the grey dimness outside having tipped into a wet black, and having put my brother and me to bed, Jenny was sitting in front of the fire, kneeling close to the hearth on the rug, absently picking wood chips out of its spark-pitted fibres and flicking them into the flames. Lark had been dozing on the sofa, but now suddenly pricked up her ears, growled and barked. She stared at the curtained window, in the direction of the yard.

'What is it, Larky?'

Even as she asked it there was a deliberate double knock on the door. Lark barked furiously and leapt up. Jenny's heart thumped in her chest. There had been no sound of a car. Whoever was outside had walked up to the house, through the rain and dark. Knock knock, it came again. More barking.

Jenny was on her feet now, approaching the front door. The walls were two feet thick and the door was bolted, but it was only a few old wooden planks. She thought, for an instant, of the shotgun, upstairs under her bed. Too far away, too terrible.

'Who is it?'

'Only me.' A man's voice, low, local.

'Who are you?' Jenny heard anger in her own tone, and a sort of archness, not quite disguising her fear.

'Huw, Jenny.'

'Huw!' she cried. 'Goodness sake, you gave me a fright.'

Huw was a surly but not unfriendly farmer who lived two valleys away. Even as she reached out to unbolt the door she thought, almost said aloud, what on earth does he want?

Huw was wearing his cap, tweed trousers, wellingtons and an old jacket. He was soaked, smelled of damp and mothballs and tobacco. He grunted about his boots, and slipped them off.

'What is it, Huw?' she asked, as he brushed away Lark's enquiring nose.

He straightened, looked at her, sharp dark eyes in a thin weathered face, and said sorrowfully, 'I miss her something awful, Jen.'

His wife, Mary, was two years dead.

'Oh, dear. Dear Huw. It must be awful for you.'

'Aye,' he said. 'Terrible lonely.'

He went and stood with his back to the fire. 'Have you anything to drink, Jen?'

'Erm, no,' she said, thinking of the whisky, 'I'm afraid I haven't. Tea?'

'Proper wet out there,' he said, turning slightly to one side, as if to warm his thighs. 'You must get lonely, Jenny, don't you?'

She ignored the question.

'Well, you must go home and get dry, luvvie. You shouldn't be out in it.'

'Don't seem to care what happens,' he said quietly, shooting her a look, 'since she went.'

'Poor Huw. You get warm for a minute and I'll make us some tea, then you must go home and look after yourself.'

She ducked into the kitchen, shutting the door behind her. She put the kettle on, shaking her head. How to make him go without making an enemy of him? She lit a cigarette. The kettle boiled, she made a perfunctory cup of tea and went back to the living room, determined to be brisk.

Huw was standing in front of the fire in his socks. His trousers were stretched along the hearth, there was no sign of any underpants. His penis was long, and pointing at her feet. He looked her in the eye.

'Don't mind if I dry my trousers, do you, Jenny?'

She stood absolutely still. 'Actually I do rather, yes.'

He continued to look at her. She didn't know where to put her gaze, so she looked at Lark, who was looking at Huw, with her head on one side. I absolutely must not laugh, Jenny thought.

'Do you want it, Jen?'

She shook her head. 'No. I don't.'

'Don't you miss it?'

She shook her head again, looking at her feet. 'Please put your trousers back on, Huw.'

'They're all wet.'

'Put them back on, please. You must go now, dearie, please.'

For a long moment they both stood still, then he turned towards the fire.

She looked away while he picked the trousers up and put them back on, with a wince. She was still holding the cup of tea she had made for him, she realised, and put it down. She moved his wellingtons a couple of inches towards him and stood back while he put them on, then she opened the front door, and stood back again.

'Go carefully,' she said.

He gave her a brief, still look.

'Goodnight.'

He said nothing. She shut the door behind him and slid the bolt across. Then she turned round, stared at Lark, put her hands to her head, her jaw dropped and she gave a silent squeak of horror, relief and near-hysterical amusement. Lark barked and wagged her tail.

'Oh my Lord, Larky! Did you ever . . .? I mean to say . . .! My GOD! Shh now, you'll wake the boys.'

While she was downstairs, 'listening to the wireless', my brother and I talked, occasionally raided each other's beds for a pillow fight, and read. Once we cracked it, and with no television to distract us, reading became a shared addiction. Mum brought hundreds of books with her from London. Everywhere there were books, and since we loved to re-read there was never a chance of us getting through them all before we grew up. We were both awake and preoccupied when Jenny came up, carrying her wireless under one arm, not missing a moment of Radio 4's evening schedule. Roald Dahl's *Charlie and the Great Glass Elevator* was the first novel I read, from first word to last, for pleasure and without being prompted.

'I've just read this book,' I announced, as if I had just learned to fly but was trying not to show off about it.

Mum was gratifyingly delighted, and I remember the elation coursing through me, as I lay in the dark, listening to the Shipping Forecast murmuring out of her room. 'Scram!' the murderous space egg-worms had spelled out to Charlie, as he stood gawping at them. 'Scram!' said the Vermicious Knids.

Enid Blyton and her ideal children, with their absent parents and their adventures, which always began with the discovery of a hoard of tinned peaches, and always ended with a lift home from their grateful friend in Interpol, came next. Willard Price's boys, Hal and Roger, became favourites – they were in the business of capturing and shipping dangerous animals to zoos and safari parks, on behalf of their absent father. It was reassuring to find that many books featured children in the wild, answerable to no one, and that most of our heroes were as emotionally close to animals as they were to humans. Tintin had Snowy, Obelix had Dogmatix, and the best thing about Enid Blyton's interchangeable children was their parrot, Kiki. Animals were just as good as humans, we felt, if not better: you could not read Roald Dahl's *Fantastic Mr Fox* without siding for ever with foxes against certain kinds of men. The essential elements of adventure, our books suggested, were wilderness, diminished authority and animals; we had the lot, and soon acquired the animal companion to beat them all: Toss.

Including the cat, Thistle, a thin old tabby with terrible teeth, and Lark, and Vivian (the mouse which turned up at breakfast, and sat behind me as I guzzled cereal, and watched us eat, chewing companionably on spilt lentils), there were six of us, until Lark became pregnant. She gave birth on the sofa to four moley little creatures, two black and two grey. Jess, Toss, Floss and Tess were all, supposedly, given local farm dog names. During one of their early moves around the sitting room, Toss fell off the low sofa and landed gently on his head. This, Alexander maintains, explained what happened subsequently. Though his siblings grew up to be bright, talented dogs, and his elder sister Jess became the star of a large farm in mid Wales, Toss never seemed to notice sheep. Inevitably, he was the puppy we kept. When his mother ran around to gather a flock Toss went too, bouncing along at twice her speed, snapping happily at her ears, trying to knock her over. He had small, topaz eyes which shone with mischief and mystification; he was as quick as a greyhound (timed at 40 mph for a few flashing moments in the wood, going downhill), he was very friendly and he never threw a fight. His missions in life were to beat the car and attack anyone he thought an intruder. He confirmed his complete rejection of his ancestors' genes one afternoon, scorching ahead of us up the lane, when we ran into a group of Derwyn's strappers. Toss did not check his speed, but tore straight into the middle of the terrified sheep and jumped clean over the biggest ewe, who had no time to get out of his way. He had a broad curious nose, twitching ears which never stood up for long, and huge paddy paws. His sex drive never definitively surfaced: either he was gay, and all those fights were the fallout of failed advances, or he never progressed beyond puberty. Toss was like a third brother to us, and with his arrival the crew was complete. It came as a comic shock, later, to discover that his name was crude slang. I muttered my discovery to Alexander. He did not believe me at first, then his eyes widened as he saw I was serious, and he began to laugh and laugh in amazement and glee. 'Oh Toss! Typical!' The innocence, foolishness and offence of it all seemed characteristic of the animal. 'Toss! What have you done now!' Toss took a break from licking himself, and grinned. No wonder people looked startled when we shouted at him in town.

By the time we came down to breakfast Jenny was already up, pushing back the curtains and boiling water. On warm days, with the kitchen door open – it led out to the rough ungrazed area we called the garden or the back patch – all the light and buzz of the day would slant in, calling to us. We ate fast, with our eyes glued to books or the backs of cereal packets. These were important spaces of cultural encounter – I discovered pop music, in the shape of The Police and Abba, on the backs of cereal packets. It all looked very good, but as it was silent, or merely rustled, I missed its point. Having no television or commercial radio and there being no billboards in town, the toys and tie-ins on cereal packets were the only advertisements we saw. Their hyperbolic claims and colours were intriguing but, without tunes, toyshops or other children to expand on them, utterly mysterious.

When we had done, and with our trousers tucked into our wellies, Toss and Lark busy on reconnaissance ahead of us, plunging along dozens of scent trails, and our favourite sticks swinging in our hands, we set out to see what we could see.

Fallen trees and old machines were bases for endless games. We were pirates, or German soldiers on the point of changing sides. We were snow leopards, Romans, wolves, highwaymen, Highland clansmen. We climbed trees, wormed our way into hollow trunks, used an old sheep dip as a moated fort. Sometimes we based ourselves on or near one of the old machines.

Tangled thickets of rusting iron sinking slowly into the earth, the old machines were probably seed drills, hoppers and ancient mowers, but it was hard to tell; they spoke obscurely, in a lost language, of all the complexity and exoticism of past time on the mountain.

Ranging over the acres we found empty shotgun cartridges in the wood, windscreen wipers stuffed into a hedge and the shell of an old boiler in the stream. There were several implements of unknown function, and on the mountain, if you knew where to look, there were unexploded mortar bombs.

Our father once brought a couple of these projectiles home, presumably to entertain my mother, who was horrified, and called the Bomb Squad. Robert was amused. The squad arrived, after a while, in combat jackets and a camouflaged Land Rover which got stuck halfway across the meadow. (It always infuriated Jenny when someone, baulking at the track, attempted to cut across our best grazing and got into trouble. So on top of their disrupted evening and the humiliation of their mishap, the soldiers received a brittle welcome.) Jack rescued them with a couple of planks and a bit of sacking under their wheels, and the soldiers took the oxidised, but still intact bombs away with them.

Years later I went far along the mountain alone and with great delight, in conscious emulation of my father, brought three home, muttering something to myself about how once upon a time a man went out on a winter's day and came back round the mountain with some bombs, and now today, that man's son was coming around the same mountain with some more bombs. I knew my mother would call the squad again if I blundered into the kitchen with them, so I propped them against the hill fence, quite precariously, business end down, tail fins tangled in the wire. She found them, and called the Bomb Squad again, who came again, and made off with my trophies. I hoped they might detonate them there on the hill, but no luck. Alexander and I loved the idea of explosions: we often heard the hillsides echo with the crump of artillery and the hammering chatter of automatic fire, but we made the racket in our heads as much as our hollering mouths.

We ran around, shooting up cohorts of invisible enemies, the whole mountain transported, in our imaginations, to central Europe, until someone real appeared, whereupon our first instinct was to level our sticks and shoot him too.

'Someone's coming up the track!' we shouted.

'I see him,' Jenny called back, from the yard. 'Get hold of Toss!'

Visitors to our outpost were often themselves people of the margins, or those who wished they were. A motorcycle gang appeared in the wood and set up camp around the abandoned cottage. 'Who are you then?' Jenny demanded cheerfully of their leader, as we peered over her shoulder, eyes on stalks at the wings and skulls, the leathers and spikes, the chrome, ponytails and exhaust. 'We're the Surrey Hogs,' came the reply.

'Well hello, Surrey Hogs,' she said gaily, before muttering to us, 'Everyone's terrified of them, but they're sweet really, see?'

Then there was the man who came to sell us iron ware. 'It's the gypsy,' Jenny said, as his van approached. 'A dear man. I wish I could afford all his hurdles . . .' He had a nose like a Roman and eyes like an eagle and a soft-burred voice. After they had done the deal the gypsy lingered by the gate for a moment, staring into the view. He had a look, at once peaceful and longing, that we recognised; Derwyn had that look when we ran into him, standing on the track, tamping tobacco into his pipe. There was something about that wide, deep prospect, the way it fell and climbed, like a symphony, to the peaks of the furthest mountains, that made you both happy and wistful.

'Isn't it beautiful, Derwyn?' Jenny said. 'Aren't we incredibly lucky to be living here? Aren't we blessed?'

He put a match to the pipe and drew on it. 'Oh aye,' he conceded. 'But you can't eat the view, can you?'

A reluctant, thoughtful look spread across our mother's face. 'No,' she said slowly, 'I suppose not.' It was as though she did not believe him, as though she was thinking 'Of course you can!' but trying not to be rude. 'We can be jolly grateful for it, anyway!' she concluded.

— * —

Jenny began ringing around the local schools. Now we were here for good, she was determined that we should attend the best available. She found one she liked, and started trying to talk the headmaster into taking us, though it was a good nine miles from door to door, down the valley and over the river, a drive that would take us past the village school and the large primary in town – both perfectly acceptable, in the headmaster's eyes.

'You'll never keep it up,' he said over the telephone, having established that she was a single parent with a sheep farm to run.

'I will, I will,' she vowed. 'Please Mr Williams, I really want you to have them.'

'Well, all right then,' he said, doubtfully. 'If the children are prepared for it too.'

We were mucking about in the sitting room behind her as she spoke to him, and she turned around, her hand over the mouthpiece, and said, 'Mr Williams says he'll take you. Are we going to do it? Everyone sure?'

I remember then, at seven years old, the sense of a world balanced on the end of my tongue, the future suspended between yes and no. 'Yes,' I said, and that was all it took. She turned back to the telephone. 'Yes, Mr Williams, yes we're sure,' she cried, and I marvelled at how easy it was to choose a new life, and how strange it was to do so, when you had no idea of what it might hold. I shrugged and went back to the game.

'Come on, come on, get up,' Jenny exhorted us, on the first morning of school. We had already been up once, piled our clothes on to the battered brown radiator in Alexander's room and dashed back to our covers to wait for our vests and shirts to heat. We dressed, then presented ourselves in the kitchen. Jenny attacked our chaotic heads with a brush, which had the effect of making our hair stand on end: the soft water, the complete absence of pollution and Mum's money-saving home haircuts (administered with the kitchen scissors and styled, apparently, after the Beatles) combined to give us a look like startled hedgehogs. 'Hopeless,' she cried. 'Put water on it! Come on, we can't be late . . .'

We piled into the car, fighting for space with the dogs, and rattled down the track. 'Buzzard! Buzzard on the post!' we shouted, in the wood, as the great bird watched us approach his telegraph pole, his gold-ringed eyes disdainful, launching himself into space only when we were right beneath him. I wished I could change places with him, and spend the day cruising the air currents, and he looked as though he knew it.

'This is better than the London traffic, isn't it?' Jenny exclaimed, waving a hand at the dappled valley, the cloud-shadowed hills and the pitching fields. 'So much better than the tube!'

'Shut up, Toss!' we yelled, in town, as the hound went wild at the sight of another dog. There was a terrier he hated who lived on a certain corner. He associated its appearance with the use of the indicator, and then, with beguiling but infuriating logic, associated the indicator with the idea of the terrier. Every time Jenny turned left or right he would leap at the windows, whining and barking, wondering where that terrier had got to.

'Now children, here we are. Be good. Have a lovely day, and I hope you meet lots of nice friends. And remember, we're getting free school meals, so eat as much as you possibly can. Gobble it all up! OK? Good. Off you go.'

\*

Mr Williams met us, a round bald Welshman who kept a cane on hooks above the girls' entrance. He never had to use it; its only reported sortie was supposed to have involved a boy who threw a book. We did not throw books. We were introduced to the deputy head, Mrs Morris, a woman as loud and warm as summer thunder, and as terrifying as two storms, when she was angry. After assembly my brother and I were separated and introduced to our new classes.

'Stand up and tell everyone your name,' the young teacher said, and smiled at me encouragingly. I gave her an unenthusiastic look and stood. The class craned for a better look at the new kid with his ludicrous pudding bowl haircut.

'Hello,' I said, in my plummy, imitated-from-my-parents, BBC tones. 'My name is Horatio.'

My classmates' faces ranged the spectrum from puzzlement to delighted disbelief.

'You *what*?' they seemed to say, as one.

We sorted out our relationships according to a set of principles, the authority of which was both mysterious and somehow self-evident. I had a silly name and both my brother and I had English accents. We were therefore posh. Everyone else had normal names and normal (south Welsh) accents – they were normal, we were still posh.

'Mum,' I complained miserably, 'they call me posh!'

'Well . . .' She didn't seem worried, indeed, she smiled gaily. 'Well, you are!'

'I am not!' I howled. It seemed the greatest possible betrayal.

'What does "posh" mean?' I demanded.

'It's about the passenger ships, the liners. The best cabins on the voyage to India were on the port side on the way out, and the starboard side coming home – facing the sun. Port out, starboard home – P-O-S-H!'

I stared out of the car window, imagining us in our cabin, in the sun, with everyone else on the other side, calling us posh. For ages I considered the difference, in one way and another, and it never quite made sense. For one thing, all my friends and classmates had better cars than we did, and televisions and, when they came out, video recorders. We could not afford any of that, I was sure, even if the mountain had not been in the way and we had been able to get a TV signal – how then were we better off? They had carpets, suites of furniture, kitchens full of gadgets, stereos; even the kids had modern record players. What was so posh about our cabin?

When finally I heard the mysterious term 'class' I asked my mother about it – what class were we, middle?

'Upper middle, Granny would say. Upper middle,' she said, with complete certainty. That gave me some confidence, anyway. There was obviously something ludicrous going on: it sounded as though Granny, famed in the family for a certain battiness, was making the whole thing up (not just our place – the entire class system) but at least the solution seemed straightforward. Presumably most people were 'middle'. If we kept Granny's 'upper' bit quiet we should fit in fine.

As well as free school meals we had Child Benefit, a state payment for single parents on a low income, which Jenny collected weekly from the Post Office. 'We're on the bread line,' she said, 'but we'll do just fine.'

'Marrowbones!' she flourished. 'It's a brilliant wheeze. If you're ever poor and hungry, go to the butcher and ask for some marrowbones for the dog. They'll give them to you for nothing, then you take them home, boil them up, and you can make a delicious soup!'

We economised in every way she could think of. 'Shut all doors and turn off all lights,' she chanted. Curtains were drawn at the first hint of nightfall. 'Just as good as double glazing,' she explained. Mouldy food was salvaged whenever possible. 'It's only penicillin,' she exclaimed, with withering humour, if you objected.

Any unfinished food at the end of a meal made her miserable. It was a contrast we always noticed when we stayed with our father.

'If you don't want it, you don't have to eat it,' he would say, after a first attempt to encourage us to finish. But he was less familiar to us, and we were ever anxious not to disappoint him. Jenny had to work much harder.

'Please finish your supper. Come on! Clean plates!'

'Don't want any more – full up.'

'Oh, do! It's a long time until breakfast. Have a little bit more, just to please me . . .'

'No I don't want to – '

'Finish your supper!' she shouted, banging the table.

When she was not looking we slipped leftovers to the dogs. Consequently, we ate our meals with Toss and Lark by our chairs, sentinels at attention, watching every forkful travelling between our plates and mouths.

'Oh these dogs! These endless mouths to feed . . .' Jenny lamented.

There was no question of the sweets and crisps everyone else munched at break times, so Alexander and I pretended we were buzzards, and scavenged off our friends. Sometimes we appeared to be worse off than we were: I broke a shoelace, one morning, found it frayed beyond repair, and replaced it with white string. It looked ludicrous by itself so I replaced the other with the same string and hurried to the car, where my mother waited, rolling her eyes. The dinner lady who supervised us at break time was scornful. 'Look at you! Look at the state of you! Got your shoes done up with string!'

I snarled, but one of my friends came to my defence.

'It's not your fault, it's because your mum's poor, isn't it?'

There were few secrets in the small town, where the contents of Jenny's shopping basket revealed us as clearly as a daily interview: cat food, dog food, milk powder for the lambs, frozen battered fish fingers for supper, bread and cereal for our breakfast, whisky and cigarettes for Jenny's nights alone in the kitchen. We all became thin. On one beach holiday my aunt watched us, as we emerged blue and shivering from the sea, and took her sister aside. 'They're not getting enough to eat, Jenny,' Ursie said solemnly. 'You simply cannot economise on food!'

'Oh Lord, Ursie! Do you think they're starving? How terrible . . .!'

We may not have been overfed, but we were extremely healthy, and barely ever ill. If I wanted to miss school, I had to feign, and I was adept at it, particularly on school sports day.

'I don't feel very well, I think I've got a temperature . . .' I ventured, and sucked with all my might on the thermometer.

'Well, this is saying normal but . . . (her cool hand on my forehead) . . . if you don't feel up to it stay where you are – I'll tell Mrs Morris.'

My brother wished me a dubious 'Get well.'

'Thanks,' I returned humbly, and while he was driven away to win races I jumped out of bed, dressed and set off up the mountain. Reflected in the puddles around the hill gate were vivid fragments of the sky. The bracken was taller than me, a sunny forest of green stalks and fronds, all its fingers uncurled; wherever I trod on it sticky white sap leaked from the broken stalks. Beyond the skyline, where the ferns thinned out, the hummocks of pin-thin grass smelled of dew and peat, as though they steamed invisibly in the sunlight. Protruding here and there were pale rocks already warm to the touch, and higher still were the whinberry bushes, exquisite collages of tiny red and green leaves, the berries like purple pinheads brushed with a fine silver bloom, so small and so deliciously sweet they stained my lips and fingers purple-red. When we climbed the hill together Alexander and I rolled around in these soft-spiked bushes, eating constantly, guzzling like legless sheep, uncaring which way up we were, and particularly pleased with the vertiginous effect of lying on our backs with our feet higher than our heads, so that the distant mountains formed an upside down horizon and the clouds became great vapour zeppelins, their fat bellies close above us. I rolled around for a while, nibbling, then doubled back to the edge of the ridge. From here the farm was a kingdom to admire, a perfect toy couched in the side of the hill. Every sheep we owned seemed to be visible, spread evenly over their fields, grazing or sitting in the sun. The sky was a blue silk doublet, slashed across with the white foils of jet trails, and around me the grasses sighed, a wishing sound, under the long, soft wind. The muttered boom of the Concorde setting out for America rolled in from behind the Beacons, and there, coming up the pitch and then along the track, was Mum in her little white car. I felt like a young eagle, with the world at my feet, and I had a feeling of utter completeness, strangely conscious that this scene, this moment, was fixing itself in my brain. I was caught out, of course: you could not climb the mountain with a temperature, but I would say, wanly, that I felt a bit better, and my mother would let me off.

Mrs Morris knew I hated school sports, and she was not fooled for a moment. She probably thought Jenny was too soft on us, and in many ways she was. Jenny was aware of it too, and used to explain it to us.

'My mother never hugged me,' she would say, 'and she never told me she loved me, and I'm just not like that. I love you both with all my heart, you know that, don't you?'

'Yes, Mummy,' we chorused. 'And we love you,' we said.

'Granny was a hopeless mother,' Jenny continued. 'She had no idea. And I think she missed out terribly. The wonderful thing about having children is that you can at last forget yourself, forget your own wretched problems, and love and be loved back. And you never have to worry that they're going to turn round one day, and say "I'm off, I don't love you any more," not like boyfriends when I was young. It's just wonderful!'

We nodded, and thought about those boyfriends, and about our father. She was at pains to remind us that she and he were still friends, and that she wanted him to see us as much as possible, and that he was a good man in many ways. But when she was cross or desperate, or when the money was tight, and he had turned down a request for higher maintenance payments, she would rage against him; how cruel he had been, his dark side, how weird he could be. 'I mean, if it was me, making all that money, I'd want to give it to my children!' she burst out. She never believed that he was not making a fortune in journalism.

'The problem with him is, he always, always puts himself first,' she said darkly, and Alexander and I became very grave. We did not know what to do with the criticism; he was in London, following his life, and Jenny was here, struggling for the benefit of ours, and yet – and yet.

'She's living her fantasy with her sheep, while I go to work every day. I can't afford to give her more money, and why should I, even if I could?' he said, when I asked him about it. He looked hostile, his face cold. I quailed. 'I'm not getting at you,' he said, more softly. 'But seriously, if Jenny wants more money, she should think about earning some.' I could understand his argument, as I understood hers, but in my mind I automatically defended whichever parent was absent, excused them from any attack, whether I could articulate a defence or not. It caused a kind of speechlessness, a flat, internal denial. An attack from any other quarter was a comparatively easy thing to repel.

'Your mum can't drive,' someone said, at school. It was not the first time I had heard this. There was a small roundabout on the way to school she considered ludicrous and irrelevant and she liked to go the wrong way around it, if no one was about, then nip up to the school gates, especially when we were late.

'Yes, she can!'

'She can't. She's mad – goes the wrong way round the roundabout!'

'Shut up,' put in one of my friends. 'She's just a bit – eccentric, isn't she, Ratio?'

It made me almost tearful. It was sweet that he thought that, and felt protective and sympathetic about it, but was it true? Was it sad, if true?

There was teasing, but no bullying; it was a kind and gentle little school, and nobody really hurt anyone else. And they made good use of my brother and me, with our inability to sing, severe hair-cuts, clear speaking voices and those English accents: come Christmas and the annual nativity play, one or other of us was guaranteed the role of Herod.

On the very rare occasions someone came with us after school, all the way home, by special arrangement with their parents, they loved it. Darren, the class bad boy, came home with us one evening. This was a slightly mad child my brother and I liked and feared – he had dark eyes, which glinted like an adder's when he had it in for someone, and he was big, and pretty fearless.

'Come and help me with Penis,' my mother said briskly. Darren looked at me, eyes widening slightly.

'Penis is a ram, Darren. There's something wrong and he can't get his penis back in, so it hangs down and gets covered in mud. See, he's in here. Hello, poor Penis.'

Darren helped her catch the stricken animal, and watched, fascinated, as she washed the mud off with soap and water, leaving the offended organ shining pinkly. Mum said he had done very well, catching and holding the sheep, and Darren enquired solicitously after the animal's health the next day, having told everyone the full story. There was generally some drama to show people, and if our mother was guaranteed to reconfirm the Posh thing, then at least she was popular; our friends always liked her.

I do not think Alexander had my class complexes, but he had his own problems. He went through an unhappy and bad-tempered patch when he threw a chair at another boy – they were both in the Infants at the time, and no damage was done. He had problems with his work: in the face of endless English and maths exercises his dyslexia made him confused and frustrated and his handwriting was a complete mess, as was mine. His teachers, my mother and even I took him aside and gave him talkings-to; extra lessons and a special needs teacher were arranged, and Alexander rapidly came around. He was an unusual child. He outraged Mrs Morris, when still very young, by calling another boy a parasite, an insult so effective it made the target cry.

'Alexander called me a parasite, Miss!'

'Did he? Well, Alexander doesn't even know what that means. He's just saying something he's heard. He doesn't know what a parasite is.'

'Yes I do,' my brother put in. 'It's something that lives on something else, like a flea.'

Tintin, of course – Captain Haddock, to be precise. Parasite, poltroon, guttersnipe, picaninny, jackanapes, bashi-bazouk, we had them all off by heart, and we knew what most of them meant. We learned to swear too, of course, but idiosyncratically. Someone, Darren or Shane, called someone else a wanker. What a word! I had no idea what it meant. That night, during a tussle over a boat in the bath, with my mother lightly scolding us and both giggling, I tried it on Alexander, who was amused and impressed by its sound. The effect on my mother was dramatic and terrifying, but it now seems she was not sure of the meaning either.

'Oh you wanker!'

She whirled around. 'What did you say?' she hissed, furious. I froze, terrified of the change. 'How dare you?' she shouted. 'Don't you ever say that again!

'Wankers go to prison,' she added, threateningly.

Alexander adopted slang from Asterix; he particularly liked the confused and stammering Roman legionaries, receiving a beating from Obelix.

'Quid? Quid?' he stammered.

Soon we swore like brigands. Though adults regularly complimented Jenny on how polite and well brought-up we seemed, she knew how fluently crude we could be in private. She often chided Jack for swearing in front us, because 'bugger' and 'bloody' were two of his standbys, but our vocabulary plumbed deeper than that.

'I think you picked it up from Mr Evans,' she sighed.

Mr Evans farmed beyond the larch trees. He kept sheep on the mountain most of the year; from the back of the house we watched him riding up the ridges on his pony, with his dogs hurtling through the bracken, and his sheep bundling away,

fleeing desperately. As Mr Evans worked his animals the mountain rang with fantastic bellows and wails, growled cautions and
sudden roars of fury. The sound came to us in long ropes of vowels
looped around occasional consonants, but though it seemed wonderfully strong you could not actually make out any words.

Jenny told a family friend that we were swearing too much. In
what must have seemed a clever piece of reverse psychology, he
informed us that the worst word in the world, much worse than
the f-word, much worse than anything, was 'quark'.

'That's the one you mustn't say,' he told us soberly. 'That's the
real baddy.'

Alexander and I stared at each other, awed. We hardly dared
ask its meaning, and readily accepted his refusal to say any more
about it. Of course he could not tell us, it was the worst word in
the world.

When he had gone we discussed it. We tried to think of what
it might mean, but our minds would not supply images to match
the appalling syllables. 'Imagine saying it at school,' Alexander
marvelled. 'That would get them!'

'Yeah, you bloody quark!'

We giggled, scandalised. 'You quarking quark,' we whispered,
fiendishly. It was like being entrusted with a nuclear weapon for
the playground, or being shown an entirely new colour. At last,
the ultimate word. 'Quark!'

'Don't say it!'

'No, you're right, we mustn't.'

'We can't.'

'Imagine if we did, and they told Mum.'

'Terrible!' Alexander said. 'Imagine if Mrs Morris heard you
say it. She would tell Mum, wouldn't she?'

'Definitely.'

'What do you think would happen?'

'You'd be expelled.'

We shook our heads. 'Right,' I said. 'Whatever happens, we
must make a vow that we will never, ever say it. We will never
say quark. Never. OK?'

'Yes,' he said, 'I promise I will never say quark.'

'Me too,' I said.

And we never did.

— * —

At school we guarded our tongues, watched the classroom clocks and waited for home time, half term, and best of all, the holidays, which began with the battered car at the school gates, our mother's smile behind the dirty windscreen and the dogs grinning out at us.

'Up the airy mountain,' Jenny sang, as the car heaved us back up the hill. 'And no school tomorrow, hurrah! Look, mackerel sky – a change of weather.'

The barred armada of silver clouds really did look like a shoal, combining to form a huge speckled fish-belly, hove-to over the hills. Below it the martins and swallows were a weaving, twittering swarm which copied the tumblings of their prey: the flecked, tottering towers of flies and midges above the fields.

'You see, nature is all patterns,' our mother pointed, waving her finger, as if tracing echoes in the air.

Looking for patterns, Alexander and I lay face down in the meadow, staring into the microscopic universe of the grass, where, if you kept it up, ants became as big as cats, and beetles were rhinos, and a grasshopper was Pegasus. We were careful with grasshoppers, because my grandfather said he thought he might come back as one in his next life. Wasps, though, were the enemy, because when he was very small my brother trod in a nest of them in the back garden in London, and they nearly killed him. The discovery of a nest in a tumbledown wall behind the house made us itchy with fear and affront; we were relentlessly drawn to the insects' stone gateway, where they alighted for two seconds before crawling inside. We dashed in and struck, fled and circled, dashed in and struck again.

'Will you PLEASE grow up and stop being so stupid – live and let live, or they'll sting you,' Jenny shouted up from the yard. 'You're asking for it, and you'll get no sympathy from me.'

But the little warriors with their gasmask faces seemed to be asking for it too; there was a brutal excitement in squashing them on the stone, and a horror which you could only assuage with the thrill of another attempted murder, in the same way the ghastly broken struggles of an injured wasp demanded another blow. When they came out in a swarm we ran for our lives.

'Boys! Come here please, we need you to come and help.'

Shamefully relieved, we went. Jack was in the kitchen, sipping tea. He seemed in a rightful place there, at the pale kitchen table which his grandfather had made from planks of beech, relaxed in the high-backed chair, puffing his pipe, his fat rubber boots resting on the flagstones.

'We're putting them up the mountain today, children, so it's all hands on deck.'

The old man smiled slightly with his eyes as he watched us listening to instructions. On the wrong day, he knew, we could take as much marshalling as the dogs. But 'putting them up' was a thrill, and we had a responsibility to behave. 'It will be tremendous fun,' Jenny said, 'as long as we all keep our tempers . . .'

The flock was gathered into the yard, all the best ewes assembled in a belling white crowd, their ears twitching, their urine puddling, as they nibbled tops off the nettles and gaped hungrily into Jack's garden. We shooed them around behind the Big Barn, up through the long grass under the larches and on towards the hill gate. They streamed like a routed army, following one or two leaders, treasured animals, cleverer and calmer than the rest, which always seemed to understand our intentions. After the leaders came the younger ewes, over-excited, pushing to the front but too timid to break away. Then came the body of the flock, their heads nodding with their strides, cropping grass as they went, occasionally adding their tongues to the racket. At the back were the tamest sheep, one or two pets which waited for my mother, charged the dogs and never stopped bleating.

'Go on, Hoppy! Get on with it, Snowdrop,' Jenny shouted, flapping at them with her jumper. Jack yipped, the dogs yapped and Alexander and I ran about, cutting off the escape routes of bolting troublemakers. At the hill fence we held them, as Jenny went ahead, wrestled the old gate open and counted the flock through. Counting sheep is a trick, because though some file through at a steady pace, most dash in twos and threes, and others stop dead in the gap and bleat, as if trying to make you count them twice or not at all. As the last two passed her Jenny lifted her head and nodded.

'Eighty-four it is, Jack. Remember everybody, eighty-four. Right, let's go! Boys, someone, stop that lot . . . Go on, Lark, get-away-out!'

The dog bounded up through the bracken, turning a party of escapees which came haring back on pounding feet, uttering strangulated bleats. Following their leaders, most now seemed to remember where they were going, taking the uphill path in a flowing, fly-blown stream. Whenever one threatened to break away Jack hissed and swished his stick; Alexander and I uprooted and stripped long stems of bracken to wave in emulation. The path climbed alongside our Quoiker then bent along the top of the field in a flat contour. The view now seemed to start at our feet, plunging hundreds of yards down the Quoiker, into the wood, and on down to the valley floor. And we felt part of the view, working within it in the most pleasurable way, striding along with our bracken-stalk switches and our trotting charges. Though its features, like a bone structure, were fixed, we looked at it always with expectation, for its expressions changed daily. The framing mountains had different personalities. To the left were 'the tops', the flat green hills lying along the Heads of the Valleys. You went 'over the tops' if you went that way, up a switching road, to a flat moor Jenny called 'the roof of the world'. They quarried there and the sound came to us over the dome of the sky, rumbling up and rolling down. The tops were industrious but old fashioned. Life went on there, but not quickly.

In the middle was a mountain of the kind we drew with our colouring pens, a huge, lazily conical hump like an ancient, long-retired volcano. I believed a Lancaster bomber had flown into it during the Second World War, and I imagined a flare of yellow light, and a twist of smoke like an extinguished match, and the mountain, then as now, massively, mournfully impassive.

To the right of it were the ridges, peaks and plunges of the steepest Beacons. The Beacons were dramatic, powerful and God-like. Wodin or Thor might live amongst them, making weather. They were mountains that could make your spirit sing in May and kill you in December. To stare at them was to face fate, beauty and terror. To their right was the Pisspot of Wales – a gentle, U-shaped valley, so-christened by Jack, because, he said, if it was raining anywhere in the country, you could be sure it was raining there.

At a certain point, where the bracken was short and the sky appeared low down between the hills at the head of the valley, Jack and Lark pressed forward. They overtook the leaders and turned the flock uphill again, aligning their course with the toes of the successive ridges which receded, up and further up, all the way to the top. For a while the path was lost, the sheep scattered and we shouted and ran back and forth as Lark did her best, barking and rushing, pursued by Toss, the white tips of their tails marking their charges through the fern.

'Stop it, Toss! Good dog, Lark, get away out! NO! She's missed three there, get away FAR out, far out dammit! Boys, go and help her, quick or we'll lose them, QUICK! Well done . . .'

By the time we regained control the flock was split in two, with Jack in the middle, but now the paths were wide and clear and they led straight up the ridges. We panted and smiled; the tricky bit was over. Now the ewes walked steadily and we followed, matching the rhythm of their climb. There is a strain of ancient peace in this, the droving of animals towards their summer grazing. Attuned to the flock, which is calm now, you relax your watchfulness a little, and take in more of the mountain's day. On the highest saddle three specks cross a cloud; walkers on the skyline. Below them, notches of oil paint on the wide grey scree, are two horses and a foal. To the right a kestrel dips, rises, slides and stills, as if she wrote music over the hillside. High to the left a glider scuds, riding the long ridge winds.

We drove them in a rising zigzag, following the sheep tracks up the side of the first ridge, back across its top, through long blond grasses, then up the next. Now we were higher than the hill which formed the western wall of the valley and the lands beyond were revealed: a gently pitching sea of fields, old Radnorshire, cross-hatched with hedge lines, fading into the haze of mid Wales. Here, above the bracken line, the sheep began to fan out, their bleating silenced, replaced by the soft ripping sounds of their grazing.

We caught up with Jack above the prow of the second ridge, and all took a breather, Alexander and I sprawling on the hummock-sprung turf, the world on each side dropping down and away; we lay on a lip between giant bowls of air and stared at the mosaics of the valley. Toss sat down, tilted his head back and fixed his gaze on the clouds. He watched their slow turning, twisting and tearing, as if he too wished for wings.

'What do you think, Jack, a bit to pick?' Jenny pinched out some bright blades and tried one between her teeth. Alexander and I plucked bents, and bit without severing them, halfway down, so that the ends stuck out of the corners of our mouths. By smiling repeatedly we forced the ends together, so that they opened and closed like the mandibles of giant insects. We sat face to face and battled with our mandibles, giggling as we tried to get the ends into each other's nose and eyes. Jack prodded the ground with his stick.

'Aye, there's a bit about if they'll look for it. Should do for a while, anyway.'

'Yes, it should. What a relief,' said my mother. 'We should go now, and very quietly, because if they see us they'll follow. That's enough, boys, please. Come on, dogs, down we go, nice and quiet.'

We set off at a trot, Jenny and Jack following. At the bottom of the steep ridges, where the ground sloped less fiercely, Alexander and I broke into a jog, then a run, going faster and faster until we hit a breakneck charge, the bracken flying by on both sides, our feet slapping the paths in a wild drumbeat. Toss passed us like a missile, his long pink tongue waving crazily around his open jaws, grinning up at us as he overshot, skidded around and came pouncing back, ready for combat.

'Oh no, Toss, no!' Alexander cried, and we laughed in wild despair as the hound went for us, and we all crashed into the bracken, panting, rolling and scuffling.

Jenny made furious 'be quiet!' gestures so we stopped fighting and started down again. But by the time we reached the hill fence the first plaintive bleats could be heard from beyond the ridges, and soon after that the first white beetles appeared on the sky-line. After a moment's pause two of them started trundling down the path.

'Oh blast. BLAST!' Jenny moaned. 'They're after us, the bloody things. Rusty and that other one. Typical! Come on, run! I just hope the whole lot don't come after them or we'll have to do it all again tonight . . .'

It was a warm afternoon. Our shoes were full of the little spines of dead bracken and under our hair we itched with midge bites; Alexander and I headed for the stream.

'Let's dip our heads!'

In the bole of shadow beneath the alders I gripped the cauldron's overflowing iron rim and received a vivid warning through my palms which made me wish I had not suggested it. The scalping plunge through the surface seemed to peel my head from crown to neck; it drove icy fingers through my ears into my brain; silver claws hooked into my nostrils and froze them and my chest heaved with the shock of it. In the few seconds I could bear, I could hear the rumble-burble of the stream flowing into the cauldron a few inches from my neck, the pressure drumming through my head, as though I pressed my ear to the mountain's stomach. I came out in a rush of gasps, rivulets of pure cold eeling down my back and front, to see my brother laughing with delight and dread.

'Aah! Aaah! Cold! it's SO cold – your turn!'

'Are you numb?'

'Yes! Completely numb!'

'Your face has gone red!'

'Yours will too in a minute. Go on!'

Alexander knelt on the wet stones. He gathered his courage and plunged, held his head under and emerged, spluttering and shuddering. We ran around, trying to warm up, then went higher up the stream to work on our dams. We spent slow hours peering into the water, at tiny jack-knifing shrimps and the chrysalises of the caddis fly: minute stones cemented into a jewelled tube, like perfect sarcophagi. Then we hurled rocks, broke bottles and killed horseflies. When we reappeared in the kitchen our trousers and shirts were streaked with red mud, our arms and nails were dark with it, there were ragged tidemarks around our necks and our feet squelched in our shoes.

'Oh no! Look at you! What a mess you've made, and those were clean clothes too! And now I'll have to wash them all again. Poor Jenny! Poor bloody Jenny! Washing washing washing! I hate washing, it's such an endless bore.'

'Sorry . . .'

'Sorry, Mummy.'

'Are you really? Or are you just saying it?'

'We are, really!'

'Well, I should jolly well hope you are. Honestly, can't you just think, if we do this, poor Mummy will have to wash everything again?'

Toss hid under the table, the cat squeezed her eyes almost shut, Lark was tactfully, typically absent and we blushed and dripped, waiting for her anger to abate.

'Huh! Well, I suppose you'd better go and have baths. And I'll slave away cooking your supper!'

We were truly remorseful now.

'Go on, go and have baths. Don't worry,' she cried, with airy sarcasm. 'Don't worry about me.'

'Very sorry, Mummy,' Alexander muttered.

'We won't do it again,' I ventured, and we all knew it was rubbish. 'We'll try not to anyway . . .'

'Huh! Just try – try – to think before you act. If you want to play in the stream, fine, but don't do it in clean clothes that I've just washed! You know the rules. Shut all doors, turn off lights, put things back where you found them and try to think of others! We all have to help each other . . .'

We made our way upstairs, and held one of our conferences. We must do better, we agreed, we must think of Jenny and try to help. When she asked us to help with the sheep we would concentrate. We would try to keep our clothes clean. We would tidy up the shoes in the hall. We would feed the dogs without being asked. We would draw curtains without being asked. We would fill the woodshed, lay fires, we could take her tea in bed . . .

I was in a strange position in our triangle, sometimes the instigator of mischief, sometimes the evangelist of improvement. I was aware of unnatural undercurrents in my relationships with Jenny and Alexander: there were aspects of the husband in the way I listened to her troubles, and a hint of the father in the way I tried to impress better behaviour on my brother and me, by bossing Alexander. My brother felt the peculiarity and injustice of this. 'You're not Dad,' he protested.

'No,' I said solemnly. 'But Dad's not here, and someone's got to say it.'

'You're just as bad as me.'

'I know, but I'm trying to be better. We must both try to be better . . .'

'All right, I know,' he growled. 'Just don't blame it all on me.'

'OK,' I said, and reached for our verbal olive branch. 'Pax! Pax means peace . . .'

'Pax,' Alexander conceded. 'Pax means peace . . .'

Robert occupied a particular place in our minds, like a ghost, sometimes present and sometimes unimaginably far away. He was separated from us by so many removes: the mountain, the Bristol Channel, the motorway and the mad warren of London, and yet he was just there, in nine digits on the telephone, in our thoughts and conversations, and in the smooth white envelopes which contained his letters, and appeared in the box at the bottom of the hill. His strong handwriting addressed us so intimately, and spoke so clearly in his voice, that you could hear him and feel his presence. 'Dear Pim,' ran the briefest note in one package, 'I thought this might be up your street.' And there was *The Machine Gunners*, by Robert Westall, the prequel to my all-time favourite, *Full Fathom Five*. He could not have chosen better. It was as though he was here with us, as though he knew what I thought and did. 'Our Father,' we said every morning at school, 'who art in London,' I sometimes said to myself.

Once or twice, at night, before Jenny came to bed, Alexander and I dialled his number from the upstairs phone extension. The first time his voice was so tired and withdrawn that we put the phone down, having said nothing. The second time, I said 'Hello' in a funny voice which he did not recognise.

'Who's there?' he said irritably, and I cut the connection.

We loved to talk about him, and best of all, to hear Jenny speak fondly of him; when she did it brought him closer. 'Your father's so clever' (or 'handsome', or 'funny'), she would sometimes say, and we loved to hear it. The better he was the better we felt, and the better we felt ourselves to be.

'Oh he used to make me laugh,' she said, the past tense moving him further away. 'When we were going to work on the tube he went through a phase of sitting opposite me and sticking out his tongue. Just a little bit, just the tip. It sounds silly but it used to make me laugh so much I cried. And people never knew what I was laughing at – when they looked at him his tongue would have disappeared, and he would be smiling, you know, looking sort of mystified. I used to beg him not to . . .'

It sounded idyllic, like a golden age, a fairy tale that should have ended happily, but which, in failing, comprised and revealed his one tragic and mysterious flaw.

'Why did he leave?' I asked the question in dozens of different ways. Jenny's answers varied. He did not love her. He met someone else. He didn't want to live at the farm. They were not complete or comfortable answers, she knew, and we could tell. She shifted around unhappily. 'He still loves you though, you can be sure of that,' she would add, with conviction and relief.

But he was with 'someone else'; a woman he had known for years, his girlfriend at university in South Africa. She was kind to us when we met, but though we found no fault with her we could not like her much.

'I expect she's very nice,' Jenny said, encouragingly. 'I suppose she's very pretty, is she?' We shrugged. We liked the woman's sons, who were older than us, and cool north Londoners, but there was something unreal about seeing our father filling the gap in their family. It made him seem more isolated than ever, more individual and alone, and it further coloured my perception of his departure.

Since it was he who was not there, who had not been there that morning, and he who had moved on to someone else, it seemed to follow that Robert was responsible for the separation. But the simplicity of this troubled us all. Jenny was anxious never to set us against him, but sometimes she fell into dramatic despair, lashing herself for our predicament. 'I'm so sorry I couldn't keep him, I'm just so sorry, for your sakes . . .'

'No, Mummy,' one or other of us would say, 'it wasn't your fault.'

She shook her head. 'I'm sure I talked too much. I used to think, you're talking too much, you'll drive him mad. And I think I loved you two too much, that's one thing. I think he felt left out. I don't know! I suppose I bored him.'

'No . . .' Alexander shook his head.

'I don't think so,' I said, faintly annoyed.

'Yes,' she said, 'I did. But I didn't leave him. I said "until death us do part", and I meant it . . .'

Seeing us pondering this she hurriedly intervened: 'But sometimes things just don't work. People can't help that. Dear Robert can't help who he is.'

And, she said soothingly, he was good really, and good at whatever he did. He was very good with sheep, she remarked, which surprised me. 'Yes, yes, very gentle. He's a dear person, really, Robert,' she would say. 'Smashing! If only he wasn't so selfish . . .'

I tried to picture him farming: I could remember Jenny going to the *Evening Standard* on the tube, but I had only the vaguest images of Dad working on the farm. When he asked after Emrys or Derwyn or Jack it always seemed strange that he knew them. One weekend, when he was visiting, he ran into Emrys, and I was struck by the affection between them, the fluency and intimacy of their conversation. In his absence I had constructed for Robert a life concerned with London, and the news, and important, faint things like the world, politics and money. I felt like the child of a distant king, so it was amazing to me that he had such an understanding of the lowly business of farming.

He was a rebel, too. When he took us to explore the riverbank we passed a sign that said 'Private Property, Keep Out'.

'Come on, chaps,' he hissed. 'Let's see how far we get before they shoot us!'

Down by the river we bombed bottles with stones, teetered along ledges and wreckage at the edge of the current and marvelled at tiny, frantic mallard ducklings whizzing across the water after their mother. We chased pheasants through the woods, trying hopelessly to catch them with our bare hands, and later whirled back through the lanes in his clean, comfortable car, listening to Mozart or Schubert or Bach.

'Your father's quite wild,' Jenny said affectionately, shaking her head, when we told her about it. 'He had to be saved by the mountain rescue people once, in the Lake District.'

Any outing with him might turn into an adventure at any moment, and I recognised him instantly in the last lines of Roald Dahl's *Danny the Champion of the World*, in which the great man wrote that what children really want is 'a parent who is sparky'!

Partly in emulation, Alexander and I were quick to scramble over fences, venture across other people's land and take liberties with the out-of-bounds. We spent a great deal of time jumping out of windows and climbing things; it was the right training, I felt, for our father's sons.

— * —

Luckily, my mother was not the only adult we grew up with, and did not always have to cope with our frets and energies alone. As well as the lambers, in 1980 her prayers were answered, and David Hughes came to be our lodger.

Guests and lodgers were given the Beast House bedroom. David's typewriter sat on the table, his pictorial map of Manhattan hung on the wall and David slept on top of the three mattresses between the curling iron frames of the huge bed – frames which Robert and Jenny had rescued from a hedge, years ago, and proudly painted white. David's routine included a few hundred words first thing, then a lope down the track to meet the morning, an exercise he occasionally underscored with joyous whooping.

'There's David, greeting the day,' we said, at a snatch of weird hollering. Then came breakfast, then feeding sheep or helping out, and a retreat to the typewriter. Around six o'clock, and the weather forecast, he would appear in the kitchen, smiling, and at some mysterious point, when the 'sun' was deemed to have dipped 'below the yardarm', he and Jenny would award themselves a whisky. They listened to the radio news, conferred and often laughed. David seemed to understand and entirely sanction the way we lived: he was not fussed or bothered; he loved the views and the space; he would stand and gaze – really looking – at the many places which made up the land, and he understood the depth of Jenny's sympathy with the animals. There was still not much money around but it went further. David struck up relationships with various food and wine suppliers, and soon boxes of 'provisions' appeared, to be lovingly unpacked. It's not just *all right*, his smile seemed to say, it's . . . *fun!*

He had not been with us long before another friend of my mother's turned up, chauffeuring a drooling setter called Humphrey in a lime green Renault 4; a beautiful, gay young woman called Elizabeth. Very quickly and completely, Elizabeth and David fell in love. She moved into his room, and though David's routine did not change outwardly, the afternoon sessions in the Beast House were now sometimes accompanied by clinking glasses and the popping of corks.

Jenny felt terribly left out, in the moments when she allowed herself to be, and bemused to have a love affair ignite in her spare room. 'My nose was a bit put out, but it was a wonderful thing, of course . . .'

The Beast House bedroom had a certain power over couples. Noel and Lesley the lambers married after their term under its chill, steepled ceiling, as did Jon and Gay, also lambers. Indeed, my mother and father were the only people not to have married happily after a spell in that bedroom. It was a very romantic place, especially in the summer, with the windows under the eaves open and the light and drowsy sounds coming through them, at shin level, and spreading across the floor of the room.

We explored the bedroom when no one was in residence; it had an enduring mystery. There was the enormous wardrobe, stuffed with a beautiful fleece belonging to Frosty (the black ewe with a white-dusted back), and our parents' old clothes from their previous lives; lacy dresses, furs and flares. In a box of books I found *The Joy of Sex*, which was intriguing, though I did not linger over it, as it all seemed rather bizarre, and clearly not meant for children.

The Facts of Life were straightforward as far as they applied to sheep and adults; their implications for small boys, though, my mother was obliged to explain. The only lesson I remember clearly involved wet dreams. We were years away from them, but Jenny was anxious that the absence of a man should not condemn us to ignorance, so the instructions were given well in advance of their time.

'As you get older and your body changes, you might find, one night, that you have a sexy dream, and wake up with the bed all wet. Don't worry, don't panic. Just go to the bathroom, get a cloth and mop it up. It's perfectly normal, no big deal at all, nothing to worry about, OK?'

Unfortunately, in the mists of my mind, these instructions became confused with what you should do if the roof started leaking, and you woke with water pouring on to the bed – a much more likely event, given our ages and that of the house.

Conflating the two I formed the impression that as your body changed you might have a sexy dream one night, and wake up to find fluid dripping from the ceiling. In which case, the trick was not to panic, but to put a bowl under it and fetch a flannel. It seemed a little odd, but not impossibly strange. After all, I woke up one night to find a black-faced lamb at the foot of the bed, bleating, and sporting a pink bath towel, which it wore like an enormous shawl.

'Mu–um! There's a lamb here with a towel over its head . . .'

She retrieved the beast. 'Oh good, he's woken up! He was freezing to death so I put him in this box by the radiator. There you go, lamb, stay in there, sweetheart . . . Very good! Back to sleep everyone, goodnight, goodnight, children . . .'

David's novel grew rapidly, and he gave us discarded drafts, piles of pages blank on one side, which we welcomed with our felt-tips and crayons. I went to work on one chapter, obsessively drawing the same huge bird, body like a boat, huge scimitar wings, eagle-billed and taloned, on the back of each page. I was being read to in bed when David knocked on the door. He presented my mother and me with a sheaf of papers. There were my discarded bird drawings, but here was a story too, typed on the pages below the pictures, a poem with each stanza matching a different picture, its story reflecting the changing aspects and wonky expressions of the bird, which David christened The Brecon Beak.

THE BRECON BEAK
by *David Hughes*

The Wild and Woolly Wowl of Wales
Has a beak like a razor and wings like sails.
It gets very cross during westerly gales.
It has wool like a sheep and claws like nails,
It puffs up the hills and hoots down the dales,
When they hear it coming the family pales.
'To-whit-to-wool', cry the furious males
And the boys all hide behind buckets and pails
As across the sky in threatening trails

The Wild and Woolly Wowl of Wales
Dives down to attack small boys – and fails.

Its beak gets caught in hawthorn trees
The smell from the clover makes it sneeze
Its wings get tangled in the breeze
It trips over roots and falls on its knees
It bumps into flowers and is stung by bees
It blinks its eyes and all it sees
Are tiny things like boys and fleas.

So Wales's Wild and Woolly Wowl
Is a very pathetic species of fowl
So worry not, the Wowl you spy
Is only dangerous in the sky
When the winds are blowing cold on high.
The moment it comes down to try
And eat up boys it starts to fry
Its fleece is hot, its beak all dry
It squeaks and sweats and with a sigh
Decides it only wants to die
But if you give it apple pie
And orange juice the bird will cry
'To whit – to wool – and now, goodbye'
For fruit's the best thing to untie
Its muddled wings and let it fly.
A drink is all it needs – that's why.

The Wild and Woolly Wowl of Wales
Has a mind like a razor and thoughts like sails
It has dreams like a sheep and nerves like nails
It thinks on the hills and broods down the dales
While telling itself all kinds of tales
As across the heavens in narrative trails
The Wild and Woolly Wowl of Wales
Tells stories about itself – and fails.

I dreamed about the Wowl, but the poem's power kept fear of
the Beak at bay, even in my sleep. The assurance that the wildest,
fiercest spirit of the mountain, the sum of all small boys' fears,

was merely a fruitjuice-drinking storyteller in search of itself was entirely typical of David, and his effect on our morale. He met us on our own level; it was as though the world seemed scarcely less enormous and possible to him than it did to my brother and me. He would have appreciated my most vivid dream, in which Matty ate me, but it was so ridiculous that I only told Alexander: Matty was an unbelievably scrawny, haggard, feeble old sheep with a fearsome appetite for nuts; she adored them, and looked as if she'd dragged her splattered and matted carcass back from the grave so that she could hoover up a few nuts more. In my dream she ate me, starting with my arm, steadily rather than bloodily. 'No Matty, please don't!' I cried, but she did.

'Nuts, nuts, nuts,' the adults groaned, as they decanted avalanches of the little grey pellets from bag to bucket to bag, measuring out each flock's portion.

'They're addicted to them,' Jenny said, shaking her head. 'It's all they think when they see me, "Oh good, here come our nuts!"'

She gave responsibility for feeding the rams to David, on the grounds that he was big and strong, and the charging beasts were less likely to knock him over. David devised a new method of distribution, hurling handfuls at them over the fence, 'peppering the swine' as he put it.

It was a happy time. The cooking improved dramatically – now there were roasts and hotpots; vats of cheese, bacon and onions, padded out with golden spuds. My brother and I became 'those boyys', a rolling, mischievous appellation the way David said it, in his baritone, and we mucked about inattentively as the grown-ups discussed politics and books and their various friends. They smoked and drank and laughed at the weather and the drudgeries of farming. It was a hard winter, but there was excitement more than fear in their faces when they heard the forecasts. 'It's just so wonderful to have *help*,' was my mother's mantra, meaning it was wonderful to have company.

Then they decided to stop smoking – David went to bed a lot, and though his relaxed, amused expression barely frayed, Mum went gently mad, bursting into tears for no reason. They assayed nicotine gum and spent a lot of time comparing dosages. Mum said the little yellow cubes made her feel sick, as she chewed them ferociously, and that she hated the bloody stuff, though she was pleased to discover it set hard and waterproof, excellent lagging for ill-fitting pipes. Soon she was addicted to the gum and back on the cigarettes, alternating one with the other.

All these scenes Alexander and I saw, from the side, and below. We stared up at men like David with great attention, and I was conscious, early on, of my instinct to look to them for surrogacy.

And all the time, Robert revolved in our imaginations: sometimes he was a perfect hero, exciting, loving and bountiful; at other times, when we were unhappy, he was a remote, flawed figure, uncaring and distant. Whenever he came to see us he turned the landscape into a playground, in a way Jenny could not, but when he came to the farm, and he and Jenny were together, I watched him with nervous attention: was he happy? Was he having fun? I tiptoed around him, desperate to please, as though in fear of an angry instant when he would open his mouth to tell us why he had not stayed with us, and everything that was wrong with us would come out: we were lazy, self-indulgent, unrealistic, eccentric, on some sort of permanent holiday, he might say, in his calm, rational way. He never did. He would laugh and talk and play; he was perfect, when he was expected, and on his way, and climbing out of his car, with his beautiful smile and gentle kiss, his cheek cool and stubbled against yours and his smell delicious. And at the same time he was miserably inadequate, in his sombre leave-takings, and the smile and the long look he gave you just before he left, which seemed to say something kind and clear and detailed; at once an explanation, a confirmation and a farewell, but all in a soft silence which forbade speech. Then he was away down the track.

I distinguished between Dad and the space he left, urging my mother to marry again, for all our sakes, to fill his empty place. I understood that we were her confidants, and that I was especially, being older. And I knew we were inadequate substitutes for a man her own age, just as she could never quite compensate for our missing father. Because the adults we had most contact with, our teachers and Jenny, were women, I came to feel that I understood them better than men, and for a long time I was more at ease in their company. Men were more unpredictable, and more distant, but they were also more interesting. They understood me easily, instinctively responding to my needful gaze; I adopted many as role models. Our Welsh teacher, who was fun, with a fearsome temper; our new headmaster, who made amiable jokes and puns; Indiana Jones, whose dry humour and love of action reminded me of my father; men were strong, often solitary, wilful and very funny, I established. I remember leaning on the cooker one evening and encouraging Mum to marry again.

'Anyone! It doesn't matter as long as they're nice . . .' I badly wanted someone to look after her, and us.

'I understand, sweetheart,' she said. 'I wish there was a man in the house too, but there just isn't anybody. There's no one around who's my type, that's the thing . . .'

Someone her type? That was that, then, I decided. She obviously did not have a type, or we would not be here, like this. So there would never be such a person, I was absolutely sure.

David and Elizabeth helped Jenny with us, taking us for walks, reading to us, playing games. One afternoon when she was away they babysat us through an almighty thunderstorm. We played cards at the kitchen table while outside the daylight turned cloudy green: the sky, the air and the rain all took on a darkly glowing undersea hue, through which the lightning flashed pink-white and there came rolling blasts like mountains exploding. Alexander and I jumped, Lark tried to sit on David's feet, and David looked thrilled, and tried to keep still, but finally could not stop himself and dashed outside to revel in it. The thunder seemed to be stooping over the house, stamping its giant feet somewhere among the larch trees, beating its furious cudgel against the low green clouds.

'Come back, David,' I squeaked. 'Tell him to come inside,' I implored Elizabeth.

She was reassuringly untroubled. 'Oh don't worry, he loves it, he'll be fine . . .' You can't stop men, she seemed to be saying. They just do these things.

It went on and on. Then the rain came down with a great ripping, hissing sound, as if a dragon had doused his fiery snout in the clouds. I knew where the local beast lived – among the great compressed sandstone blocks, as mighty as any granite, which made the mountain's forehead. Reading *The Hobbit* had made dragons an imaginative reality, and looking across the valley to the Beacons on a stormy evening it was easy to see them: their smoke rising from the pine forests; their wings in the torn black clouds; the horizon bloody with their fires. Such grim nightfalls made us shiver: I would lock the front door and bolt into the kitchen, determined to get my back to the cooker.

It was not unusual to 'get spooked' at the farm. Although the whole place felt charged full of ancient, benevolent energy, there were sinister patches. A corner of our Quoiker never felt quite right, to Jenny. And she dreaded passing that dark shadow behind the barn. Some nights, when nothing moved or called, everything seemed to be waiting for something. On certain days, when no birds sang, the slightest noise in the wood would set your heart racing. Sometimes under a cold moon we heard weird cries and terrible shrieks – a fox, my mother would say reassuringly, but with an odd note in her voice, or 'Don't worry, it's just a rabbit, caught in a snare.'

Coming down from the hill one night, Alexander and I took a short cut across the fields, following a path which led into a small wood. We were penetrating it, going slowly, able to see nothing, when suddenly there was a crash in the branches above us, and an alien, grating squawk. The hair on my neck stood up, and Alexander froze.

'What was that?' he demanded.

'A bloody crow or something probably, I dunno,' I said, and heard in my voice that same note of lightness, tinged with dread, that I feared in my mother's speech.

'Didn't sound like a bloody crow to me,' he retorted, and we ran.

On a dawn walk along the sunken lane between our village and the next I came across a sheep, a perfect young ewe, lying across the very middle of a track, unmarked and quite dead. Peering at her, in the slowly brightening light, I could see she had a scrap of twine around one hock. It was like discovering the scene of a murder. The mud was smoothed into semicircles under her feet where she had kicked, but there was nothing to suggest what had killed her. No bird sang and the atmosphere around that part of the track was malevolently eerie, heavy with unnatural death. I felt the presence of some dark and unimaginable purpose, and fled again.

David and Elizabeth stayed with us through the winter, the lambing, and on into early summer. Warmth and excitement surrounded them; they gave off gaiety like light. They took Alexander and me to the reservoir one day, and while we swam, they laid out a feast of foods and wine, and kissed each other and laughed. When we emerged from the water there were rosy prawns heaped on a plate, with tiny black eyes like berries, crackling pink armour and extraordinary insect legs. We had never seen prawns like this before. We watched, amazed, as David cracked one open, peeled it, raising an eyebrow at us in conspiracy, before devouring the white flesh with a lip-smack of pleasure.

'Haven't you had prawns before, boys?' Elizabeth asked.

'No . . . Not like that!'

'Here, this is how you do it . . .'

We stood up to our knees in the reservoir, and littered the bank with shells and legs and heads. We told Jenny about it later, with great excitement, and she rejoiced with us. How lucky we were to have lodgers! They seemed to me to dissolve all our money worries, our fears of ghosts and strangers, and to applaud our isolated, unworldly life.

When they left we felt more alone than ever; Jenny's isolation was underlined, and I understood that our friends had not extinguished our worries, merely sheltered us from them. Now all that remained of them were rituals, like the sun-downing whisky. Jenny began to lean on it more heavily.

I woke one night to find my light still on, and crept down to bring her upstairs. She was in her nightie and a threadbare orange dressing gown, pacing the kitchen, with a cigarette and a whisky, and she was weeping.

'What's wrong?'

'Oh, dearest, I just don't know what will happen to us. Sometimes I feel so worried, sometimes I just despair,' she wept. 'Oh dearie me . . .'

'But it's going to be all right, I'm sure it is,' I pleaded. 'You mustn't worry, it will get better!'

'Yes, I expect it will, of course it will . . . Oh . . .' She wiped her eyes and nose, but now the tears came again, and she spoke through heaving sobs, her expression terribly broken, like a child wailing in a playground. 'It's just sometimes . . . I think it was a terrible mistake . . . bringing us all up here, up this mountain . . . I don't know how we're going to manage . . .'

'It wasn't, Mum, you know it wasn't. It's wonderful really, isn't it?' It sounded hopelessly thin.

'Yes, yes, it is, but . . . ohh! Dear me!' She smiled damply. 'It's just the drink making me cry. We'll be fine, we'll survive some-how. Don't worry.'

She stopped pacing and returned to her station by the cooker, sniffing, wiping her eyes. Now I began to pace, moving over the flagstones in the way I always did, one, two and one to the side, the way a knight moves in chess. I curled my feet so that I walked on my heels and the tips of my big toes, keeping the soles away from the cold floor. My gaze roved over the kitchen, the thick walls, the ranks of jars on the shelves, the empty wine rack, the cobwebs slung like dusty hammocks in the corners, the calendar on the back of the door . . . It all seemed so secure when Jenny was happy, and so terribly vulnerable now.

'Is it money?' I asked, tentatively.

'Well, yes. It is partly money . . .'

'But, so, how much do we have?'

'Well – not much. A bit. Enough to be going on with. We'll be OK if we get a good price for the yearlings.'

'Do you think we will?'

'Yes, yes, we should do. They're jolly good little sheep, anyway,' she said, with defiance in her voice. 'I should think they'll do just fine. Come on, it's no use worrying. Go back to bed before you freeze, I'm coming up now too.'

It was one of the bleakest things I ever saw; this strong, brave woman, pacing as if caged in fears, in her poor, thin dressing gown. Not long afterwards all three of us addressed the question of happiness.

'Life is all ups and downs, think of it as hills and valleys,' she instructed us.

'Why do there have to be valleys?' Alexander asked.

'Yes, why can't it all be hills?' I demanded.

'Because you can't have hills without valleys, my darlings. Because life goes down as well as up.' She drew a series of humps in the air. 'The important thing when you're down is to remember that it goes up, too. However bleak things seem, remember, you must face with courage whatever the future brings, and trust that things will get better. All Will be Well.'

'But will it, though?'

'Oh yes,' she nodded, over the top of her coffee mug. 'Always!'

The day of the yearling sale came; Jenny and Jack gathered thirty-two of the best into the pens. The buyer was a friend from mid Wales who ran an extensive farm. He would not buy as a favour, but if he liked the animals he would give a good price for them, and by coming to us he saved Jenny the auctioneer's fee, and the cost of paying Gwyn to take them to market.

Jenny and Jack hovered anxiously by the gate as the shepherd made his inspection.

'Do you want my honest opinion?' he asked, after a while.

'Yes,' said Jenny.

'They are very good,' he said.

'Oh Jack,' Jenny cried. 'What a compliment to you!' Jack tried not to look too pleased.

'How much do you think they're worth?' Jenny asked the shepherd.

'How much do you want for them?' he returned.

Jenny took a deep breath. 'Well, last year they sold for £38 each, but I thought, well, I wouldn't *mind* £40 this year . . .'

'Right,' said the shepherd. It was done. When he had gone Jenny did a little wiggling jump for joy and hugged Jack.

'I know what! Let's go to the pub. I'm going to buy you a beer to celebrate.'

'Oh, no, can't really,' Jack demurred. 'I haven't shaved, see.'

'No, I insist, I'm kidnapping you. Come on, boys, everyone into the car! It's a celebration!'

We sat in the near-empty pub. Alexander and I had juice and crisps, and Jenny worked out 32 x 40 on the back of an envelope. When the cheque arrived a few days later she propped it on the kitchen windowsill behind the sink.

'Look at that, boys! £1,280! It looks good enough to frame!'

It was a double celebration, because the yearlings had been sold to breed; they would have happy lives on their new farm, Jenny said. When sheep went to the abattoir it was a miserably different story. Then their panic at being chased into the back of Gwyn's trailer was terrible to witness. When the door was slammed shut behind them they peered out through the slats in the sides and cried, and Jenny's face was haggard as she turned away, drawn and haunted. 'They know I'm betraying them,' she whispered, 'they can tell.'

'Don't think about it,' we urged her. 'It will be over very quickly, Mummy . . .'

But she shook her head, and as the trailer lurched away down the track she wept.

'I'm a hopeless farmer,' she wailed. 'Robert always said I was much too sentimental, and he was right.'

The worst were the old biddies, old friends going for a few pounds. She held back as many as she could, more than she could afford, to spare them the horrors of slaughter. 'I want that one to die at home,' she would say, 'where I can look after her.'

She had a large collection of these old animals, and whenever Jack or Gwyn raised an eyebrow at them she was loud in their defence. 'They make lovely mothers. They have perfectly good lambs, and they're much easier to work with than mad young ones – I don't know why everyone doesn't keep a few . . . You're laughing at me, Gwyn!'

The last days of the old were spent in the Patch, the steep field below the pens, where they could be watched from the yard. Under the hazels at the bottom of the field the ground was chequered with their graves. When one died as she hoped it would, quietly, without pain, Jenny was as happy as if she had witnessed a new birth. 'She went in her sleep! No fuss – just perfect. Wonderful! I so wish they all went like that . . .'

Found dead in the morning, the corpse would be left all day, to make absolutely sure, as Jenny said, that the old biddy was definitely, definitely dead. At some point in the late afternoon the body would be transported, wobbling, bouncing and beginning to smell, to the bottom of the Patch.

The burial party consisted of the corpse, swelling gently, its weight swaying the wheelbarrow, which was pushed by Jack, and followed by Jenny and Alexander and me, dragging tools.

Mum reconnoitred the ground. 'We don't want to put her in on top of any of the others, and we don't want too many stones. How about here, Jack? That's not too close to Calpurnia, is it?' Jack cast an eye at the gentle depression of Calpurnia's grave, shook his head, and set to work, cutting foot-square turfs with the spade. He removed each with great care, setting them in a stack like a pile of parcels, leaving a red rectangle of naked earth. This he attacked with the pickaxe. 'Stand back, children!' Jenny ordered, as we pressed forward to watch the spike stab and rip. Jack paused to rescue earthworms, which writhed between his gentle fingers.

'Good for the ground, worms,' he explained, and I nodded, as if knowledgeably. In my eyes Jack was the ultimate authority on this mysterious, almighty thing, the ground, and Jenny was his apprentice. He was the source of our most common mantra. 'Good for the grass,' someone was sure to say, quoting him whenever it rained.

'Jack says there's liver fluke in the L-Shape,' Jenny said. Even after she explained that this meant there were bacteria in the marshy grass of that field, it still sounded like a kind of spell, a rune in the turf which only Jack could read.

He began heaving out hills of red soil with the shovel. When he rested we joined in; he watched our efforts tolerantly before reclaiming the grave. The thumps and scrapes of the pick and shovel drew the attention of the hedgerow birds. A party of great tits passed squeaking comment, and a blackbird chinked, indignant at our presence here, in the quiet at the end of the day.

When he was up to his hip in the pit Jenny said, 'I think that's enough, dear Jack, don't you? Such hard work, you've done wonderfully well . . .'

'Bit more, I should say,' Jack grunted. 'Don't want any resurrections.'

Jenny laughed at the question marks on the faces of my brother and me.

'The foxes will dig them up if you don't put them deep enough,' she explained.

'On the third day she'll rise again,' Jack intoned.

The climax of the enterprise was the moment when the body was lowered into the pit. Nearby sheep stopped grazing and watched, incuriously, as the stiff white form, with its clouded eyes and mucus-trailing mouth, was swallowed by the field, leaving a whiff of rotten egg.

Alexander and I recoiled, protesting.

'It's only methane,' Jenny sighed. 'Perfectly natural.'

'It stinks!'

'Yes, and if you hung around for three days and nights you might see a green cloud of it coming out of the grave,' she said. 'Sometimes you see it burning in marshes – people used to see the light and think they'd seen a ghost.'

Wrinkling our noses we took up spades and joined in with the conclusion, heaving the cones of soil back into the hole. It was sombre work at first, as the earth fell on fleece, shovelled lumps bouncing hollowly on the inflated ribcage and settling around the head. When the body disappeared it was better, and when the hole was nearly filled Jack did a grave dance, stamping, bouncing, packing down the earth with his boots. At last the turfs were replaced, and trodden in, and we loaded the tools into the barrow.

'Thank you so much, Jack, and well done, boys! Well done, everybody!'

In the gloaming we made our way back up the Patch, my mind swimming with green gases, ghost lights and sheep's souls, ascending on the third night.


We drove Jack back to his cottage, and returned to the now dark farm. 'Do you think we've got ghosts here?' I asked, as Jenny bolted the front door.

'Oh yes, I should think so, very friendly ones,' she smiled. 'You can feel the spirit of a place when you go into it, and I felt wonderful when I first came here.'

'Who do you think they are?'

'Some lovely old farmer and his wife I expect, keeping an eye on us, keeping us company. You're not scared are you, boys?'

'No,' we said. 'Never!'

It was nearly true: we were more often enchanted than scared. Doing a round of the meadows one night, Jenny was amazed to see a fiery orange light, like a big blazing fruit, which appeared over the wood and cruised across the meadows, rising up to follow the contours of the Quoiker before disappearing over the northern skyline. It made a rushing sound, she said, and it was climbing parallel to the rising ground: it was no meteorite, nor ball lightning. Perhaps it was the Tanwedd, a legendary Welsh apparition like a flying saucer.

We saw the great shimmering pillars of the Aurora Borealis, one winter, like pink and green searchlights probing the northern sky; another night, to the west, we watched Halley's Comet on its weird, stationary plunge through space. Derwyn showed us the entrance to a hidden tunnel, leading straight into the mountain, and high up above us on a distant ridge was the split gravestone of the notorious villain Macnamara, whose shade, it was said, haunted the lonely heights.

'Don't worry about ghosts,' Jenny used to say. 'We've more to fear from the living than the dead.'

It made sense, and though the lengthening of the shadows and the coming of night made me prickly with the sensation of awakening spirits, in daylight the sown ghosts of the landscape made it rich and fascinating. The heap of rocks in our lowest field, all that remained of Ty Newydd ('New House'), seemed to await the return of its builders. The abandoned cottage in the wood was so perfectly sited, under the arm of a tree-topped bank, that it was almost an effort not to see smoke curling out of its cracked chimney. The crumbling stone exclamation of the ruined castle still commanded three valleys, and demanded that all travellers acknowledge it.

On the other side of the mountain lies Llyn Syfaddan, a lake which abounds in fish, particularly large pike and eels, and myths. It was said to change colour – to a livid red, 'as if blood flowed partially through certain veins and small channels', as Gerald of Wales reports, and to an eerie green before times of war and desolation. The lake has also been seen covered in buildings, pastures, gardens and orchards, and, when frozen, heard to emit terrifying sounds, as Gerald says 'resembling the moans of many animals collected together'.

There are stories about drowned villages, and archaeologists have discovered evidence of extensive ancient settlements around the reedy shore, including the canoes and tools of Bronze Age lake dwellers, who built their homes on stilts above the water.

Gerald also tells of a prophecy which said that if the natural Prince of Wales were to come to the lake and order its birds to sing, they would immediately obey him. In the reign of Henry I, Gerald writes, three men, Gruffydd son of Rhys ap Tewdwr, Milo lord of Hereford, and Payn Fitz-John lord of Ewyas, were passing the lake, and jocularly discussing the prophecy. Milo and Payn went down to the water's edge and took turns commanding the birds to sing, and were ignored.

> And Gruffydd, perceiving that it was necessary to do so in his turn, dismounted from his horse, and falling on his knees towards the east, as if he had been about to engage in battle, prostrate on the ground, with his eyes and hands uplifted to heaven, poured forth devout prayers to the Lord: at length, rising up and signing his face and forehead with the figure of the Cross, he thus openly spake: 'Almighty God, and Lord Jesus Christ, who knowest all things, declare here this day thy power. If thou has caused me to descend lineally from the natural Princes of Wales, I command these birds in thy name to declare it'; and immediately the birds, beating the water with their wings, began to cry aloud, and proclaim him. The spectators were astonished and confounded; and the earl Milo, hastily returning with Payn Fitz-John to court, related this singular occurrence to the king, who is said to have replied, 'By the death of Christ (an oath he was accustomed to use), it is not a matter of so much wonder, for although by our great authority we commit acts of violence and wrong against these people, yet they are known to be the rightful inheritors of this land.'

Gruffydd's people have always looked at incomers with mixed feelings. At the bottom of the scale, in our time, were the second homers, who bought beautiful farms, sold off the land, and visited but rarely, in the summer and at Christmas. They inflated land prices and denied homes to the next generation of locals. Theirs were the houses that were targeted by Meibion Glyndwr, the self-proclaimed Sons of Glendower, nationalist arsonists who burned out a few second homes during the 1970s.

Next came the weekenders, who would keep a few acres around the house and rent out the ground; befriend the farmers; boost the pub's takings and buy a few pet horses or sheep. They were tolerated or welcomed, as were the straggling lines of walkers, pony trekkers and holidaymakers.

We were of the third kind, immigrants who had exchanged their distant lives for Wales. My mother reckons it took her twenty years to be accepted, as a fixture, if still an incomer. Amongst our peers my brother and I were identified as incomers by our accents, which seemed to bar us from ever being Welsh. But as we became accustomed to a permanent life on our mountain, which we had known on and off all our lives, we felt ever more at home, and as rightful inheritors of the territory as any true Prince of Wales.

One bright morning I stood in the back patch and stared at the spiny, tousled crowns of the larch trees above the house. I could not see him, but there was a cuckoo in there somewhere, making an almighty racket. In between shouting his name he was rattling out a series of clucking squawks; he plainly wanted everything with ears, near and far, to hear and admire his hullabaloo.

I felt an amused aggravation. Who did this bird think he was, turning up on the finest morning of the year so far and shouting as if it was all somehow his doing, this paradise of warmth and promise, the fresh sunlight and the dreamy view?

'Cuckoo!' he shouted.

'CUCKOO!' I answered.

'Cuck-coo?' he replied, before he could stop himself.

'Cuckoo,' I affirmed.

There was a doubtful pause.

'Cuckoo,' I prompted. 'Cuckoo!'

And then he let fly. 'Cuckoo! Cuckoo!' he cried, and I answered him, and he answered me and chatted off a squawk for good measure.

My mother came out of the kitchen, laughing. 'He was talking to you!'

'Yes,' I said, coolly. 'He was, wasn't he?'

Talking to the birds did not seem in the least strange to me, in a world where everyone talked to their dogs and their sheep, but not necessarily their neighbours. Every little mountain farm is a kingdom, as particular and unalike in character as each farmer is from his neighbour: all were in some sense eccentric, but some were definitely more eccentric than others.

# 7

# The Realm

O N THE WALL behind the bathroom door, at eye level when you sat on the lavatory, Jenny had pinned the speech given by Elizabeth I to her troops at Tilbury:

> . . . though I have the body of a weak and feeble woman I have
> the heart and stomach of a King, and a King of England too, and
> think foul scorn that Parma or Spain or any Prince of Europe
> should dare invade the borders of my realm . . .

Our Parma or Spain was Idris Baines, who farmed the mountain miles beyond us, but whose ragged animals were forever appearing on our precious grazing.

'I bet he's putting them in on me again,' Jenny hissed, 'the little bugger.'

And there he was, in his cap, a still shape on the skyline, waiting for her to do something about it.

'Come with me, children. He's better when you're around.'

Idris's face was a red tide of broken veins; his voice spiralled up from shrill greetings when he was calm to enraged shrieks when he was angry, and he was nearly always angry. His memory of the insults his family had suffered stretched back to his grandfather's time; his grudging eyes seemed to be calculating your good luck against his misfortune. Animals belonging to Idris went in terror of all humans: his sheep ran for their scraggy lives when you stepped into the field and his dogs were savage and scared. At his most relaxed he puffed on the tiny butts of roll-ups which he carried in his pocket in a tin; Alexander and I stared, amazed, at the little glowing buds which stuck to his lip, leaking smoke into his moustache; he was like the pirate Blackbeard who wore tapers in his hair. When our cars passed in the valley his lips moved, but you could see he was not mouthing greetings.

'They've jumped in again, Idris,' she called, as we approached him, allowing herself the thinnest note of bleakness, which sounded like provocative sarcasm to me, as her voice chimed loudly across the top of the Quoiker, over the tops of the thistles. Was she trying to set him off?

'Aye,' Idris shouted, in his wavering way. 'Bloody things won't come from there!'

'I'm fed up with it – they're eating all my grass.'

'Ah. Can't do nothing with them. Seem to like it though, don't they?'

He watched with a half-smile as we chased his sheep, which bolted over the fence like fleeing thieves, dashed into the bracken and kept going, hectic in their fear. Idris's dogs stiffened, pointed their muzzles at the strays, but did not move.

'See? He runs them at the fence,' Jenny muttered to us, under her breath.

'Do you think they'll stay out this time?' she demanded, plaintively, as she tugged the rusty wire erect once more, and began to knit its top strands together with a length of baler twine ('farmer's friend', Jack called it: bright plastic string which holds hay bales and the poorer part of the countryside together). She looked at him and raised her eyebrows, emboldened by his silence.

'Might do,' Idris smiled.

When the rain and sleet came for days you would see his animals standing on mud, bleating to be fed, but no Idris.

'He lies in bed watching the television,' Jenny sneered. 'And his animals starve!'

'I'm scared of him,' she said, after another encounter on the hill fence, just the two of them under a beaten grey sky, by the dripping blackthorn, Idris hysterical, screaming something about being cheated by the Davises and the bloody Joneses too, as his dogs flattened themselves to the rain-fattened hill and Jenny looked at her feet, her voice quiet, soothing, 'Yes Idris, no Idris, I don't know about that . . . poor Idris, look, I've got to go now, the boys will be worried . . .'

'I'm sorry for him, really, but I'm scared he'll hit me one of these days,' she said when she returned.

'No he won't! He'd better not!' Alexander and I said hotly, as if our glowering tempers were enough to hold him back. We were only ten and eight but if he ever touched our mother, by God, we'd go at him together with our fighting sticks, from two sides at once . . . We went out the back to hack and swing and roar, exorcising our impotence against phantom Idrises, and practising for the day.

On your own ground you could almost believe you might win a fight like that, but in someone else's farmyard you went very quiet. Going to see Idris – when we absolutely had to, to return a lost lamb or a sick stray – was like volunteering for a nightmare. The road went up over a ridge, past polythene feed bags strewn about like oil-slicked birds, past rusting rolls of barbed wire, past a dead car, drunkenly tilted on blocks, and on, into his yard, into the blast of barking dogs and the gaze of broken windows, patched here and there with more feed bags, some of them ripped. As you waited for him to come out you tried not to stare at the torn corrugated iron roofing and the streams of oiled water running straight into the buildings, and you avoided the yellow eyes of the maddened dogs running around the midden-cum-scrap heap, and you smiled in your most friendly way when Idris appeared. He never asked us in, and we never guessed aloud at what might go on in there, in the gloom over his shoulder. Squalor and weirdness, I imagined, which was exactly what some visitors must have thought when they came to us.

'Oh Lord! Look at the dirt,' Jenny cried, when the year's first proper sun came out and illumined the blotched downstairs windows, where Toss had pressed his nose against the panes, and where Alexander or I had squashed flies, leaving their innards in little yellow smears on the glass. She was happier drenching fifty sheep than cleaning a room. 'I know it's grotty, but the fact is I haven't got time most of the year,' she announced, one sleeve rolled up, flushed and flustered by the annual spring clean in a way that she never was in the pens. 'Life's much too short for housework – it's just so boring!'

Our agreement was stiff with self-interest, since we made a great deal of mess and hated hoovering. 'I suppose I ought to do something about those cobwebs,' she sighed. 'But why should I?' she brightened defiantly. 'I love spiders!'

She shrugged at the trail of mud which followed her into the kitchen. 'The point is, this is a working farm.'

'Yes, Mum,' we affirmed, and knew that we colluded with a wildly idiosyncratic set of values. Mud, sheep shit and broken furniture were dismissed with a wave of the hand. No one ever made a fuss about dirt or germs. 'Oh, microbes,' Jenny called them, 'what can you do?' But a brash dress, an ugly vehicle or a nasty piece of new building in town caused shrieks and retching noises. At the other end of the scale from the farm was the mysterious and ludicrously disinfected and over-clean land of the 'bijou' and the 'chi-chi', the capital of which, for some reason, was a particular London suburb.

'Golly, it's like something out of *Virginia Water*,' she exclaimed, in the face of certain objects and attitudes. Fussy clothes were bijoux; smart cars were chi-chi. Expensive flats in London were bijoux; microwave ovens and duvets were Virginia Water: ugly things, conspicuous bad taste, suspiciously – dangerously – convenient, and devoid of class.

I had no idea what Virginia Water might actually be like, but I had a clear picture of what it was not. Vivian on the kitchen shelf, nibbling red lentils and depositing piles of his little black droppings. Toss, stretched out across the entire sofa, on his back, fangs grinning, paws kicking gently in the air as he dreamed of catching squirrels; fleas pinging off him. Ranks of penicillin and antibiotics fighting the milk for space in the fridge door; giant syringes of colostrum in the freezer, snuggling up to the fish.

My mother squatting in the grass out the back, keeping an eye on the skyline in case Mr Evans should catch a half-mile glimpse of her urinating. My brother lying flat on the ground in a tantrum, pounding the mountain with his feet and fists. Me, with a hammer, smashing one of the old hen houses to pieces in an act of entirely gratuitous vandalism, for the sheer pleasure of it. My brother and I play-fighting so fiercely in his room that our combined weight drove the leg of the double bed right through the carpet, down between the floor boards and out through the ceiling below, into the living room . . .

'Oh no, oh no, oh no,' I gasped, trying in vain to heave the bed back up through the floor. 'It was an accident . . . ' Alexander began, shakily, before tailing off. An agonised, amazed noise came up from below. We exchanged a look like a farewell, then slunk downstairs, trembling like curs. The small but darkly ragged hole in the middle of the ceiling seemed to drain all prospect of normality out of the house; the bed leg, jabbed through it, punctured any hope of completeness.

Our mother stared at it, then at us, in silence. We braced ourselves for the tempest, but when she spoke she was terrifyingly calm.

'Well, you've finally done it, haven't you?' she said. We flinched. Enunciating every word with a terrible clarity she said: 'Pushed the bed through the ceiling!'

Our stammered apologies were utterly inadequate. She gave a defeated shrug.

'It's pretty well the final straw, I reckon.'

The coming of the Final Straw had been threatened before, but this was surely its moment: the dark wooden limb poking obscenely into the room even looked like it. Shocked and remorseful, Alexander and I pulled the bed back into the bedroom and turned in all our savings, which came to about eleven pounds.

'Well. That's not going to help much, is it?' she said tiredly. We were already so distressed that further chastisement must have seemed pointless. The ludicrous hole, gaping like a mouth, dumb and irreversible, made everything seem futile.

The next day she climbed on to a chair, holding a rectangle of white cardboard, which she carefully taped over the hole. She seemed to find it quite funny.

'There you are. That'll have to do, I'm afraid! Looks sort of all right, doesn't it?'

We nodded dubiously.

'Good,' she said brightly. 'Perhaps you'll be a bit more careful in future. It would be nice if we could keep the rest of our ceilings . . . you pair of prunes! Luckily it's quite a small hole. It will be fine, as long as no one looks up – trust your mother to sort it out,' she said, with a laugh, and tapped the side of her nose with a finger.

We laughed, but as I looked up at the cardboard and the sticky tape, part of me longed, silently and treacherously, for something like Virginia Water. Alexander and I shared occasional moments of weakness when we fantasised about warm houses in which all the doors were left open, the stairs were carpeted, white bread was toasted for breakfast and the days ended with television and warm duvets. Jenny dreamt of a life free from wellington boots.

'I hate wellies,' she groaned. 'I hate tramping around in them all day. So boring and ugly and your feet get so hot . . . oh, I used to wear lovely shoes!'

Sometimes her previous life jangled into ours through the telephone.

'Hello? Hello!' she cried. 'Golly, how are you?' and there would follow a laughing conversation, conducted in warm and excited tones. 'Well,' she said, when she had put the phone down, 'that was my dear friend Angus, the Canadian oil millionaire. Ringing from Calgary Alberta to make sure we're all right – isn't that just amazing?'

Her past did seem amazing: there were Christmases in Welsh castles; spine-chilling episodes in a Boston terrorised by a figure called the Strangler; precarious travels around Europe in a tiny plane . . . There were E-type Jaguars, famous boyfriends, proposals of marriage, last-minute changes of heart on airliners. When she washed our hair she would lather it and then tease it into vertical spikes, so we looked like the Thai children she had seen in Bangkok. She knew how to live, and she knew how to tell stories. They came with morals, and not boring ones either.

'When chances come, my darlings, you must seize them with both hands. Grab everything!'

There were one or two simple formulas for the most enjoyable kind of life: Cambridge or Oxford, followed by London in your twenties, and lots and lots of parties. She did not seem to have many regrets, except when she knew there was a party some-where. 'It's awful thinking of all that fun, and not being there,' she would say, wistfully.

These longings fell with sudden intensity, like cravings for honey or chocolate; they surfaced on our returns to the moun-tain after we had visited our cousins or friends, to be rapidly sub-merged under the farm's next requirement, whatever it was.

'Boys, would you mind, I need to put a post in – would you mind giving me a hand?'

We groaned.

'Come on! It won't take long!'

All of our friends were probably watching television or riding around on their bicycles to see each other, and here we were . . . Nothing would ever take long, according to her, but we knew that everything did.

Patching up a stretch of our boundary took a couple of trips back and forth across the fields, between the tool shed, the yard and the collapsing fence, carrying – when Mum was not look-ing, dragging – posts, the sledgehammer and the iron bar. When everything was ready, and she had chosen the spot where the wire was feeblest, we took turns wiggling the crow-bar into the earth, then positioned the post above the hole. One of us knelt down, praying, and steadied it, while Jenny hauled the sledgehammer up to her shoulder level, and half dropped, half lowered it on to the target, the small flat head of the post. We could all imagine what would happen if she missed: the lumpen hammerhead arcing down towards your skull, shoulder and restraining arm, the thud, the shrieks.

'I'm so scared of hurting you . . . I hardly dare hit it . . . ' she gasped.

You said little, staring down at the grass, with the damp seeping into your knees, and waited for the thuds to stiffen the post sufficiently for you to let it go.

'There, it's going in,' Jenny puffed. 'You try.'

Alexander took my place, giving me a wary look. 'Watch it, OK?'

'Don't worry, I'll try not to kill you,' I grunted, and raised the sledge. I could not swing it, so I copied Jenny, tap-thumping it up and down, until it jumped in my grasp and the post splintered.

'Oh well, never mind. It's pretty good,' Mum said. 'Actually, feel that, boys! It's really sturdy!'

We waggled it; it did not move that much. Jack would shake his head when he saw it, but for now it was declared a triumph.

'That will keep you out for another week, won't it?' she shouted at one of the Norsters' ragged ewes, which stared insolently at her, the wool trailing off its unshorn back.

'Blooming strappers, Jack says they leave a bit of wool as a marker for their friends,' Jenny remarked, tugging the tell-tale strands off the sagging wire. We eyed the strapper, which snorted and stamped its foot at the dogs. Lark twitched one ear, Toss ignored it completely. 'Go home!' we shouted at the sheep.

— * —

It was impossible not to identify shepherds with their sheep: a glance at Jenny's coddled, vociferous white bundles spoke tellingly of her, just as the whistling, fleeing figures belonging to Idris or the Norsters betrayed them. When farmers fell out they prosecuted their disputes through each other's animals. In one incident a man enraged by his neighbour's continuing failure to keep his strappers under control seized an intruding stray and broke one of its forelegs, snapping it with his hands. One of Gwyn's enemies imprisoned a pregnant ewe belonging to Gwyn in a barn and starved it almost to death before slipping it back,

little more than an animated corpse, to die in front of its horrified shepherd. Another trick was to round up offending animals,
put them in a trailer and drive them miles away, then let it be
known on the grapevine where they could be found.

'It's bloody medieval around here,' Jenny said, shaking her
head.

Warring neighbours tore down one another's fences, stole hay
and hurdles from remote barns. Or they marched, toting a shotgun, into a hostile farmyard, to murder dogs suspected of attacking their sheep. At the climax of one confrontation over a
collapsing fence, two sets of brothers fought a battle on the hill.
In a perverse, self-spiting insult, the losers chained one of their
own dogs to a stake on the mountain near the disputed boundary and left it there, eating its own faeces to survive.

The police and the animal protection authorities were never
involved – to inform on a rival, however hated, was simply not
done. Jenny's love of animals was well known, and she grew used
to being suspected of telling tales.

'You'd better feed them soon, or someone will see and report
you,' was her ultimate sanction. When someone did see, and did
make the call to the RSPCA, she would naturally be blamed,
though the reporters were almost certainly walkers, appalled by
the starving or mistreated victims they had stumbled upon.

— * —

When Jenny had finished knitting the wire to the new post with
baler twine she declared the job done.

'Aren't we brilliant? We did it! What a team – we're the three
musketeers,' she exclaimed, and we laughed and felt bigger; a
little chipped, like the post, because we were unwilling volun-
teers, but a little heroic too.

'See? We can do anything if we put our minds to it, and all
help each other,' she continued, as we made our way home,
lugging the tools through our own private evening: the valley
filled with shadow half an hour before the sun left our uplands;

up here every thistle cast a long shadow, midges still danced in the lanes for us, and our bats came out to hunt them, skiing wildly through the warm air, little black flickers against the still sky.

From the meadows came the thrum of pounding feet: the lambs were running races, forty or more hurtling along beside the hedge towards an invisible finishing line, some leaping, kicking and twisting, others pouncing in a joyful, stiff-legged dressage, before they all turned and bolted back the other way.

'Look at the moon!' Alexander pointed. It was waxing, a silver crescent supporting a blue shadow.

'Oh, yes,' Jenny sighed. 'Isn't that wonderful – the new moon with the old moon in his arms . . . Goodness me, aren't we lucky?' she breathed. We paused and gazed about us: she encouraged us to stop and drink in beauty, to set sights in our minds like post cards. Two herons, standing on the church tower one morning, seemed to be doing the same thing. Wild sentinels in grey morning dress, their drooping crests like warriors' plumes, they looked like pagan conquerors who had dressed for a wedding then seized the church, and were now surveying their demesne.

When the three of us stood like that, attempting to grasp, in the glow of each moment, the true, full being of the place, as we tried to open our senses enough to embrace it, widening our eyes and ears, it was as though we were all the same age, child–adults, knowing nothing but wonder.

We all sensed it but Jenny made it explicit. 'Age doesn't mean a thing, you know,' she said. 'In the great scheme of things we're only here for a millisecond – if you look at it that way I'm pretty well the same age as you.'

I turned this thought over. It had serious implications, which I broached one night in the kitchen, as she struggled through the sheaves of paper in the cardboard box which somehow directed our lives: her 'admin'.

'I don't understand how you become an adult,' I said. 'How do you know how to do admin and pay bills?'

'I don't know, darling! But don't worry about it – as you grow up you will understand. It just happens.'

'Can you teach me now?'

'No, I'm afraid I can't! I'm hopeless at it – that's why I have an accountant.'

It was as though the gap between our ages changed constantly. When she attempted admin, pulling her hair, muttering to herself, piling heaps of cigarette ash on the floor on one side of her chair, and torn envelopes on the other, she did not seem much older, or more competent, than a sixth-former. But once she had passed the front door, the moment she confronted the farm, she became, in a trice, commanding. Then she was in charge again, at the head of her troops: like any good officer, she was keen to develop their capacities.

We began as little more than self-propelled barriers, slightly cleverer than dogs but not as fast. We progressed, via fencing, nettling, gathering wood, grave-digging and lamb-feeding, to catching and holding. This was properly useful, and could mean hours in the pens, sliding around in the muck, buzzed by the flies, infuriated by the sheep, and subjected to the long, soothing monologue Jenny kept up, talking to and about each animal as you grabbed it, subdued it and presented it for drenching, maggotting or vaccination.

'Hello, lamb, aren't you beautiful? Who's your mother then? Oh I know, you're one of Hippo's twins. You've done very well considering your mother is so hopeless. Dear Hippo, I've never known a sheep with less of a clue about parenting. First she tried to adopt someone else's, then she abandoned it, and then she damn near abandoned you, didn't she, sweetheart? Hold still!'

The monologue was broken occasionally with terse commands to me: 'Watch out!' 'Don't hurt her!' 'We've already done that one . . .' Her mind was entirely absorbed in the task, and each animal's well-being. Your tiring limbs, shortening temper and circling mind did not exist. Many, many times I raised my eyes towards the sticky canopy of the sycamore tree which shaded the pens and thought darkly of my father's departure and decided that there was no mystery to it at all. He probably resented being used as a sort of sheepdog with arms . . .

'Good! That's the last of this lot – only one more lot to go and we'll have done it! And you can stop looking so sorry for yourself . . .'

'I hate sheep,' I shouted. 'I hate farming and I hate sheep, they're so stupid!'

'They are not,' she shouted back. 'Some of them are very clever, as a matter of fact. Now, stop fussing and come and help, please.'

'No! Why should I? I don't ask you to help with my home-work, do I?'

'If you won't help me,' she said, bending towards me slightly, with narrowed eyes, 'I won't help you. Then you can cook your own supper, and wash your own clothes, and get yourself to school. Or you can go and live with Robert. It's absolutely up to you . . .'

She turned back to the sheep. I sent a beam of pure fury at the quilted back of the green body-warmer she always wore, a tatty sleeveless thing with pockets full of nuts that the sheep adored, and were forever nuzzling, and did as I was told, impotently, pointedly sulking, like an angry cat.

It was not quite true, though: I did not hate sheep. I loathed one or two, when we could not catch them, and detested small bands which insisted on running the wrong way. I devised an imaginary instrument for herding them, like a machine gun which would fire clay pigeons. As the operator and inventor I would enjoy setting it up in the corner of the field, and demon-strating it, firing streams of bursting, leaping projectiles in a flail-ing ribbon across the field, a line no sheep would ever dare cross. A burst on the left, a burst on the right to turn them, a little squirt behind them to get them going, and as for any that broke away . . .

'Will you please concentrate! Think what you're doing, sweet-heart, or we'll be here all day!'

I gave up that fantasy, guiltily and for ever, the day one of our rams was faced with a real gun. He was dying in the First

Meadow. I did not know what was wrong with him, but Jenny was quite unequivocal, and very busy.

'He's a goner, I'm afraid, the poor old boy. He's in pain too, so I've asked the vet to come and kill him,' she explained. She was being deliberately brisk. 'Jack doesn't want to, and I don't blame him.'

Jack shook his head. I felt a shameful disappointment, having hoped for a glimpse of his famous Humane Killer, the bolt gun which he used for stunning pigs, a darkly precious instrument which he tried never to let me see, lest I should try to touch it. His reputation would not permit him to turn down a pigsticking but he would not kill a sheep if there was any choice: the Humane Killer remained wrapped in its oily sack. 'We've got to deal with a minor crisis in the barn,' Jenny went on, 'and the vet is on his way. The thing is, I'm worried about that ram, lying out there by himself. I'm scared the crows will come and get his eyes. Would you mind going down and keeping them off him?'

It was a gritty grey day, spits of rain in the wind. The ram was the only animal in the First Meadow. He lay on his side, bloated and wretched. As I approached he shifted a little but he could barely kick his short legs. His flanks heaved as he watched me come; we stared helplessly at each other. I was sure he knew what was going to happen and feared he thought I might be his death. His bleat was a rough gargling.

'It's all right, boy,' I said, 'it's all right.' I sat down next to him. He looked at me, and I imagined appeal in his dark yellow eye, and pain. I stroked his head. It was a queer, desolate sensation to sit with him, beside all his size and smell and plight, and feel the warmth of him through his wool, and to sense his senses, his snorting nostrils, his licking tongue, and know that a man was coming to make an end of him, to put out all this life. I looked at the mud between his clees, and thought it would still be there when we dropped him into his grave, and marvelled that death should be so certain, and so near.

Three crows glided down from the hill fence to the Lower Meadow, thirty yards below, shouting angrily as they came overhead. In the Lower Meadow they shouted again — Kaaa! Kaaa! Kaaa! — then they came back up, turning their heads towards us as they flapped past, lascivious and impatient.

For a while I talked to the ram. I told him it would be over soon, and that I was sorry, and I burst into tears. He stared at the dank field. I felt ridiculous, stopped crying and picked a handful of dull winter grass which I held under his nose. He did not want it. I was horribly relieved when the vet arrived — ashamed at my sentimentality, which I suspected I had stoked — and still bleakly sorry for the ram.

The vet brought a pistol. Jenny was appalled: why not an injection? The vet had some reason. Mum hustled my brother and me into the car, contriving a mission to town, but as we came down the track above the First Meadow she slowed, unable to pass the sight of Jack and the vet standing over the animal. I understood: there was something unconvincing about the tableau, about the way the vet held his gun. Jack retreated.

'Oh hell, he's going to make a mess of it,' Mum blurted, and the vet fired. Jack started to approach the body but the vet held up a hand to stop him, and bent over the animal again. He fired another shot, and, after a word with Jack, a third.

'The stupid — incompetent — wretched —' Jenny ground out, 'hopeless — bloody — fool!' she shouted, to us, with the car windows up, in an unclenching fury. 'Goodness me, I'd like to give him a piece of my mind! But if I do he'll never come back. And one day we'll need him again, heaven forbid. Don't do it, Jenny. Bite your tongue . . . '

We all adopted this sort of running commentary, which was part conversation, part performance and part self-instruction, so although there were only three of us we lived in a babble of conversations. There was barely any distinction between talking to a dog, a cat, a sheep or to yourself. Alexander could often be seen talking to Toss, I murmured to myself whenever I was alone, and Jenny, when she was not chatting to the sheep, thought aloud as a matter of course, especially when problem-solving.

I discovered the many merits of this as soon as I was old enough to be sent alone into the lambing fields at night, to do a late round.

'There's one thinking about it in the Far Meadow, just the other side of the hedge,' Jenny said. 'If she's having trouble give me a shout. She's a very good little ewe though, so it should just slip out. Wake me if there's anything. Wrap up warm!'

Outside, under the protective yellow penumbra of the yard light, I tried out the heavy lambing torch. The sliding switch was temperamental.

'Not too far forward and not too far back,' I muttered at it, and flashed the long white wand into the cavern of shadow behind the Big Barn before heading down the track. One of the old biddies at the top of the Patch belled a question. 'Good biddy, only me,' I answered. She repeated herself. Her noise seemed to expose me and I was already jumpy. As I passed her I tried to sound quietly confident. 'It's only me, I'm just going out to look around the meadows, and then I'll be back, all right? Be quiet.' She called again.

I kept the torch off but my thumb was tense against the switch. There was some scattered bleating from the hill fields. 'It's just a fox . . . passing through,' I announced, to the night breeze, making it so. The Middle Meadow gate made its familiar double rattle. I advanced into the dark field. The hedges whispered, tapping their twigs and creaking.

'Now, where are these sheep?' My voice sounded warm and orderly, pushing back the not-quite-formless dark; my sensible tone reducing the impenetrable conspiracy of the night to nameable things: low cloud and light wind over a wet field.

I switched on the torch and turned a slow circle. Molehills looked black-red, like fat scabs; sheep's eyes glinted blue-green. Beyond the range of the torch the darkness thickened, seemed to contract. I stared down the blade of light. The flock were settled and peaceful. I spoke to them, reassuringly.

'I see, you're all down there . . . chewing your cud . . . so you're not doing it . . . nor are you . . . everyone's OK . . .' As the eye of light fell on them they stopped chewing for a moment, turned their heads slightly, and waited for it to move on. 'Good . . . very good . . . what was that?'

A choked, whickering sound from the middle hedge. 'She's doing it,' I thought, with a surge of adrenalin. 'Don't run,' I told myself. 'Don't frighten her.'

She was down on her side, a bulge of flesh pinkly distending under her tail, which was bloody and wet. As I approached she tried to stand. 'It's all right, sweetheart, all right, girl. Stay there, don't get up, don't get up,' I gabbled, but at least the tone was right, low down, part reassurance, part supplication.

I was with her quickly, on my knees, hand on her side, and she was not trying to get away now; there, bulging out of her, yellowish and covered in slimy fluid, were the nostrils and the tiny clees of her lamb. The night seemed to funnel down through concentric circles: in the vastness of the dark was the tiny splash of torchlight, in the torchlight was the little puddle of flesh and fluid, and in the middle of that was . . .

'Nose and feet together, that's good,' I said, my heart thudding, knowing I was not going to go all the way back to the house and fetch my mother to what looked like a perfect birth. 'Good girl! I can almost get my fingers . . . push! There–there, there you are, good girl, push!'

I worked at the tight ring of muscle, easing it back a fraction, just enough to get finger and thumb purchase on the soft, tiny feet. The ewe groaned; I heaved. 'It's coming! It's coming, good girl, very good . . .' Now there was an inch of leg behind each foot and a centimetre of nose above the nostrils. A gentle pull had no effect at all. The ewe was panting like a runner and I was shivering with nerves. 'Right, I don't want to hurt it, but it can't stay there . . . this lamb needs to come out and breathe . . . I'm going to give it a proper pull . . . are you going to help me, biddy? Come on, girl, come on!'

Wincing – to ward off the possibility I might pull the baby's front legs out of their sockets – I pulled, building up the draw until it took all my strength. 'It's coming,' I cried, and there it was, long and yellow and sliding out now, an entire lamb, perfect from end to end, finished with fleece, ears, tail, toes, eyes and even lashes, flopping out on to the dark wet grass, a small, impossibly complete sheep, half in and half out of the glistening cape of its amniotic sac.

'Clear the nose and mouth,' I told myself, and pinched the slime away from its head. 'Now it has to breathe,' I added, 'or I have to rub it to get it going . . .' But there it was, a miraculous, spluttering cough, and the lamb threshed, and its legs seemed to engage suddenly, like gears, and then it was wriggling up on to its knees and trying to stand. The ewe was on her feet in a moment, all over it, whickering and muttering, nuzzling and licking madly, nudging and kissing and guzzling the slime, and as she talked to her baby it answered; a high bewildered cry, which carried far across the dark fields.

I poked my head around my mother's door before I turned in, and proudly told her what had happened. 'Wonderful!' she said. 'And did it stand and . . .'

'Yes,' I said, because I knew the last line, 'it suckled. It had its first drink!'

We were taught by this sort of mnemonic narrative in an eclectic range of subjects, Jenny's interests. We both became quite good at stars. On a cloudless night the three of us stood outside, a little way down the path towards the hill, so that we were clear of the towering ash tree which guarded the house, and tilted our heads back, like the dogs when they had treed a squirrel. Jenny pointed up as if the heavens were a great blackboard.

'The big W?' she prompted.

'Cassiopeia.'

'Good. Easy one – that group of little stars, how many are there?'

'Seven! Seven Sisters.'

'Good, what's their other name?'

'Pleiades.'

'Good. Alexander, what are those three?'

'Orion's Belt,' he said, and went on to quote her precisely. 'And there's his bow, and there's his dagger hanging down.'

'Very good. And what's that saucepan?'

'The Plough.'

'Yes. Now, where's the North Star?'

'There!'

'Good. So why can't either of you learn flowers?'

We laughed. We were intimate with foxgloves (and the trick of gently pinching shut one of their pink trumpets behind a visiting bee, for the outraged buzz the insect made before you released it) and with honeysuckle, which we suckled. We all delighted at the lemon-cream eruption of the primroses in the exhausted, after-winter Lower Meadows, and the harebells which appeared behind the house, pale lavender and exquisite, tiptoeing, tremulous as fairies. But we were hopeless at hedge flowers. In May or June, as we bowled along the lanes in the car, the questions would start.

'Now, what's that white plant, children?'

'Uuummm . . .'

'Oh do wake up! It's Queen Anne's lace! My favourite!' She brought the car to a stop.

'Twinks, what are those white stars in the hedge?'

'Celandines?'

'NO! You know they aren't! White stars in the hedge – come on!'

'Stitchwort?'

'That's right, poor man's buttonhole. Pim, what's that?'

'Vetch?'

'No, it's Herb Robert.'

'Herb Robert!'

'Yes – so what's that lovely thing?'

'Campion?'

'No – that's Vetch!'

'Ahh! That's Vetch!'

'I don't know, it's hopeless,' she sighed. 'You can do fauna, why not flora?'

\*

Fauna was more exciting. Animals and birds did things, ate things, moved, died, left traces. I became obsessed with tracks and signs, picking up egg shells in spring, feathers in summer, poking at droppings and prizing owl pellets. 'Shit Exploring', my brother called it. 'Oh no, not Shit Exploring,' he moaned, wilting, as I made haphazard guesses at the kind of bird that had left this particular turd. 'Why can't we play a game?'

I was merciless in imposing my crazes upon him, and he was normally forgiving. He did get very fed up with my insistence on walking everywhere quietly, though.

'Shhh!' I hissed. 'Step around the sticks, and don't let these branches brush you.'

'Why? Why do we always have to sneak about?' he roared. 'We're not hiding from anything, are we?'

We knew the land so well that we often wished we were hiding: if only an enemy would come and chase us, we could use our territory to defeat him. I spun a monologue out of how it might go: you could skip across the deep stream on the fallen tree which would not take his weight, and tiptoe across the steepest slope above the rotting corpses – he would probably break his neck. And then there were the fences he would take an age to climb, because he did not know the crossing points, and if that did not work there was always the gully: you could go straight up to knacker him out, then . . . but Alexander was not listening. He was pointing straight up.

'Wow! Look,' he yelped. 'Balloon! Hot air balloon!'

And there it was, vastly red and bright, its extraordinary swelling sides somehow cupped in the palms of the air. Now its burner roared magnificently, sending Lark scrambling home for shelter and Toss charging up the hill for battle. Alexander and I laughed and shouted after him and waved at the enormous, fatly elegant thing.

Jenny came out of the kitchen and said, grudgingly: 'Terrifies the sheep of course, but never mind . . .'

I saluted the basket. I knew how they felt up there, suspended over the breathless world. And I imagined them passing envious comment, as they looked down on our realm. Bird-men in hang gliders also came to visit us, and watching them I felt barely earth-bound, as free and more free than they could be, in permanent residence on the mountain, while they had to turn for home.

'Good dog, Toss! You see him off,' we laughed at the hound, as he bayed at the retreating alien. He failed to catch any hot air balloons, but turned into a first-rate guard dog. He established a fearsome reputation for biting people and we were not sorry. When friends and neighbours came they telephoned ahead, or waited in their cars until assured 'that dog' was inside.

The only unannounced intruders we had now were those who did not know what they were getting into, and the police, who came once or twice, cautioning us to keep the dog under control. It was our fault. At first we thought it very funny, when the dots appeared on the skyline, to see Toss take off like a rocket, hurdle two fences, streak straight up the mountain, and, moments after his little black arrowhead intersected with the silhouettes, inspire distant shrieks and screams.

'Bloody walkers! Good dog!' Toss went for the colour red. Anyone wearing red hiking socks and blundering across our fences was in trouble. Jenny developed a redemption strategy, which involved running victims to the hospital for jabs and then pressing cash on them, to pay for ripped trousers and bloodied socks. They might also get the standard lecture, if they had been caught on our ground, about trespassing.

'Where do you come from?' she would ask.

'Luton (or somewhere),' came the reply.

'Well, how would you like it if you found me climbing over your garden fence in Luton?'

It was not a robust strategy, and Toss lived, obliviously and near permanently, on his final warning, and we all dreaded the day he would go too far, and 'they' would come and get him.

'They' were a puzzling enemy, comprised of all the faceless human forces who were not on our side. They dug up the roads in inexplicable places, making us late for school. They wanted our sheep to be ear-marked, an identical mutilation of every animal, which was supposed to make them harder to steal. They cut the hedges with vicious flails, destroying birds' nests and leaving thorns in the lanes which punctured our tyres. They cut down trees, ripped up the old field boundaries, set snares, hunted foxes, trapped and baited badgers. They flew fighter jets low over the mountain, terrifying our animals and us. They were wedded to fertilisers and chemicals, forcing us to dip the sheep in poison twice a year. They believed in the Bomb and nuclear power stations; they beat and broke the miners. And then they had the gall to traipse across our fences, practically inviting Toss to bite them . . .

No one we respected ever spoke up for them, except our father, whose clear-eyed comments could cut through all our peculiar philosophy. During one of his visits we were walking down the mountain on an inclement day when we encountered some walkers: before we could stop him, Toss had nipped one of them. Dad made a mortified apology, then turned to us angrily and said: 'Your dog's a bloody menace.'

There was suddenly no denying it. Toss was a savage, and we were savages too.

Another time, driving with him further up the valley, I looked at a particularly wild stretch of mountain and announced that I wanted to live there.

'But how would you make your living?' he countered, curiously.

I had no answer. The idea of making a living had barely occurred to me. As I understood it, you did what you wanted to do and your living somehow made you. He was the only person we knew who had an office job, and we questioned him on it: what do you do when you get to work? What's it like, where do you have lunch, what happens after that? He answered us patiently, but the world he described seemed unreal. On one visit to London he led us at a jog up a long, dirty spiral staircase out of the Underground, remarking, 'I don't take the lift – this is the only exercise I get every day!' He laughed sadly as he said it, which allowed me to take it as a joke. I could not seriously believe that anyone, least of all my father, could live such a deprived life.

He bridged the gap between us and them, and however perverse 'they' seemed, anything associated with him was, to me, sacrosanct.

The farm was scattered with his doings: Robert's roof, Robert's bit of fence; the swings he set up in one of the larch trees behind the house, which were amazing, allowing the rider to hurl himself off a collapsing old wall and fly out, with the shed roofs, the yard and the whole valley whirling away between his feet. Even the bulb in the yard light was his, since only he was tall enough to approach it, via the extendable ladder; it was an annual ritual that on one of his visits he would climb up to replace it. I loved to be compared to him; if one of my jokes made my mother laugh she would sometimes say, 'That's so like your father. Gosh, he could be funny, so dry . . .' In the Lower Meadows one evening, I was standing among tall thistles, lost in some thought, waiting for Mum to tie up the gate, when I noticed she had finished, and was looking at me. 'You looked just like Robert, then,' she said, 'exactly the same,' and I tried to work out how I had done it. My brother, who is very handsome, and sometimes melancholy, was often compared to him.

We both longed that when he came he would linger, and Jenny did too, for our sake. 'Can you stay?' we always asked, though we knew, and even now, the word 'London', the summons and finality in its heavy syllables, reminds me of his answer.

With time, I came to accept that the three of us were sufficient to ourselves, and that it was unlikely that Jenny would meet someone else. Robert's feeling was that occasional meetings for significant periods would be better for everyone than 'little and often' – weekend encounters and truncated visits. We accepted this too, and Alexander and I would count the weeks, days and, at last, hours until he came again, and the sight of his car cresting the pitch and advancing towards us was one of the most thrilling sights of our childhood.

He always came on Boxing Day, with presents wrapped in beautiful paper. When we had unwrapped them, and eaten a second Christmas lunch, our fabulous new toys were carried back to his car, we climbed in, and the three of us set out for London, and a week of him, and theatres and cinemas and television, in a city glittering with lights and Christmas trees. On New Year's Eve we drank champagne. 'Cheers, chaps,' Dad said, and winked, as we downed the bright bubbles. Jenny spent it alone.

Almost the New Year – Rob took the children away on Boxing Day, at 3 in the afternoon, for a week in London. I am pleased they are surrounded by radiators and central heating and television and museums, and, hopefully, films and pantomimes. I am here, quite alone except for the animals (350 sheep) surrounded by tinsel and holly and ivy inside, and snow and strips of ice out. It is odd to be without the children. Awful really. But I have a battle to fight with the weather keeping all the animals alive, and that is tremendously extending and takes my mind off my loneliness. And I think of John Eskell now that Betty is dead, and he so lonely now, and also, there are the desperately brave and valiant Poles holed up in their mines hanging on to their Solidarity. Being alone on a Welsh mountain is rich really. I'd rather be here than alone in a flat in Chelsea. And I remembered to buy a bolt before Christmas, and when the children went away I spent some time trying to nail it to the bedroom door. I feel much safer now when I go to bed even though I couldn't get the screws to go right in. A freezing fog. The yard unfrozen and awash in deep brown sheep droppings (because I've allowed 70-odd to live in the buildings during these three weeks of blizzard and cold) and outside the back door and blowing in billows a thick white fog. In the morning I heard a sheep bleating high on the hill, so, in thick mist and dusk, walked the hill fence. Followed the four-leaf clover tracks of a small fox. In the Quoiker Lark discovered a perfect, fresh sheep's front leg. It was white, loose, no smell. A murder. A world of pathos in this beautiful, softly fleeced limb. I looked, slipping on ice, the dusk changing to darkness, for the rest of the animal. Like tracking a murderer, trying to read clues in the snow. But in the white fields and deep snow I couldn't distinguish it. I'll look again tomorrow. I need to know the mark on the fleece. Derwyn, and Mr Evans, I know, both have killer dogs.

I felt so hungry when I came back. I sliced off a piece of cold lamb shoulder and ate it with a cold roast potato . . .

The self-conscious pathos in the last line and the ellipsis suggests she did not write without a certain humour, but it is a pitiful portrait. When we came back from London we pulled the decorations down and threw the holly in the fire. It burned with a rush so fierce that the flames were almost white, as if all the cheer of Christmas was released and spent at once. Now we faced January together. Garnet, one of the farmers at the bottom of the hill, waved as we passed him in the lane. 'See you in March then, Jenny,' he said. 'Different world up there . . .'

One night we saw a sunset like an icy apocalypse; over mountains still as rigor mortis a flash of gold bled out of a murderous sky, as if the last hope for the world was retreating. It was to be a hard, hard winter.

# 8

## Great Snow

IN THE COLD the mountains look like clenched fists, bare, lined here and there with white, where the paths have frosted and the streams frozen. When it is clear, the icy brightness of the sky seems to yell, almost blinding in its cold blue infinity. At night the stars are crushed diamonds, scattered winking across the velvet black; planets like tiny fires blaze – red-blinking Mars; Venus, the evening's fiery pearl. In the morning Sirius, the Dog Star, shines brighter than the fading moon. Snow is heralded by a slight alleviation of the cold, and a certain yellow light on the far horizon, which we learned to take as a warning. I was out when snow clouds came suddenly, roiling in from the northwest, tumbling over themselves like angry waves, a vast white tide, submerging the sky, drowning the stars and dousing the full moon. I hurried inside as the moonlight faltered, faded, and the hills disappeared, and the flakes came spiralling down.

Jenny listened to bad winter forecasts with dread for our fortunes as much as those of the animals; we could stand any rain or wind, but ice and snow meant leaving the car in the valley and walking down to it, then lugging ourselves and our supplies back up. We did it for weeks when necessary: Jenny walked us down and drove us to school, then did the shopping, climbed back up with carrier bags, fed the sheep, then walked down again and drove to fetch us, before finally shepherding us home.

The trek to school was wonderful, first thing, all downhill, with rabbit tracks and fox's prints to identify and untangle. Jenny showed us the tiny footmarks of mice and the four-twig tracks of crows. We pictured all the night's goings-on, as the sheep greeted us hungrily, looking strikingly yellow against the snow. Down the lane we slithered, and on into the wood, where we found rooks turning over the snowy leaf-litter beside the road: they exploded up from the cover as we approached, ragged, wet-looking purple shapes, like djinns incarnated from the dark mulch under the snow, cawing protests about the interruption of breakfast.

The walk back up was not so good; tired at the end of the day, wanting nothing more than to settle down with our toys, we clambered out of the car at the foot of the hill and started up the opening section, the thigh-searingly steep first pitch. My brother, with his little legs, found it particularly tough, and as any youngest child knows, it is twice as hard to walk uphill as the last of the party than it is as the first.

The glimmering wood seemed to listen as we trudged through it, following our own tracks. The tangled trees darkened against the stippled white; somewhere amongst them snow slipped off a branch with a noise like a poacher stumbling.

'Come on, darlings,' Jenny said. 'It won't be long now and you'll be bigger than me, and I'll be saying please, please wait for me!' Alexander stumped along, grumbling at the pace, until Jenny clipped Toss to a lead and handed it to him: the dog pulled him on like a husky.

When we were not at school Alexander and I hurled ourselves into the drifts, snow in our sleeves and hard-packed down our boots, snow down our necks, the cold crystal taste of it in our mouths, our cheeks burning, our bodies hot under layers of clothes and coats.

When it had not snowed for a week, and days after most of the area's roads had been cleared, a plough would arrive, spurting gouts of white, or a council digger appear, patiently scooping the drifts out of the lane and dumping them into the fields. Ice might keep us walking for days after we were dug out.

Jenny developed a winter routine: at the first threatening fore-cast she stocked up supplies, lagged the water tank and the pipes above the bathroom, turned up the radiators, moved the sheep to fields best sheltered from the expected direction of the wind, and waited. She called on Jack and warned him not to try and reach us if it snowed. The village cottages seemed to huddle together for warmth, smoke rising from their chimneys like breath. 'Wish us luck, dear Jack,' Jenny instructed him. 'And make sure you keep warm, for goodness sake!' We knew she dreaded the snow, but Alexander and I looked forward to it: she was in control, what did we have to fear?

'Gritter!' Jenny shouted, as we drove to town for supplies. The sight of one of the council's bright-striped lorries was an omen as powerful as the yellowish light in the sky. 'It must be bad if they're out,' we agreed, as the vehicle rattled past, flashing its orange strobe and pelting the road with reddish lumps of salt. On the way back from town the first flakes came; we eyed the ground and studied the sky. 'Will it stick?' we pondered. 'Too wet, I think,' Jenny decided. 'We'll chance it tonight.'

We cheered. It was a miserable sleety night to have to walk all that way, with the shopping too. The next morning the fields were mottled, snow covering the roots, the grass like green fur on the back of a white beast, as if winter was pushing itself up through the ground. Still the flakes fell, sometimes fast, sometimes slowly, sidelong slipping through colder air, careless, unhurried, as if the weather was shifting from foot to foot, waiting.

'I'm taking the car down to the bottom,' Jenny announced, after she had heard the lunchtime forecast. 'It's coming, my dears . . .'

As she walked back up the hill it began to fall heavily; now there was nothing warm anywhere in the world, except her sheep in their coats. They called to her as she passed.

'Good girls, sensible sheep, you stay there. You'll be warm under that hedge . . .'

As Big Ben struck six, Jenny turned away from the radio and towards the supper she was making, frowning. The forecast was not good – we might well be walking for a week, she thought. Had it given any true impression of what was coming, she might have been tempted to evacuate us and drive the flock off our land, down to our neighbours' lower fields. Instead we ate, played and built one of our great fires. We filled the grate with a wigwam of branches over crumpled newspaper and twigs, lit it, and basked in the heat of a roaring conflagration, which sent skirls of sparks swirling up the chimney and flung ruddy light into the cold sitting room. We perched as close to it as we could, until our clothes were almost too hot to touch and our clammy backs felt feverish, as though they too were glowing red. The crackling branches spat sparks on to the rug, and we stamped them out, tutting mildly at the little black pits that remained. With the draughts on one side and the fire on the other you could feel two temperatures at once. When the blaze had burned down to its embers we went to bed, and the next day the storm arrived.

'Blizzard,' said Jenny tersely, peering out through the bedroom windows.

Term had not yet started, so after breakfast we kitted up and went out to see what was happening. It was a near-whiteout. I got as far as the bottom of the yard before turning back. The wind was coming from the north and east, driving the snow off the mountain, straight down the gully and on to us. It was like being under a pressure hose of snow – snow blowing horizontally, vertically and diagonally, snow coming up at your face from the ground as you bowed your head under the blasting, strengthening wind. And the cold was like a punch in the ear. As Alexander and I retreated to the living room, arming ourselves with toy guns and preparing to exchange fire between defensive positions behind the sofas, Jenny set out to feed the sheep.

It was already drifting in the lanes, forming waves against every wall, hedge and bank. The world was changing shape. The cold soon drained the strength out of Jenny's arms and legs, but she did what she could, dragging out bales, and cutting their restraining strings. The wind spun armfuls of hay away into the white, swirling it off like so much dust. She made it as far as the Lower Meadows, ducking lower and lower under the blizzard. Peering about her she realised she was nearly lost, in a field she knew intimately. She turned back. She followed the gradients back up towards the First Meadow with nothing but the feel of the ground underfoot to guide her. There was a cold tapping against her cheek: icicles were forming in her hair where it escaped from under her hat.

Halfway across the First Meadow, she stopped briefly to rest and get her bearings. But there was nothing to tell her where she was: the whiteout was complete. The field, the gentle little meadow nearest the house, was gone. There was nothing now but wind, and the infinite, clinging snow. She staggered on, going slower as the freezing air plucked her strength out of her and little drifts tugged at her legs. She sat down for a moment to recover her breath – 'I'll just get my strength back,' she thought peaceably, and the moment stretched, and she was less cold now, almost warm, everything was better. Sitting there in the snow was strange and beautiful, and the wind was a little gentler nearer the ground. Perhaps she might close her eyes for a minute.

She jerked suddenly, lifting her gaze to the mazy whirlpool of flakes.

'My God,' she thought, all at once. 'I have to get back to the house right now. I have to get back.'

She stood once more, bent her head, and began to trudge slowly up across the field, towards the place where the house must be.

We looked up from our game as she came in, pursued by a gust of snowflakes. Her hair was clotted with icicles.

'Look!' she cried. 'Look, children, I've got icicles in my hair!'

'Wow!'

'I think I nearly died in the First Meadow . . .'

We did not know what to make of this, so we stared at her, and her icicles, and made sympathetic noises. 'Truly,' she said. 'It was touch and go, I promise you! It's really dangerous out there. Batten down the hatches, we'll just have to wait until it passes.'

The storm came on all that day. It attacked the house like a legion of furious, freezing ghosts: licking under the doors with its white wet tongues; pouring down the chimney; coming up through the drains. The plug holes and overflow holes in the sinks and the bath spat icy draughts. Finally the windows froze over inside and out, and the world beyond them disappeared.

As the light began to go, in mid afternoon, Jenny scratched a hole in the coating of one of the panes and peered out. For a moment she could not comprehend what she was seeing: huge white shapes moving across the back patch. Then she realised what they were: whirling off drifts, which stirred like waves, were twisting pillars of snow, stalking silhouettes, circling the house.

'Golly!' she muttered, and closed the curtains. 'I think we might be here for the duration, my dears,' she announced, tugging the curtain tight. 'Just listen to that wind . . . have you ever heard anything like it?'

As we looked at one another the pause between us was immediately swallowed by a roaring noise like a train, a noise which rose to fall and rise again, on and on, raging and tormented. How puny and temporary we felt, as we listened to it, and how thrilled too, in our little fortress of stone and wood, as it defied the terrible elements.

'I hope it won't pull the roof off,' Jenny said, rolling her eyes, partly in mischief, partly from nerves.

'No, Mummy . . .' Alexander said, smiling uncertainly. 'It won't, will it?'

'No, it won't. It's stood for centuries. Nothing to worry about. Except the poor sheep!'

The fire hissed and twisted in the grate, battling the draughts and flakes in the chimney, and my brother and I went back to playing with our toys and messing around with the dog. There was a fizz in us which did not just come from being inside all day: it was a rare feeling, gleeful and nervy, as the wind howled – really howled, like an animal – to be safe but not secure from the danger outside. Jenny listened to the radio, the wind and our bumps and bangs, and quietly prayed that the electricity would not fail.

The lights stayed on, the phone still worked, we had supper and went to bed as normal. While we slept, Jenny lay in bed, listening to the wind. As it flailed the corners of the house the stone moaned, raising a wuthering, fluting song. She wondered what we would find outside, the next day, and then she slept too.

She awoke puzzled. Something had changed. As she shook off her sleep, she realised what it was. The roaring had stopped. In fact, all noise had stopped. All was perfect silence.

In the bathroom she noticed there were no more draughts coming up through the pipes. She hurried back to the bedroom and woke us.

'Time to get up, boys. It's not quite as cold as it was yesterday but it's still pretty chilly . . .'

In winter it was always cold, even with the radiators on, the fire going and the cooker turned right up. When Robert came to stay, one Christmas, he went to bed in the Beast House bedroom fully clothed, with a woolly hat on. Jenny was in the habit of keeping her coat on when she came in from the fields, which always made me uncomfortable. We ought at least to act, I felt, as if there was a distinction between the sheds and the house. Jenny was impatient with such niceties. 'But I'm cold,' she said, when I objected. 'Put a jumper on then,' I retorted, smugly: it was one of her catchphrases.

Getting out of bed that morning we were sensitive to every degree, selecting from multiple vests, shirts and jumpers.

'Layers,' Jenny said, throwing us each another vest. 'Layers are the key!'

Downstairs reeked of dog: Lark and Toss grinned at our appearance. Jenny tried to let them out, but the back door was frozen shut. The windows had thick white curtains drawn across them from the outside, so when I went to open the front door I had no inkling of what might be there.

The door often stuck, as it did now, so I put my back into it and heaved on the handle. It opened, but I did not move. Before me was a vertical white wall, containing a perfect imprint of the doorknob and the knocker.

'Mummy! Twinks! Look!'

We stared at the snow wall. It was as though a great polar beast had died in the yard and was now lying with its flank slumped against the house. Or it was a variation of *The Lion, the Witch and the Wardrobe*: our front door now led to the back of someone's fridge. It was ludicrous, somehow. We laughed as if it were a practical joke.

'Crumbs,' Jenny said. 'Buried alive!'

Alexander and I exchanged thrilled glances.

'Upstairs,' Jenny said. 'We'll get a view from the landing window. Unless we're completely covered.' She led the way. On the landing we scraped and scratched at the windows and peered out. The entire front of the house was drowned in drifts. They came up as far as the upstairs windows, huge lapping white waves with snow still falling on to them. The blizzard had swallowed us.

We went back downstairs and ate breakfast. The phone was dead, there was no more dry wood and no way of getting to the woodshed. Under the overhead lights, which we needed, because the snow smothered the daylight, Jenny's face looked drawn. Her gaze shifted uneasily from us to the opaque windows.

'I don't know if I should try to go out or what. I ought to go and see how they are, but I don't know if I'll be able to do anything for them. It might not be very sensible . . . I don't even know how I'll get out of the house.'

'Don't go,' Alexander said. 'It's too dangerous.'

'Yeah,' I agreed. 'We're snowed in.'

'Stay here and wait for it to melt?' Jenny exclaimed. 'It could take weeks! We'd starve, and what about my sheep? We'll have to think of something . . .' She put the kettle on.

Reassured that she was not going to try anything straightaway, Alexander and I made our way up to the attic. Leading the way up the small stone stairs, I got as far as poking my head up above floor level.

'Snow! Drifts!'

Low, perfectly smooth white dunes had formed all the way up one wall, where the draughts had penetrated the eaves. We retreated to the sitting room and began a game there.

'Snowdrifts in the attic,' we explained.

Jenny nodded thoughtfully and made herself a series of cups of coffee while she recalculated the food supplies. Soup for lunch, cauliflower cheese for supper, soup again for lunch tomorrow and pasta tomorrow night, then what? Cereal, if there was any milk left . . .

The wireless said the army were rescuing people with helicopters, and urged anyone who needed help to write SOS in the snow.

'Fat lot of good . . .' Jenny murmured. 'They'll never look for us up here.'

There was a shout and a thump from the front of the house.

'Hey! What was that?'

'Rescuers,' Jenny exclaimed, rushing to the door and opening it. As we stood staring at the white wall it chipped at the very top; a small semicircle fell away, revealing a red face, hatted, whiskery and smiling.

'Happy New Year, neighbours,' Mervyn greeted us. 'Stand back!'

He had come up the hill with his daughter's boyfriend, wading across and around a white-changed world, found the house, found a single fencing stake protruding from a drift near the Big Barn, and with this he was now digging a hole in the blockade by our front door.

'Dear Mervyn! Happy New Year! You've come to save us.'

'You can't stay here, Jenny. Best come down to ours for a bit. Better get these boys out, eh?'

'Yes! This minute! Right, children, we're being rescued. Gear up! I want you to put on the warmest clothes you have.'

We did, and Mervyn pulled us out through the hole, one at a time. Then we set off.

We walked down the yard, stumbling along, six feet above ground level. The world was unrecognisable. The five-bar gate to the track was reduced to two inches of iron sticking out of a drift. The fences had disappeared. There was no sign of the sheep. Here and there were the tops of hedges, the trees transformed into little bushes, poking out of the white. All the planes and angles of the fields had changed, whimsically rearranged by the storm. We could not walk along the usual routes, but slalomed slowly around great dunes of snow, tripping, sinking and sliding, every step a struggle. In the Horse Fields I strayed slightly and sank immediately into deep snow, floundering helplessly, panicking, until I was dragged clear.

When we reached Mervyn's house, halfway down the mountain, we were all exhausted. Avril, Mervyn's wife, fed us baked potatoes and showed us our room; then the adults held a conference. Jenny was appalled by what might be happening to her sheep, but they agreed that it was too risky to attempt to go back to them today. Alexander and I had already found the television.

The next morning Mum and Mervyn set out after breakfast to rescue the flock. The mountain had swollen, a great pregnant shape, white and huge, its woods like stiff black hair. Jenny struggled up the hill as fast as she could, terrified of what she might find.

The thought of what might be waiting for you out there is one of the things that keeps farmers going, year after year. If you have been negligent, or slow to rise, you will see the crows have gathered well before you get there, and you will know there is horror waiting, and you will find yourself praying, please, let it be dead. Please God, let it be dead . . .

Spurred on by her imagination Jenny plunged uphill through the snow, along the edge of the wood, and Mervyn had to hurry to keep up with her. They crossed the Horse Fields and the Lower Meadows and arrived at the buried fence line which marked the boundary of the Rough Field. There had been more than thirty animals here, Jenny knew, but as they stared across the field they could see nothing but waves of unbroken snow. It was as if the mountain had swallowed the flock, or the storm swept them away, sucked like spindrift into the blizzard's maw.

'Christ, they've disappeared! They've been buried alive.'

They began investigating likely areas of the field, around the banks and hedge lines, in places where Jenny knew the ground dipped, scraping and digging here and there. The drifts were a dozen feet deep and more. Mervyn cut sticks from the hedges, and they poked and prodded the snow. Where the probe met resistance they dug, and found the first victims; stiff, stuck, but alive. Jenny used her scarf as a sling, working it under the bellies of trapped, cramped ewes, then Mervyn and she tugged and heaved them free. Lark began making discoveries, barking, wagging her tail and digging furiously. As they uncovered more ewes they began noticing bare patches on their flanks and rumps: denied food or movement, the animals had nibbled their own and each other's fleeces, presumably for comfort, and whatever nourishment there might be in the wool. They moved the weakest cases up to the farm; the outhouses and sheds began to fill with the reek and press of sheep, just as they would have done in the old days, when the inhabitants lived directly above their animals, profiting from their warmth.

The searching and digging and feeding went on for two weeks. Jack came up to help. I remember all three of them coming down the mountain, returning from their expeditions full of stories about sheep nose-to-tail deep under the drifts, and full of amazement at the animals' endurance, and I remember too my mother's utter exhaustion: every evening she came back shattered. Mervyn was a tough man, a builder and a farmer, but my mother matched him, stride for stride, shovel for shovel, driven on by will and worry and care. Not one sheep was lost.

The snow still fell at intervals but the ferocity of the first storm was not repeated. When the road to town was opened and term started again, Alexander and I went to stay with friends near school while Jenny returned to the farm. The attic and the roof spaces had filled with snow; when it began to melt the house rained inside. First in the bathroom, then on the landing, then in the bedrooms, water began to drip and run out of the ceilings. Jenny hurried around putting a pot, pan or bucket under each new leak, until the whole house rattled like an orchestra pit, trickling, tip-tapping, drips, drabs and drops plinking and plunking in different tones.

When the pitches thawed she came to reclaim us. She blew into our friends' warm house, where we were glued to the television.

We hugged and kissed and returned immediately to the screen, where the Nazis were about to do something terrible to two members of the Resistance. 'Oh no, children, switch it off please,' she exclaimed.

'It's OK, Mum, they won't show it.'

'No, no, it's terrible. It'll give us all nightmares, turn it over please.'

We switched over to *Ski Sunday* for a minute or two, then flicked back. Post interrogation, the Resisters – I think it was Violette Szabo and her lover – were now talking gingerly to each other.

'They pulled their fingernails out,' our mother explained. 'With pliers. Can you believe it, with *pliers*! And their toenails. I mean, just imagine the absolute torture . . .'

Alexander and I stared at one another, sharing this hideous thought. Our friends, Rhiannon and Gareth, looked horrified.

'Just terrible. And they used to drown that poor man, the White Rabbit, in a bath, and resuscitate him, so that they could drown him again. Unbelievable what people will do to one another. Sorry, I'd better not go on . . . We'd better be off, boys. Gather up your things. I shouldn't think you want to leave this beautiful warm house much . . .'

On the way home she told us about her adventures. 'The water! You've never seen anything like it! It was just pouring, pouring through the ceilings. Everywhere. It was amazing going to sleep – my bed was all right, by some miracle – but listening to it dripping into all the pots and pans . . . There were so many drips I ran out of buckets and bowls. Hopeless really, everything got soaked.'

'Did our beds get wet?'

'Not too bad, actually, and I've had everything on full blast to dry them. I think you'll be OK. I've put the electric blankets on . . .'

The weather abated but the snow did not leave the mountain; it hung around on the ridges in white flashes, 'waiting for its butty', as Jack said, ominously. (Sheep have butties, a particular friend in the flock, whom they butt and nudge playfully.)

'Oil!' Jenny exclaimed. 'Quick, while the lanes are clear, we must get some more, we're low . . .'

But neither Mr Ferguson nor Mr White could be persuaded to pit their nerves against the mountain. She telephoned every vendor who served the area, but none would come. Tankers were now too big, they said, very sorry, but it was out of the question.

'Oh Lord, if I can't get oil, what on earth will we do? No cooker, no hot water! I'll try Mr Ferguson again.' She called him back.

'Please, Mr Ferguson, please! You're our only hope.'

'No, I'm sorry, but the insurance won't cover it,' said Mr Ferguson. 'I can't help you.'

'But what am I going to do?' Jenny cried.

'Well, I could let you have some barrels and a pump . . .'

The barrels were hauled up on a neighbour's tractor and trailer. The red and black drums were positioned on the bank above the house, and their contents hand-pumped into the tank. We all took turns working that pump, and quickly came to hate it. It was a cruel labour, and we worked at it until our arms and shoulders were exhausted, sweating and swearing, the view swimming in our vision, the oil soaking our wrists and impregnating our clothes. After days of pumping, the level in the tank had risen by a dispiriting fraction.

'It's murder! But we've done frightfully well,' Jenny encouraged us. 'It's just to keep us going. I'm sure we'll get a tanker to come when it thaws properly.'

The frost returned, and now we worried about the water. Was there enough in the tank? Would it freeze? Jenny went up the Quoiker to check. She bent over the cover of the catchment tank and heaved at it: her fingers burned against the cold iron, but the cover did not budge. 'Come on!' she exhorted it, and tried again; no movement. She stamped on it, kicked at it, pulled from different angles: nothing, not the tiniest shift. She glared at the hatch cover, furious with it and her weakness. Frost sparkled at her from the rusty surface. She fumed. Defeat by physical weakness made her furious. 'It's just weights,' she would exclaim to us. 'If only I had stronger arms! I could do anything then . . .'

Her hand went to her pocket for a cigarette, and paused. Slowly, carefully, she extracted a bundle of dry hay, left over from a parcel for an old biddy. She arranged it on top of the hatch cover, together with a tissue paper hanky and handfuls of dead bracken and gorse. She squatted over the little heap, tenting it under her coat. The lighter snicked, the tissue paper smoked and the hay caught.

She fed it and sheltered it, blowing gently and tending. 'Come on, fire,' she whispered, as the little red worms investigated the edges of the bracken. 'Yes!' she said, and there was a single, iron ticking sound, and she thrust her hand around the rung, and heaved, and it shifted. 'Ha ha,' she said, to the gathering night, 'I'm the greatest!' She peered in. The tank was less than a third full, and there was nothing coming in. 'No worries, children,' she said when she returned. 'But we'd better go easy on baths.'

The freak weather brought splendour too. After another spell of fearsome cold we found that one of our woods, the tangled, stream-riven spinney, had frozen into a slanting, chaotic fairy rink. A foot of ice lay locked around it linking every tree and bush, forming an undulating crystal floor, a perfect playground so long as you did not try to stand up. The whole spinney now sprouted from a bed of curved and corniced ice, bubbled and pooled, perfectly petrified, every form of the water captured, as though stilled, instantly, by a spell. We slid around on our backs like big hockey pucks, spinning and sprawling, giggling at our own and our dogs' helplessness, then set off to explore the glaciers on the mountain.

We were moving carefully along the skyline, marvelling at the sculpted, precipitous drops, when a young dog-fox appeared ahead, his ears twitching as he watched us. Toss and Lark immediately went for him, but the little fox was unconcerned. He trotted off, unhurried, leading the dogs straight up one of the steepest sheets of ice. Lark, ever intelligent, suddenly stopped, turned, and regretfully retraced her steps. Toss paused, but the fox paused too, looked over his shoulder, and seemed to taunt the dog. Ignoring our shouts Toss went on, but he was too heavy, too clumsy, and as his dainty prey circled around above him, coping easily with the ice, Toss began to lose his grip; barking and whining he started to slip. The fox sat down, tucking his tail neatly around his feet, and watched as his hapless pursuer struggled, floundered and slid, helplessly frustrated. Enjoying himself now, the hunted circled the hunter, so steady and sure he might have been wearing crampons. Unable to go higher, unable to turn and intercept him, Toss roared and howled, as if his barks could bring the mountain down; the fox seemed to raise his eyebrows, as though disappointed at his pursuer's ineptitude. Finally, with a couple of amused and scornful backward glances, he skimmed away over the crest of the glacier.

You could almost hear Toss vowing vengeance.

All living things came closer together, under the rule of the cold. In the afternoons the fox trotted past the house, quite careless of being seen, sniffing the air, scenting our fire and food. Jenny's birds assembled; finches, tits and the robin waited outside for handouts of seed or cereal. Every morning, there was Vivian, on the shelf directly above the fan heater, looking at us over his lentils with a shrugging frankness.

Upstairs his cousins were even less discreet than usual: a family of mice lived behind the bulges in the wallpaper of my bedroom. They were forever rattling off on a forage, or returning from one, squeaking and scrabbling.

It could make reading in bed quite difficult. 'Will you please be quiet,' I demanded, staring, vexed, at the wallpaper.

'Sorry, what's that?' my brother answered, from his room.

'It's these mice! Running about and shouting – I can't concentrate!'

'You should trap them, then.'

'I will, if they don't shut up.' I went back to my book, *Sagittarius Rising* by Cecil Lewis; biplanes fighting in the skies over France.

The mice counted to six, then went back to their bustling.

It was easy, in the cold, to nab them with an upturned cereal bowl propped on a pencil over a piece of cheese. In the course of their feasting they would dislodge the prop and spend the night under the bowl. We always freed them in the morning, though. 'Live and let live' was our mother's creed, and the rule of the farm, except in the case of the crows, of course.

'A murder of crows' is the old proverb, and it has them right. In the snowy fields there were only the sheep: nothing else warm, bloody or exposed anywhere; no grubs, no worms, and, before lambing, nothing young. Now only death would feed the crows, and they called and called to it, waiting. The ravens came over more often, flying lower-level patrols; magpies cackled and the buzzards sat around in bare trees, puffed up like turkeys, watching.

'You have to be so quick,' Jenny said. 'If something goes down for a second . . .'

If something weak went down it would be lucky to get back up. The knife of a beak in an eyeball would kill it through shock, and then it was a free-for-all: the yellowish corpse a berry-burst on the snow; buzzards in their shaggy pantaloons tearing off strips; magpies raiding titbits; ravens squatting and hammering on the ribcage and the crows cursing them all, triumphantly.

'Oh well, she was an old one, I didn't think she'd see the cuckoo,' Jenny sighed. 'What a job they've done on her already! It will feed the foxes though, which I'm pleased about.'

By the next day the corpse would have travelled down the field, fragmenting; by the thaw there would be nothing left but scraps of wool and scattered bones.

'Food for the foxes' was always said jauntily: it was a final compensation, a bit of good news on the other side of death. A hill farmer's relationship with death is matter-of-fact; as we grew up we learned that the horror lurked on our side of mortality, in the bloody business of preserving life.

'Horatio, could you help me for a minute, something rather awful . . .'

She was looking very serious. Even for a hail-black lambing day, which had never seemed to get light properly, she looked bleak.

'What it is, I've got a little ewe with a dead lamb inside her. I've got her in the shed. The problem is, it was a head, and it's come out and it's awfully swollen, I don't know if I'll be able to get it back in . . .'

I held the ewe and Jenny set about trying to draw the corpse. The protruding head was so swollen it could not be pushed back beyond the cervix; after a struggle, Jenny decided that the ewe could take no more – if we were not to lose her too, the lamb would have to be decapitated. She fetched the wicked little kitchen knife she normally used for preparing vegetables.

'Oh God, please let it be dead,' she said, as she knelt down and prepared herself.

'It is, isn't it?' I demanded, cloaking my queasiness in impatience: why did she always find something worse to imagine? Wasn't this bad enough?

'Yes,' Jenny said slowly, feeling the mouth, prising open the eyes and peering into them, 'I'm sure it is. Oh dear, this is going to be absolutely ghastly.'

'Don't think about it, just do it!'

'I have to think about it a bit,' came the reply, and there was a harder note in it now. 'I don't want to cut the ewe. How's she doing?'

'She's fine – well, she's OK . . .'

'Right. Here goes.' As she worked I stared at the wet, stinking floor and vowed I would never be a farmer. I listened to the knife sliding back and forth, and Mum's single grunt as she went through the spinal cord. At last there was a fleshy, tugging sound. 'Done it,' Jenny said. She tied off the neck with a loop of twine and dropped the head into an empty feed bag.

'Hold this,' she said, presenting me with the string and the pinched end of the neck, 'and on no account let it go!' Wincing, I did as I was told, as she worked her hands inside, pushed the body back, adjusted the position of the forelegs and, finally, drew out the headless lamb. The ewe would live. We retreated into the house. Jenny washed her hands and reached for her cigarettes. I described what had happened to my brother. He was gratifyingly revolted, and I milked it.

'I had to hold the neck while she drew it . . .' I repeated, but now Alexander was philosophical.

'Oh well,' he said, 'food for the foxes!'

As the foxes know, most farms have their evil secrets, gloomy places, far from boundaries and footpaths, where the farmer disposes of his dead. On one walk, which had taken me far from home, into a great dark fir forest (I was looking for goshawks) I stumbled down a bank, into a sunken lane, and suddenly found myself surrounded by corpses, skeletons, white spines, skulls, torn and rotting ribcages; it looked like an entire flock of the dead, and in my swollen imagination I had stumbled into the ovine equivalent of the Somme after the battle; I fled in terror.

We had two such secret places: down below the badger setts, and below the road through the wood. Compared to assisting with grotesque surgery, disposing of bodies was easy. I was unperturbed to find myself, on the way to school, dragging one by a stiff cold back leg, the head bumping over molehills behind me, towards the dizzy edge where the badgers lived.

'Bye bye, sheep!' With a last heave the corpse went crashing and tumbling down the near-vertical drop into the dell, foul fluids spurting from its mouth and nose, filling the air with the dreadful eggy stink of putrefaction.

Jenny heaved an old one after it. As the second carcass began to tumble Jenny suddenly screeched, retched, spat, swore, and finally vomited.

'What's happened?' we yelled.

'Eeeyuch!'

'What is it?'

'The most disgusting thing! The most – uugh, yuk! I can hardly bear to tell you – as Elvira went over the edge a gobbet of something flew out of her mouth – and landed in mine!'

She raced the car into town, moaning and gurning.

'It's just typical! It's the end! A parting kiss from a dead sheep . . .'

She presented herself at the chemist's, and told her latest tale.

'Only you, Jenny, only you . . .' the pharmacist laughed, through her grimaces.

— * —

It was illegal to dispose of corpses like this. The Ministry, that remote, ignorant and all-powerful force, insisted that dead sheep should be buried. When we could we did, but often we had neither the time nor the strength for grave-digging. The visits of the man from the Ministry were nervy occasions. Jenny would flatter and charm, offer tea and snacks, lay out the accounts and tallies of sheep born, dead, sold or fled, and then would lead a tour of the farm, so that the Ministry Man could count the animals, and establish how many of each age we had, to check that we were claiming and receiving the correct payment: 'The Subsidy', as it was pronounced, with significant weight, between farmers.

This annual payment, provided by the European Community's Common Agricultural Policy, was the thread by which Welsh hill farming dangled. So many pounds per ewe and per ram, combined with whatever a farmer could make at the lamb sales, plus a few quid for the wool, comprised the annual income. As its many critics have pointed out, this policy not only flew in the face of economic logic, and defied all the principles of fair trade, but also encouraged farmers to overstock, cramming the hillsides with thousands of underfed ewes, skinny and worthless to the market. Now the Subsidy has been replaced by a single farm payment, calculated on the basis of each holding's acreage. The link with production having been broken, it is only a short matter of time before the smaller farms go out of business, and are absorbed by the bigger ones.

Most of the men and women who make their living farming the mountains will die out, their farms will either fall down or be bought by weekenders, and future governments will find other ways of paying less for a new kind of countryside. For the hill farmers who have survived thus far, relations with the authorities have become ever more involved, and more fractious. A dead sheep now represents more of a setback than ever before: not only does the farmer lose the value of the animal, and the potential value of any lamb it might have had or sired; thanks to disease scares and European legislation, burial is now illegal, and the law demands that farmers bag the corpse, seal it in a special bin and inform the authorities, who will come and collect it and charge the farmer for the service – at a rate higher than the value of the sheep. So the hidden graveyards of Wales grow larger, and the crows and foxes fatten.

— * —

'Just because it's all blood and guts out there', Jenny said firmly, 'doesn't mean we're going to be savages in here.' When we had taken our coats and boots off, and after Jenny had cooked our supper, we sat down to our daily lesson in civilisation. Meals were punctuated with instructions: hold your knife and fork properly, close your mouth when you chew, never speak with your mouth full, sit up straight, look people in the eye when they talk to you, and answer clearly. Do not overload your fork, if you're doing it properly your knife should be stained towards the tip, not all the way to the hilt. Leave a clean plate, say please and thank you, wait for everyone to finish before you get down, don't say 'can I', say 'may I . . .'

'But why?' I demanded petulantly. 'What's the point? There's no one watching, is there?'

'Because good manners are very important.'

'But why? Why are they important?'

'Because otherwise people will judge you and they will think you're ignorant louts.'

'I don't care what they think . . .'

'You will. Manners are keys, that's the thing. I am trying to give you keys which will help you in your lives. It's for your own good. Now hold your knife properly or go to bed without the rest of your supper. I'm warning you!'

Beyond the warning, if you ignored it, lay a furious shouting, which would leave Jenny on the verge of tears and the offender in red-faced silence, and beyond that, when the offence was grievous or compounded by the great but sometimes irresistible mistake of Answering Back, there was the ultimate sanction: an open-handed slap to the cheek.

Then the dogs fled, Toss glancing backwards, guiltily, as if apologising for his cowardice, and the cat stared at the floor with a magistrate's air of distaste: not a minute too soon, she seemed to say. I sat with my head ringing, more in shock than pain, as Jenny administered a final admonishment, 'Behave yourself in future!' before turning away to conceal her distress and face her guilt: now she tormented herself with a picture of a woman drinking too much, smoking too much, losing her temper, and hitting her children. Am I a rotten mother too? she wailed, silently.

Alexander looked at me appraisingly: when it was his turn, one morning, in the instant Jenny's temper snapped and we all knew a slap was coming, he dived under the kitchen table, scooted out the other side and hared into the back patch. She went after him but Alexander was lightning quick, and kept the woodpile between him and her, circling it rapidly and defiantly.

'Come here, you wretched child,' she cried, but he would not. She darted left, he darted left, and seeing that she could not catch him, Jenny paused, her anger deflated, and she was overcome by the giggles. Alexander stumped off, more upset by her laughter than her rage.

Beside our mother's efforts, the other constant voice of civilisation came from the radio. The complexities, triumphs and disasters of the world beyond the mountain were related and explained to us in the even tones of BBC Radio 4. Mornings began with the *Today* programme, presented by two of Jenny's heroes, Brian Redhead and John Timpson. 'Good on you,

Redhead!' she would cry, when he was getting stuck into Some Bloody Tory. 'Go on Timpers, get him!' she would urge. When the *Thought for the Day* slot was conducted by the Rabbi Lionel Blue she would hold up her hand for respectful silence and we would all listen carefully.

'I think he's a wonderful man,' she would conclude, when he was done. 'My pin-up!' (I think the good Rabbi would be surprised but not in the least alarmed to find himself in the company of the rest of her pin-ups, who included Gregory Peck ('Oh, Pecky!'), Harry Andrews, Jonathon Porritt, Chris Patten (the only decent Conservative, in our book), Misha Glenny, Mikhail Gorbachev, Nelson Mandela, Robert Redford and Michael Foot.)

Sometimes our father's voice issued from the box – he was a radio reporter now. It was a tersely musical, familiar voice, which, unlike everything else we heard, did not seem to be speaking to us. During the Brixton riots he covered Race Relations. His dispatches were clear and calm, but underneath the professional dispassion we could hear a tight-held anger, at the Brixton councillors who watched the riots from the town hall, like spectators at a football match; at a society which crammed its poor minorities into concrete high-rises, then goaded them, through the police, to breaking point. We knew how apartheid had banned him from South Africa; I recognised, in his description of the riot, the unequivocal tones in which he had explained to me what racism was and how it worked. We looked to Jenny when his report finished. 'Phew,' she said. 'Fantastic! Isn't he good?' We swelled with pride and vicarious achievement.

With other reporters we splashed ashore with the British forces as they landed on East Falkland; we heard of burning ships. We listened, spooning Weetabix paste into our mouths, as wisps of the horrors of Sabra and Chatila leaked out of the box near the sink. Later we followed the course of the Miners' Strike, and took our anti-Thatcher convictions to school, where a game called Police and Pickets sprang up and was swiftly banned, involving as it did pitched battles between groups of struggling boys. We were transported to the desperate scenes of the Zeebrugge Ferry disaster, the Brighton and Harrods bomb attacks, the Iran–Iraq war and many other of the decade's convulsions.

Then it was half past eight, and time for *Yesterday in Parliament*, and if we were not heading for the car when the sonorous voice of the Speaker of the House, George Thomas, intoned 'Order, Order,' then we knew we were late for school. Scrambling into our coats and shoes we grinned at the thunderous hubbub of Parliament, and grimaced at the high, sword-waving bray of Margaret Thatcher, which seemed to rear up and taunt the mob of voices.

This narrow access to a single medium made me simultaneously precocious and ignorant: I could name most of the European leaders, and their political leanings, and I knew who Reagan's Secretary of State was, but I would have to wait years to discover Monty Python.

At the other end of the day, we had our supper with *The Archers*, and when my mother came up to bed and put out the lights, the last sounds we heard before sleep were the chanted psalms of the Shipping Forecast, lulling us into unconsciousness, accompanying my last sight: the rectangle of light on my bedroom wall, a refracted beam from our beacon, the yard light, a little burning brooch on the dark breast of the mountain.

Finally Jenny turned the volume right down, as the National Anthem played, and it was as though Queen, country and world were reduced to a tiny buzz, somewhere at the bottom of the mountain, and we slept.

At the weekends all three of us bounced in our beds to the jumping jingles of *Sport on Four*, and the holiday programme, *Breakaway*. *The Lord of the Rings* sent Alexander and me rushing outside for our swords, to slay cohorts of invisible Orcs, and one afternoon we sat around the kitchen table, transfixed, living the nightmare of nuclear war through the radio adaptation of *When the Wind Blows*, by Raymond Briggs. When it was finished I went outside and stared at the silvered leaves of the ash tree, whispering and turning in the breeze, and the sagging woodpiles, apple logs dusted with lichen, and the mighty cerulean sky and the distant, anvil-red hills, and felt terribly frightened for it all, picturing everything blackened, poisoned and destroyed.

'What would you do', I asked, soon afterwards, on the way home from school, 'if you saw a mushroom cloud behind that hill?'

'Well,' Jenny said. 'If it was coming I would get some injections from the vet, and we would go into the Beast House, if it wasn't too bad, and I'd block up the door, and if we started to get sick I'd put us all to sleep, just like we do with the sheep. It would be just fine – it's barbiturates – it's wonderfully quick and you don't feel anything.'

It seems strange now that our suicide was to have taken place in the Beast House, among the woolsacks, beneath the gaze of the family of bats which hung from the rafters, swinging gently on their little hooked feet, but at the time it was very reassuring. We had a plan for Armageddon, that was the main thing.

Shriller than the rumblings of the Cold War, the noise of bitter national division came angrily through the radio. Pro or anti nuclear; for Thatcher or against; the country was polarised, opponents united only in loathing and contempt. During the General Election the hedges sprouted red 'Labour' and blue 'Conservative' posters.

'The big farmers are always Tory,' Jenny said, slowing the car. 'Why?'

'Money . . . Get it!'

I jumped out, grabbed a Tory board and dived back in. It was not particularly democratic conduct, but Britain did not feel like a particularly democratic country. Glimpses of friends' televisions showed battles between police and miners, ranks of strikers, chanting pickets and marching columns of the soon-to-be unemployed. You could tell friends instantly, by their 'Nuclear power – No thanks!' or 'Ban The Bomb' car stickers.

One of our friends, Sue, drove a car coated in them. Her boys were our age, incomers like us; they too had English accents and an absent father. Our mothers thought we should play together.

While we held fir-cone fights and small riots in hay barns, Jenny talked politics with Sue and her second husband, Guy. A tall, angular, white-haired man with a quiet voice and a great many interests, Guy ran an environmental pressure group. He researched, wrote and distributed pamphlets with titles like *Nuclear Power – The Facts They Don't Want You to Know*.

One afternoon, as they sat in the sunny gardens of his house, Guy told Jenny the story of Hilda Murrell, a retired Shropshire rose-grower who became interested in nuclear power. Hilda Murrell was preparing to deliver a paper to an anti-nuclear conference when she was murdered in bizarre circumstances, having apparently disturbed an intruder or intruders who were ransacking her house. An inadequate police investigation convinced many in the anti-nuclear lobby that Hilda Murrell was the victim of a vicious and bungling arm of the secret state.

Incredulous and appalled in equal measure, Jenny told us the story. We made disbelieving faces at one another. Could it possibly be true? A little old rose-grower in Shrewsbury? Had 'they' finally gone mad?

'N-o-o!' said Alexander. 'Boller!' (He had trimmed down a longer word for use in company.)

I was less certain. From our mountain, overlooking the hazy valley, it did not seem impossible. The world at the bottom of the hill was clearly in terrible peril: the good and true, Guy and Hilda Murrell, were trying to save it, but they seemed frail and tiny, compared to Thatcher's faceless, atomic-powered cohorts.

If it came to nuclear war I was certain the Russians would bomb Hereford, the nearest English outpost, and the home of the SAS. When we needed something special, like a new consignment of pants and socks, we piled into our battered vehicle and set out for the border. Expeditions to Hereford always began in a spirit of optimism but often degenerated into fractious farce, as our hill-billy spirits clashed with the norms of that genteel little market town.

First there was the business of finding somewhere to leave the car: there was no question of 'wasting money on parking', as

Jenny put it, so we crept and crawled around the side roads, occasionally scorning the system and reversing up one-way streets, until Jenny found somewhere cunning and close to the centre. We emerged from the car, lightly dusted in seeds and strands of hay.

'Tuck your shirt in! And you do your shoelaces up! Please try and look respectable, boys, for goodness sake . . .' She slapped seeds off our backs and winced at the state of our hair.

Clothes shopping afflicted me with truculent depression: in Marks & Spencer's I lurked, muttering crossly about not needing any more socks, while Jenny roamed the aisles. On finding something suitable she shouted brightly: 'Pimmy darling! Horatio! Come here please, look, they've got some really good pants,' which covered me in furious mortification.

After this came trial by women's clothes shop, which meant Alexander and me squatting, sullenly, on the edge of the window display, or listlessly drifting around the rails as Jenny hurriedly tried things on. So hurriedly, for our sakes, that she sometimes eschewed the changing rooms and stripped at the back of the shop, to our further horror. She was suspicious of being sold to, but interested in the people doing the selling. 'Well, it's not my thing, dearie, really, is it yours? Honestly? With that funny frilly bit? Not me!' Prices were always outrageous, since she had no money. I remember her holding up a scarlet dress and asking, desperately, 'Have you *anything* for under a hundred pounds?' The assistant was sorry, but no, she hadn't. 'What do you think, boys?' she demanded, twisting and turning in different outfits. 'Very nice,' we droned. The rare decision to buy something brought further complications, since she refused to use cash points, and so wrote cheques for everything. Cashiers' demands for a cheque guarantee card were regarded as insults to her trustworthiness and means, and soon the whole of Hereford seemed to teem with petty and pathetic obstructions to our progress, designed to wind her up.

'Look, they've closed the whole street. They want us to walk all the way down there – perfectly stupid! Come on, children, follow me!'

'No Mummy, NO! They're working on the road, don't!'

But she did, sweeping aside the barriers and charging across the forbidden strip, to the impotent agitation of the road menders. It was as if she was sent from God to test officialdom, and it drove my brother and me beyond embarrassment, through flaring rage, into semi-hysterical giggles.

Finally, we arrived at the bookshop, and at last peace descended, as we entered an environment we understood.

'However poor we are, I don't mind spending any amount of money on books or paints,' Jenny decreed, and so we spread out, stooping, reaching and craning between the stacks, kneeling, pawing and poring over the selections, absorbed and happily torn over which new treasures we would add to our collection.

I loved Just William, Robert Westall, Peter Dickinson, Rosemary Sutcliff, Robert Louis Stevenson and Biggles, and the wonderful nature writing of 'BB', Denys Watkins-Pitchford, whose stories, told from the perspective of wild geese and foxes and runaway boys living in forests, chimed exactly with my imagination. Many of my heroes were tearaways, Red Indians, highwaymen, pirates, bandits and other outlaws, and I always thought I would make a good one. Never in my daydreams did I place myself in the position of a terrified householder, menaced by a marauding brigand; I never considered the awful fear of the unarmed, law-abiding citizen when a barbarian came down from the mountain, looking for plunder and who knew what else, until one hot summer night, when an outlaw came for us.

# 9

## Intruders

THE MAN APPEARED in the vegetable garden, wearing emerald green shorts. Jenny jumped when she saw him, standing still between the neat rows of Jack's bean poles, watching her, and her first reaction was anger.

'Can I help you?' she demanded, in the brisk and confrontational voice she used when her hackles were up, an attitude she would describe as 'shirty'.

The man continued to look at her, and said nothing. He was big, barrel-chested, with dark hair in a ponytail.

'That's not the way to the mountain, you know,' she continued.

'I know,' the man replied, slowly, 'I'm trying to get away from THEM.'

Oh my God, she thought, wishing the dogs were not shut in the house, and immediately became more conciliatory.

'OK, well, if you come down the steps and follow the path up around there, behind the barn, you'll see the gate to the hill on the other side of the trees. It's just there . . .'

The man said nothing, but after a moment he descended and disappeared behind the barn. Jenny fled inside and watched from the windows as he re-emerged, climbed over the hill gate and began to walk away slowly, up the hill. It was a bright June day, the bracken was high and bursting green, tall enough to conceal him when he sat down, which he did, before he reached the skyline. She lost sight of him then, and waited a while, watching, but he did not reappear.

'Has he really gone, dogs?' She let the hounds out. They rambled around, sniffing and peeing, but neither of them more than glanced at the hill.

She went about the business of the day, wondering whether she was being watched. She topped up the water trough in the Patch with a hose from the yard and gave one of the oldies a drench. She fed the orphans bottles of milk and patrolled, looking for signs of maggots. Her suspicion fluctuated but did not dissipate. Sometimes it was a thin, paranoid whisper, but at intervals it came as a conviction, which sent her scurrying back to the kitchen to scan the hillside through binoculars. There was no movement. There were a few of Evans's sheep scattered across the ridges, but they were grazing quietly. Perhaps she was imagining it. At half past three she collected us from school.

'Funny thing,' she said. 'Some weirdo turned up in Jack's garden.'

'What did he want?'

'He said he was trying to get to the hill. Didn't like the look of him much.'

'Mmm.' Walkers were common in the summer; as far as Alexander and I were concerned most of them were weirdos, so we thought nothing of it. We ran about and played outside as usual, making the most of a lovely evening, until Jenny called us in.

'Time to feed the dogs. I think we'll have them in tonight.'

The dogs were moved between the barn and the sitting room, depending on the weather and occasional hygiene campaigns. Feeding them was our job: they lived on a yellow mixture of lumps and flakes, which was served with water in precise proportion, because any uneaten mulch caused Mum almost as much despair as our leftovers: 'Look! Look at the waste! And it's so expensive, too!'

It was an iron rule that animals ate before humans. 'How can you be happy, how could you enjoy your supper, knowing an animal is hungry?' she demanded, when one of us, lazy or ravenous, objected. 'The animals must come first.'

'But why?'

'Because they rely on us. It's our duty.'

So we all ate, then Alexander and I withdrew to the attic, which smelled of warm wood and stone, and mucked about until the shout came from downstairs that it was time we had our bath. We ran it and climbed in together, fitting easily into the great iron-footed tub, which stood on planks intended to stop it falling through the floor.

Shortly before midnight Jenny checked that the back and front doors were bolted, collected her radio and came upstairs. She shot the bolt on the bedroom door, turned out my light and went to bed.

At a quarter to two she heard the first bark downstairs. Toss and Lark often barked, especially if they were quartered in the sheds, where they could hear all the night's noises. We were accustomed to their various sounds: droning, repeated barks if they had heard another farm dog somewhere; suspicious growls for a rat rustling in one of the outhouses; long howls in answer to a keening fox. But normally they were quiet when they were in the house – partly because outside sounds were more muffled, and partly because they were within range of our retribution if they kept at it.

They began with a couple of interrogative, questioning barks, then paused, in a listening silence, in which you could clearly picture them with their heads tilted sideways, mouths slightly open and ears cocked. Then suddenly it came, a volley of furious sound which escalated, both dogs baying.

Again there was a pause, but it was briefer this time, and now came a fusillade of noise, each cry tearing open the night, driving all sleep, all comfort, all gentleness out of the dark, filling the air with alarm. We lay in our beds hoping it would stop, wishing that whatever it was would go away, but the dogs were incensed; they hardly paused for breath between their outraged arias. They only ever made this kind of noise when someone had walked into the yard or driven up the track to see us, and their meaning now was clear – Enemy! Enemy! Kill! Kill!

I climbed out of bed and Jenny turned her light on.

'What is it, Mummy?'

'I don't know,' she said. She looked shaky and alarmed, and small, in her pale nightie.

The noise downstairs now was ferocious.

'I think there might be someone outside,' she said. 'I'm going to call the police.'

It was a warm night; all the bedroom windows were open. The upstairs phone was on the windowsill. Jenny dialled 999 and spoke loudly into the handset, projecting her voice into the yard in the hope that the intruder would hear her.

'Police, please,' she said clearly.

She was put through to an exchange in Brecon, and then handed on to the station in Newtown, a good hour's drive away.

The officer who finally answered said he had two cars within range of us, one in Brecon, which was busy, and one in Newtown. (We discovered later that thanks to the Miners' Strike the coverage of our area had been reduced to almost nothing.)

'He'll be with you as soon as he can,' the officer said.

Jenny said loudly, 'Good, see you soon then,' and hung up. She backed away from the window. 'They're coming, but they're coming from Newtown,' she whispered.

Your heart seemed to jump at every bark, and your stomach tightened.

'Who do you think it is?' I asked.

'I don't know, it could be the man who was in Jack's garden.'

'Have we got Jack's gun?'

'No. He took it back.'

I thought about the rule of threes. The rule of threes was one of Jenny's. Three slips or misfortunes, she said, would take a life. One: a vicious easterly, flailing the ridges with rain, catching some of the flock in the wrong field, exposed. Amongst them, a ewe with a poor udder and a weak lamb, which you thought you saw drinking yesterday – two. You hoped that the udder might be better, but you forgot to check the lamb today: the rule of threes would deliver a little cold body tomorrow. And now there was the man in the garden, the missing shotgun, and the policeman in Newtown . . .

The barking intensified suddenly, and it was no longer coming from the front of the house.

'It's moved. It's moved to the back,' Jenny whispered.

We stared sightlessly through her doorway, into Alexander's dark bedroom, and listened. Both dogs were now jumping against the door to the kitchen: whatever was outside had circled the house.

'Hell's bells,' Jenny rattled, 'he's trying the back! How's Twinks?'

'Still asleep.'

'Well, that's a miracle, anyway.'

'I'm scared,' I confessed.

'So am I,' she answered. 'But don't worry, if anyone tries to get in Toss will make mincemeat of him. And it might be nothing, after all.'

We both knew it was not nothing. Toss was hysterical with fury. His barks were interrupted with ripping, savage growls, as if he had the enemy in his sights. I sat beside my mother in her bed, and we waited, listening for the sound that was not barking, for splintering wood or breaking glass.

'What are we going to do if he breaks in?' I whispered.

Jenny shook her head irritably, as if dismissing the possibility. Then she shrugged. 'Just pray he doesn't,' she said.

Everything in my panicked sight, the warm light of the bedside lamp, the soft sheets, the entwined flowers on the wallpaper, all, now, looked appallingly vulnerable, terrifyingly gentle and feminine, as if their fragility invited desecration.

Minutes scratched past on Jenny's little bedside clock; half an hour, an hour, and still the policeman did not come. The barking downstairs retreated from its worst frenzy but did not stop. Toss sounded certain now, frustrated and convinced. I know all about you, his tone seemed to say, and you know I know. Bark, bark, bark. As another half hour passed the dogs fell silent for periods. Each time they stopped I began to think it might be over, but each time they started again. We stared out of the window, willing car headlights to appear.

'It's very strange,' Jenny frowned. 'He can't still be there, can he? Why are they still barking? How long can they keep it up?'

'It's getting light,' she said, later. It was twenty past three when suddenly there was another avalanche of noise from downstairs.

'Oh no,' Jenny muttered, then 'There,' she jerked. 'The police! Thank the Lord! Oh, thank heavens for that.'

The car came along the lane with extraordinary reluctance, its blue light flashing.

'He's taking his time,' she exclaimed. 'Giving anyone who might be around a chance to get clear so he doesn't have to cope with them, I should think.'

At last the policeman reached the yard. Jenny was too relieved and exhausted to be angry about the response time. 'Over an hour and a half on a 999 call,' she noted wearily. 'We're all goners by now.'

It felt to me like a strange parallel of Christmas, as we went down to the shadowy sitting room to calm the dogs and welcome the longed-for arrival. We invited the officer in, strictly instructing Toss not to bite him. Jenny offered a cup of tea and the policeman, had a look around. He went out the back and flashed his torch at the larch trees and the lightening hill.

'Look,' Jenny exclaimed, when he had given that up. 'Look at the window frames!'

All the wooden sashes and struts between the downstairs window panes had been gnawed and chewed right through. Little remained of the white-painted bars but strips of wet splinters. In his determination to reach and slay the enemy, Toss had almost broken out.

'What's going on?' Alexander enquired, as we returned to our bedrooms and the policeman drove away.

'Hello, sweetheart,' Jenny laughed. 'Have you just woken up?'

'Yes, what's happening?'

'And I slept through all of it!' he marvelled, when the story had been told, as amazed at this as by what had gone on.

He gave Toss a hero's reception the next morning. Toss was Alexander's dog, and the adoring, beguiling, small-eyed savage had saved our bacon, everyone said.

'Good dog, clever dog,' we lied, lovingly, as Toss ducked and wagged under the weight of all this pleasure, his tale whipping joyfully. He flopped over on to his back, inviting a belly scratch.

When it came he expertly grabbed Alexander's wrist, nipping another hole in the sleeve of his jumper.

'Ow, Toss! Get off,' Alexander laughed, tugging. The jumper stretched, threads popped, Jenny sighed and Toss grinned, his little eyes travelling from upside down face to face, the sleeve locked foolishly in his incisors. A couple of weeks later he landed us in court.

'Mrs Clare,' the clerk said, and my mother stood up. The policeman closed his notebook sceptically. One of the magistrates had given me a gently encouraging smile, as I sat behind Jenny, praying. 'Look agonised,' she had instructed me, on the way in. 'Look as though they're going to kill your pet!' It seemed likely enough; I had been pulled from school to play the part of Alexander, the dog's best friend, while Alexander remained there, so that he would not have to hear the death sentence from the magistrates. There were three of them, two kindly-looking men and a sterner woman. They had all directed appreciative nods at the police officer, for his bloodcurdling tale of unprovoked assault on a lady from Birmingham by a berserk dog; when they looked at Jenny, however, their expressions seemed to change. Her story, of a marauding brigand who did not attack, a valiant dog, and a policeman who did not turn up, had made them frown and shift in their seats. The chief magistrate had the unblinking look of an annoyed headmistress. She leaned forward.

'You did say you let the dog out at night, to run around, uncontrolled?'

'Erm . . .' Jenny dropped her gaze for a second, realising the mistake. 'Um, yes, but . . .'

'Well, we can't permit that. We do accept that you have a need for a good guard dog, as you say . . . And if the police are unable to respond to an emergency like the one you describe, in our view it is reasonable for you to retain the dog.'

'Oh! Wonderful!'

'But we absolutely cannot allow the dog to run around out of control.'

'No . . . no, of course . . .'

'So, we are not going to issue a Destruction Order in this case, but we are going to order you to keep the animal under close control at all times. He's been very lucky, this time, Mrs Clare. Very lucky indeed.'

'Yes! Yes, he has. Thank you so much . . .'

'You did it, well done!' I exulted, as we scurried away.

'Trust your mother,' she said, risking a rascally wink. 'I can't believe we got away with it! Quick, let's get out of here and tell Twinks before they change their minds.'

We retreated back up our hill. Close control at all times, I thought. What did that mean?

That evening Alexander and I took Toss for a walk. It was raining softly, a thickening of hill mist; tickling the hazels, patting the dock leaves, making the nettles shiver and darken. We went down the green lane, listening to the birds; something in the warm mizzle and the approach of dusk was thrilling them. Thrushes floated notes across the Hill Fields; flycatchers and warblers threaded thinner calls through the spinney. Blackbirds threw comments after us, as we wandered down the tunnel of trees.

Toss ranged around as usual, checking roots, holes, boles and stumps, sniffing, spraying, scenting. We watched him, calling him back when he pulled too far ahead, though it seemed pointless. There was no one for miles. We skipped from side to side across the track, keeping to the larger stones and the drier patches, heading through the spinney to the point where the trees stopped and the lane met the Hill Fields in a splashy patch of mud. On the bank above it, under the holly tree, was a fox's earth, and here suddenly Toss paused and tensed.

'The fox lives there, you foolish animal . . .' I began.

'No,' Alexander said. 'Look what he's found.'

Then I saw it too: dangling from the holly, on a long string, so that it nearly scraped the ground, was a single glove, tied by the tip of its index finger.

We stopped dead.

'Let's rip it down,' Alexander said crossly. He knew how Jenny would take it, as did I, but in a quixotic burst of responsibility I decided we should show her.

'Poacher!' she hissed, when she saw it. 'Look at it, right by the earth. Look at the way it's tied. A noose! And the middle finger! Up yours, baby! Well, sucks to you too . . .'

Toss barked gruffly and ran a circle around the bush. 'Good dog, Toss! Kill the blasted badger baiters!'

'Perhaps someone just found it and hung it up to be helpful,' I suggested.

'Nonsense. Tied with a noose! It's some creep . . . some Mad Bomber.'

Mad bombers were a generic menace. We could see Jenny mentally shuffling suspects: it was a sign from the poacher; it was a message from one of the hunt followers; it was Idris, or the Norsters; it was another weirdo; it was the same weirdo in green shorts!

'You're being paranoid, Mummy,' Alexander said calmly. 'It's nothing.'

'I sure hope you're right,' Jenny replied darkly, with a look of bleak prophecy. 'It's hard enough without Mad Bombers.'

The suggestion of threat, the air of intimidation, was much more disturbing than overt menace. One bright morning as I strolled out into the yard my eye caught a brown, huddled shape by the gate. Soft feathers stirred as I drew closer; I bent over two large speckled ducks, not long dead, tied together by their feet with string. There was a cardboard label attached to the string, bearing a single handwritten line: *a present from brer fox*

This seemed so crude and silly that I did not show Jenny, but disposed of the corpses in the stream. It was a perfect day; the ravens flew very high, throatily discussing some distant prospect, and pied wagtails bowed and flitted in the yard, bobbing suddenly, as if they meant to catch out their shadows. So some lunatic held us responsible for the nature of foxes – so what? It was a relief to find a grievance so clearly expressed; much less worrying than the glove. I told Mum about it a week or so later, and she shrugged and rolled her eyes. We could not be hurt, frightened, or even worried like that: we were much more vulnerable to our own imaginations than anyone else's.

The oil pump had been playing up: we yanked and heaved until our arms burned, for barely a dribble of oil. After one brutal spell of pumping, Jenny vomited blood in the night. Cancer, she thought. But the doctor diagnosed a stomach ulcer and called for the surrender of the whisky bottle. The patient invested in a powdered drink called 'Slippery Elm' and checked her treasured *Dictionary of Symptoms*. 'Ulcers,' she murmured, turning the page to the light. 'I love this book, because it says things like "probably not serious" and "don't panic". . . Here we are, treatment . . . Oh! Hops!'

'Hops?'

'It says that hops are good for stomach ulcers,' she cried, joyfully.

'What's hops?'

'Hops? Hops are beer! Hurrah!'

A can of cheap lager replaced the nightly slug of Bells. There was no surrender to the situation, but there was a feeling that we might be prepared to negotiate with it.

'This would not be a good place to be if I got ill,' Jenny said, looking out of the windows at another green dusk. She had the lights off in the kitchen to save money; it was almost dark inside, tenebrous as a cowshed. 'Oh I hate making decisions,' she moaned, 'I loathe it!'

The sheep sensed it. The next morning one of her favourites, Arabella, came up and leaned against her, really leaned, pressing her warm, soft weight against Jenny's legs.

'It was just so wonderful – such love – such trust! I've never heard of a sheep that leaned . . .'

— * —

I do not remember a moment in which we first discussed leaving the farm. It became a background certainty that just as we would not be driven off our mountain, neither would we stay there indefinitely. Contained within our feelings of being custodians and adventurers, was the hazy prospect of departure. Jenny had many thoughts about where we might go – further into Wales; somewhere near the sea; Somerset; Oxfordshire or just lower down the mountain – but we had no idea when: one day, we said, one day.

'We should keep our eyes out for somewhere round here,' Jenny decreed, and so began the never-ending house hunt. Her curiosity seemed more urgent than any desire to go; we toured the district as if for pleasure, meeting farmers, inspecting their dwellings and attending farm sales. These were heartbreaking. When farmers gave up, their neighbours helped them move the entire contents of their house, barns and fields into the best meadow, where it was arranged in neat lines. On the day of the sale, somewhere amongst the tractors, sagging double beds, cutlery drawers, hayracks, sheepdogs, tables, clocks and chickens, slightly apart from the milling crowd, would be the stunned, still figures of the farmer and his wife, staring numbly across their entire lives.

It was enough to put us all off, and the idea of leaving would recede again.

'But I can't stay here for ever,' Jenny sighed. 'All alone up this tump, especially when you're away at school.'

I swallowed. We had decided that once I had finished primary school I would try for an Assisted Place: a government scheme which would sponsor me to go to a fee-paying school. I dreaded the thought of leaving the mountain and my family, and feared for the two of them, isolated up there.

'The winters are so hard, that's the thing. I don't think I could stand it when Twinks goes off as well.'

'You couldn't stay here then,' I said firmly. 'So far from everyone and alone.'

'No. So, we need to find somewhere lovely, nearer people, southwest facing and with a few acres for my sheep.'

Guy and Sue suggested a long, low farm near their house. It was haunted, thick with spirits; its barns, pig pens, cowsheds and walled garden were all frozen, agape, in the moment of their abandonment. It had too few acres for sheep farming: could we manage cattle?

'I don't know anything about cows,' Jenny said. 'How do you make them do something they don't want to?'

I knew about cows from one of her stories, about a bull who leaned, crushing his farmer slowly and inexorably against the wall of his byre, while the farmer's son screamed and jabbed with a pitchfork, and the bull took no notice. While I imagined being the son, Jenny imagined being the farmer. 'It hasn't got any sun, anyway,' she said, and we let it go.

She mentioned the night of the prowler to Guy. He listened, stooping slightly, his head inclined in order to catch every word. He took it very seriously.

'It was all right in the end,' she concluded. 'The police were hopeless, but what can you do?'

'Do you think you are well defended?' Guy asked. 'I mean if he came back, do you think he could get in?'

'Well, there's a bolt on the front door, and I screwed one on to the back of the bedroom door, I don't know . . . Thank goodness for the dog, that's all!'

She was a little surprised by his concern; her own fears had faded, though she slept very lightly, as she had done for years, alert to any sound outside.

Guy said he would come up the mountain the next day, and inspect our defences.

It was late June. In the meadows scarlet cardinal beetles flew low above a sea of seed-heads. There was a yellowhammer by the Far Meadow gate and buzzards wheeling and mewing in the blue. In the distance the mountains looked like the hills of east Africa, eternal and kind under the sun. Guy's sleek car bumped cautiously up the track. Jenny greeted him with huge gratitude and pleasure: how kind it was of him to come. She offered coffee, which they took sitting on logs out the back. Then Guy began his inspection. Doors, windows, skylights in the attic, the roof, internal and external walls were examined. Jenny accompanied him, talking. Her first impressions, months ago when they first met, had been of a rich and ineffective romantic, but she had been wrong: he was a practical man, 'a doer', she knew now. And she found him extraordinarily easy to talk to. It was as though she did not have to try.

She had tidied up, of course, but to a man who loved to work with his hands, who had taught himself masonry and woodwork, whose eyes were quick and scrupulous, the farm appeared as it was: old and primitive, cool verging on cold, even in the summer, and fragile: wormy, brittle, unkempt.

'Awful – chaotic – a tip!' he laughed, recalling his first visit, when I asked him about it years later. 'The walls only faintly divided stock from humans. It was bleak . . . a completely different climate zone.'

I pushed him: 'And what else, how did it strike you, when you first came?'

His expression softened and he chose his words carefully.

'Romantic and very beautiful. Free, most of all – it had a feeling of freedom, not just physical, it had an atmosphere of spiritual freedom that I had rarely encountered before. It was absolutely striking, and deeply attractive,' he said, and we both knew he was talking about more than the place.

The next day he came again, with wood and a serious box of tools. Jenny offered him coffee again and they took it outside. She sat in the grass and he lay down, stretched out, his eyes shut against the sun. He asked her about living there: how did she manage? She chattered away, happy but anxious. To have someone to talk to, a friend her own age, someone kind, it was wonderful . . . all at once she caught herself, and paused.

'I thought "Wait!"' she said, telling us the story. 'I thought, "You hardly know him, you are a desperate, boring woman, wittering on about your worries."'

He lay very still. Jenny looked at him, watched him breathing, and in that moment, suddenly, with a swoop of a feeling like fear, she saw him for himself. Not as a friend, and not as Sue's husband: she saw *him*. She jumped up, almost physically shook herself. He opened his eyes, stood, smiled, and began work.

He was still working when Jenny brought us home from school. There were little heaps of curly shavings and piles of sawdust scattered around the top of the stairs. There were saws and drills and boxes of bright screws. Guy was quick and unhesitating, chatting as he worked. I thought he was wonderful. He never asked any of the questions adults always asked, there was none of the old 'And how was school?' routine. He asked about what you were up to, and what you were interested in, and he listened to what you said. He had a way of squeezing his eyes, narrowing them slightly and nodding slowly when you made some point; it made you feel original, as though you were worth following closely. He seemed to place you on the same level as him, which was a huge compliment.

The bedroom door was transformed. There were thick wooden shields fixed to the back of the old planks, and hefty cross bars, and instead of one rickety bolt there were now three shiny new ones, screwed in tight, braced against reinforcing spars.

'It's really good,' I gawped, tremendously impressed. He was the first man since my father who showed any sign of taking things in hand. He knew I had been fretful since the bad night, and now he meant to allay my fears.

'Well, it looks all right, but will it work? Let's see. You go in there,' he instructed Jenny. 'Lock up, and I will try to break it down. It's called destruction testing,' he told me, with a look which seemed to promise all kinds of excitement. He backed on to the landing.

'Are you ready? Standing back?' he called.

'Yes,' Jenny cried, and then he charged the door. There was an impressive thump and nothing gave.

'Good,' he said, turning to me with a grin. 'If anyone wants to get through that, they'll need a hand grenade.'

The way he said it convinced me that he had seen a hand grenade go off, and I knew from playing with Sue's boys that he had a swordstick among the umbrellas in the stand by his front door. Around the edges of his tall, distinguished frame, and lurking in the vaults of his arched, aristocratic voice, was an impish mischief, something conspiratorial and amused. When he laughed a certain laugh you could see in his face the schoolboy he had once been; an odd one out; a curious, wide-eyed child, giggling with delight and surprise.

He swept up the shavings and sawdust and we all went down for tea. Twinks and I were on our best behaviour, taking our cues from our mother. After tea he measured the upstairs windows for a set of iron bars, which he said we should order from the blacksmith in town. We had no idea there was a blacksmith in town. We waved him off as he left, and that night we shot all the bolts and felt so much more secure that we laughed as if in victory. It seemed that help had come at last, and that we had found a wonderful new friend.

A few days later he came back to install the bars. At the Middle Meadow gate he was ambushed by Hansel, a recently weaned orphan, begging for a bottle of milk. Hansel would not leave him alone, stumbling around his feet, bleating, pleading up at him; Guy could not get the car through the gate without Hansel coming too. Jenny watched, smiling, from the farm, as he appeared to negotiate with the lamb. It did no good. Guy abandoned the car and walked up the track. Jenny noticed his walk: long, slightly uneven strides, head back, very determined.

She kept her distance while he worked. When he had finished he gathered his tools quietly. He seemed to be leaving quickly. On the way out he stopped suddenly and fixed the garden gate's wonky hinges, and then Jenny accompanied him back to his car. She told us what happened next.

'I walked him down to the Middle Meadow gate after he had put the bars in. I said, "Goodbye, then, Guy. Thank you so much for everything you have done. It is incredibly kind of you."'

He had gone very quiet. As they walked down the track he put his arm around her shoulders. She was holding a spare iron bar, which she dropped, so that she would have to move away from him. But when she straightened, the arm was there again.

'We got to the gate, and he looked at me very directly and said, "May I come again?"'

She paused as she recounted this, trying to remember precisely, to get it right.

'I was a bit taken aback. I said, "Yes, Guy, you are always welcome here, we'd always love to see you." But then he said, "I want to get this quite clear, may I come and see *you* again. Would *you* like me to come back?"'

'Well, I couldn't believe it. We gave each other a hug, and he said, "I admire your courage so much. And I admire the way you are bringing up your children." And he said he thought of me – too much, he said. And I said I thought I could fall in love with him but I wasn't sure I could take it all in.'

They sat down at the edge of the hayfield to talk about it. The grass was high and hot.

She said: 'I don't have affairs with married men. It is not my style. I'm always so careful. And I've given up sex, anyway.'

'What *do* you mean?' he said, and pulled her down to him, beside his car. She laughed suddenly. 'Is it right? Is it proper? To be lying with Guy in a hayfield?'

'It's quite all right,' he said. 'I'm just making sure the exhaust system is functioning.'

'Oh it was funny! We laughed and laughed, and it was all all right. Then he looked at his watch and said help! It's five to one and we're having people to lunch! He leapt up and off he went.'

He turned his car and drove away, raising his hand. Jenny leant against the meadow gate, raised hers, and watched him go. She walked back to the farm. She felt extraordinary, warm and excited, and peaceful, and happy and panicked; definitely panicked. And fearful: vulnerable again, she thought, after all this time.

'I hadn't felt like that for years,' she told us. 'Fifteen years! . . . I didn't know what to do.'

There was an amazement about her as she spoke, a genuine inability to account for what had happened. She hunched slightly, her hands clasped in front of her. It was a position she took instinctively when she heard something terrible on the radio, or some surprise had struck her, as if she was physically trying to hold herself together. It made her look like a tensed rabbit, unsure of which way to leap.

'I never dreamed of meeting someone like that, it never crossed my mind,' she exclaimed. 'Why would it? I've given it all up. How on earth could it happen, up here in the sticks – in the nettles!'

She pulled her hair up with her fingers and let it fall, befuddled. She wanted to see him again, and she wanted to run away.

He telephoned the next day. Could he come and see her? 'No! No. Not for a week at least, it's too fast . . .'

A letter arrived and she pounced on it. She read it over and over again. She was happy, she was dreamy, she was busy, she was skittish. It was a summer enchantment, she told herself, a brief encounter. She liked his writing so much. He couldn't possibly love her, not really, why her? She was tired, she wasn't pretty, wasn't loveable, had no chin . . .

She went to church and gave thanks for her happiness, and asked for wisdom to deal with it. It was a madness which would pass, she told herself. Midsummer magic, it would not affect Sue and Guy, not really.

The next time he came they went up the mountain. Jenny never climbed it for pleasure, but now, suddenly, she wanted to go higher. He lay down on short, nibbled turf at the bottom of the first tump. She sat near him, afraid to be too close. He talked about his past loves. A first wife, several relationships. He had been in a muddle, she decided. He had made compromises, and tried, but was still not happy – like me, I suppose, she thought.

They talked about time, about how precious and ephemeral it was, and how terribly swift. He helped her bag up loose hay in the barn. She tried to be busy, and to keep her distance. Then an arm shot out and held her. 'Is it wise to come so close to me?' he teased.

'Do you always get what you want, Guy?' she asked him.

'Yes, I do,' he said.

Then he had to go again. He changed his clothes.

'What on earth are you doing?' she asked. He was supposed to be somewhere else, at a meeting somewhere, he explained. She thought it was funny, at first, but then it was terrible. They were into lies.

It was a hot July. One Sunday we dipped 300 sheep; the next day Guy took Jenny out for lunch. She rose early, washed her hair a second time, to get rid of the smell of dip, and went through every piece of clothing she had, leaving them in heaps around the bedrooms. She put on make-up, took us to school, and they went off up the border for a picnic.

'It's terrible what happens to your confidence when you're in love,' she sighed. 'We were in a health food shop and there was this lovely girl serving us, she was wearing a lovely jumper and sexy shorts and her hair was all beautiful golden curls like a Botticelli angel and I suddenly thought that's the kind of girl he'd really go for and I found myself desperately wishing I looked like her – wishing I was her! Awful, really.'

Get a grip, she thought, I am me! Later, on a mountainside, she wanted to shout her happiness; instead, she rolled over and over, dizzier and dizzier, down a long green slope. Guy rolled too. How happy I am, she thought, how happy! I can't believe it.

Thoughts would just pop into her head, and, given any excuse, out of her mouth. Gosh, he's handsome. A real knock-out. And so kind, so unbelievably sweet! 'He's one of those people who just love to help. He can't see something that needs doing and not do it . . .' And so good at everything. A Renaissance man. Her type all right, I should say! And so silly. Thought Shakespeare dreadfully overrated. Oh he made her laugh . . .

I saw them sitting out the back one morning. Every day seemed awash with light now; the long grasses were bent and gilded. Jenny and Guy leaned their heads towards each other, discussing something, close together on the lip of the huge blue view. They looked beautiful, in the crisp sunlight, and I played at being their child, in my mind, and thought how that would be, how strong and unusual it would feel.

Between his visits she talked to us, of course.

'The awful thing is, darlings, I think I do love him, I do – I love him. But he's married! He's married to Sue!'

'But he loves you, doesn't he?'

'Yes, I think he does. He says he does. I believe he does. But he's married – it's not right.'

'Does he love Sue?'

'He says not. He says it was a mistake to have married her. He says they aren't happy but he cares for her very much and he desperately doesn't want to hurt her, and nor do I.'

'Well, I think he's great,' Alexander said, pulling one of Toss's ears.

'Yeah, me too, Mummy. He is.'

She hugged us both, but when she stopped there was desperation in her face. Alexander and I had no trouble understanding it: they were in love, but not free to love; they had to steal their happiness from themselves as much as from the world.

There is one morning, with swallows diving like thrilled swimmers, sheep nosing up through bracken towards the heights and a sky like a swelling hymn, when every bright thing seems to proclaim itself, as if all existence is in salutation to the day. Jenny is going to meet Guy while we are at school. She has not dressed up, wears a T-shirt and jeans, but there is an air, a swish about her, as she herds us into the car, something vivid and pretty and breathless.

He comes again the following Sunday afternoon. Alexander and I play in the larch trees; holding the swing above our heads, with the ropes tight, we hurl ourselves off the old wall, flinging out in a wide arc, like a horizontal parachute jump, blurring the valley miles beneath us.

Jenny and Guy wander across the meadows and down to the badger setts. They sit together in the bracken for a while, then scramble down to the stream. She wants to show him all of her kingdom; the dog roses; the old trees with their ears of fungus; the dark pebble pools and the silver falls of the brook. She feels joy like a deep gulf, something enormous, bottomless, beneath them; as they walk back it seems to carry them, to bear them up and glide them along.

They climb up the Patch, lean on the gate at the top and gaze at it all, at the late afternoon and the sun-dusted valley, at the cloud shadows and shafts of light, like God's fingers, playing over the hills.

'You may have to come and live here,' she says.

'Yes,' he says. 'I've thought of it.'


Guy tells Sue what has happened. They talk about divorce. Sue is distraught, and furious. She fights every way she can, in love and hurt and anger. She attacks our terrible squalor, Jenny's cooking, her poverty, her emotional indulgence and the way she has brought us up.

It is as though everyone in town knows. 'Half the High Street is on my side and the other half is against me,' Jenny says.

'You're imagining it, Mummy . . .'

'Am I? I'm not sure. I don't blame them anyway – I don't blame them. It's a terrible, terrible predicament. Poor Sue! We could never be happy if she's miserable, anyway. I could never be happy . . .'

Guy says he will leave Sue. Jenny says are you sure? Perhaps you should put this aside, she says, and try again with your wife. 'I know what it's like to be left,' she agonises. 'We know, don't we, children?'

Guy says he could do that, he could try again, but would she still be there, at the end, if it did not work?

Of course, she says, of course I will wait for you.

Guy vacillates. Does Jenny love him enough? Will she put him before her children, will she put him before her farm? He tells her to think about it: think about losing your independence, he says, and your autonomy. Think about losing your farm.

'Whatever happens, you simply can't stay up there,' he insists, gently, but looking her hard in the eye.

'It's not safe, it's not healthy . . .' She is making faces. He smiles sternly and grips her hand. 'It's not sane! You will become more and more lonely. You're going to send the boys off to school. What then? You absolutely must come down.'

But she resists: one cold, wide evening, under a luminous lemon sky, she watches storm clouds gathering in flocks over the Beacons, and wonders how she will ever leave.

They each fear the other has 'cold feet'. That is the phrase they use, 'cold feet', as if they are standing in the edge of the sea.

Now he says they will need money, to buy another house for Sue. Jenny calculates how many acres she can sell without destroying the farm. The Far Quoiker and Ty Newydd, she decides. Twenty acres will bring in £30,000; she will give him that. He says he is going to talk to Sue and finish it one way or another, but he does not.

They turn over and over, trapped at the confluence of their hopes, her responsibilities and his fears. He studies her, and us.

But it is not all anguished debating: they are in love, and how they laugh and kiss and court! At last she has a true friend, a confidant, a partner: in photographs from this time she looks radiant, laughing; someone has found her, at last.

And he loves to help, to make improvements. A cassette player appears in the kitchen: Mozart greets the morning. He spends hours installing a second water system, to augment our supplies.

He lugs a thick barge rope up to the attic and ties it over a beam. Thrown out of the skylight it will reach the ground: we now have a fire escape. He gives me an air rifle and teaches me how to shoot it. He buys tools for us, fits us up with a workbench in the attic, and gives Jenny a silver ring.

'It's fallen off,' she cries, that winter. 'I went up the Quoiker to check the tank and it's fallen into the snow!' We go looking for it, with a torch, following her footprints. Beside every second pace is a circular trace from the tip of her stick, but there is no sign of the ring.

When Alexander and I go to stay with our father, Jenny and Guy go to Scotland together, and then in the summer to France.

'Oh, boys, we had such a funny time, such a wonderful time. And oh it was a gas, he does make me laugh. There was one morning . . .'

I want them to be happy, want it to work, but my neediness and jealousy add to the great weight against them. One night after he has been to dinner I suddenly cannot bear the time it takes them to say goodnight at the Middle Meadow gate. I work myself into a lather.

'Why are you panicking?' Alexander frowns up from his book as I peer out of the windows. 'There's nothing to worry about.'

'But I don't know what she's doing.'

'It doesn't matter,' he shrugs. 'She'll come back.'

I ignore him and charge down the track, cursing and wailing in a brutal, self-induced tantrum: seeing the lights of his car poised at the edge of our realm has tipped me into a kind of insanity.

'I don't mind the love affair,' I shout, 'but I can't stand all this creeping about!'

'You don't have to be jealous!' Jenny cries when she returns, her voice rising to a pitch of disbelief, as though this hysteria in a boy whose mother obviously loves him is the most absurd thing in the world, and I can see that it is.

'I'm not, I'm not!' I shout. 'I'm just worried when I don't know where you are and what you're doing.'

But I am; I am terribly jealous, and torn: I want him to make her happy, but I fear displacement, a shuffling of my position.

All four of us went on holiday together, to a rented house in Somerset. Between the gentle slopes of the Quantock Hills little oak-wooded valleys wound down towards the Bristol Channel; from rocky beaches we stared back across the sea to Wales, humped, blue and hazy behind its cliffs. We had never seen our mother so happy; it was as if she and Guy were in an open con-spiracy which everyone was invited to join. Laughter burst out of nothing: a twitch of his nose; her sidelong glance; every shop assistant, tea waitress, hiker and holidaymaker was offered a part in the play. A tractor driver grinned and winked as we passed him in a lane. We walked miles, over hills and along cliffs. They held hands, and teased each other about her map reading, his appetite, her walking speed, botany (Guy never admitted not knowing the name of a plant: 'You're making it up,' Jenny would cry), and architecture, competing to date houses to the nearest year. Each seemed to have met their match in the other, and it was as though they could not quite believe it.

They dived into churches, swept in and out of shops and led us beachcombing for fossils. At supper Guy held long conversa-tions with my brother and me, discussions on everything from nuclear power to ghosts. I started to adjust to the sight of our mother beside his tall figure; it was like remembering a half-forgotten formula. We had lived as three, two boys plus one mother; now I began to see how we could live as four, simulta-neously composed of three plus one (us and Guy), and two plus two (Alexander and me, and Jenny and Guy). In this adjustment were echoes of memory from the time when Alexander was a baby, and the two of us travelled in the back seat of Dad's car, while he and Jenny talked in the front, and I daydreamed, my attention drifting in and out of their conversation, and it did not matter, because I did not have to listen or respond.

We returned to the mountain full of hope: Guy and our mother were in love; we had had a wonderful holiday; we could all be happy together. Alexander and I knew that with Guy as with all adults, we were on Best Behaviour. 'Do me proud, please, boys,' Jenny would say, and she let us know when we had, with marks out of ten, and blasting reprimands if we had not. The week in Somerset had been a success: we got ten out of ten, and it had been easy; we had had a lovely time. If it was a glimpse of our future then there was nothing to worry about, we were all blessed.

'Here we are, home again,' Jenny said, gunning the car up to the top of the yard and hauling on the brake.

'Doesn't it look green! And look, the sheep haven't got in and eaten my tubs for once, since Guy fixed the gate.'

It did look green. After fifteen years of her stewardship, nothing had been cut back. Trees and hedges bustled with growth. Gorse rambled across the Quoiker, bracken rolled down from the hill, skirmishing across the fence, sidling ever closer to the house. Armies of thistles bristled proudly in the Patch, jaunty under their cockades of purple and white, and all around the buildings the nettles crowded, waist high. Moss made bright cushions of the roof tiles and the clematis swung from blocked guttering, pushing its tendrils into the upstairs windows and peeling flakes of whitewash off the walls.

Inside, the house smelled of summer: cool stone, bracken, old plaster and must. Motes of dust danced in shafts of low sunlight. Along the collapsing shelves at the back of the living room, hundreds of children's books bulged and leaned against each other. On the pegs, coats from my father's time mouldered. There was a faint acrid tang from the fireplace, where rain had fallen on the ashes, and from the back door came a buzzing sound: large wasps were nesting in the roof. But out beyond the window the mountain waited, summoning our eyes and attentions, calling us away from all that ought to be done, towards everything we wanted to do.

'Right, children, you take the dogs out, I'm going to check on the rams and the yearlings, see what's died while we were away . . .'

It was as though the farm was beyond repair, beyond our wills, our strength and finances: it was so fiercely itself, in its beauty and dilapidation, and its reflection of our wilful carelessness, that it seemed unchangeable. Did Guy really think he might live here?

I asked him, years later: did you ever seriously consider it?

'Tacitly, I think we understood there was never a moment when that was going to happen. I never got used to the tip aspect. I've always loathed cats. There were several mangy dogs. It all took a lot of getting used to.'

He is not the kind of man who gets used to things; he prefers to change them. He glanced at the floor, then back to me.

'I tried to sell the proposition of her coming down to some-where softer, more peopled . . . She had a fluctuating degree of freedom. One day she was lonely, the next, anyone was an intruder. She appeared to be over-relaxed about things, but also she had a steely something that wouldn't make you stop to argue. I hyped the weather aspect, the snow and the danger and the loneliness, hoping she'd come down. But she never did.

'I think I realised it wasn't my life,' he said. 'I would have got terrible claustrophobia. Travel is in my blood. Then there was the collapse of my marriage, and I had to try and keep my family together, and myself on the move, and I began to feel I was being pulled in too many directions.'

I nodded. We both knew what had happened then. One day, a year after the holiday in the Quantocks, a year of inconclusive discussions, informal trials and unmade decisions, he packed a bag, put it in his car, stroked his dogs, left a note for Sue, and drove away to France. He wrote a long and loving letter to Jenny, with 'goodbye' so gently between their lines that she could scarcely read it.

'What's happened, Mummy?' I asked her. We were walking across the meadows.

'I waited for him, but he didn't wait for me,' she said. She spoke slowly, forming the sentences carefully, precariously, like someone tiptoeing along a log over a fast deep stream. 'He wanted me to sell the farm and go away with him, but I wasn't quite ready to. I didn't want to dump you both in schools and sell our safety net. I wanted him to wait, until you were settled and I was ready, but he couldn't.'

'Why not?'

'I don't think he wants a woman with children and animals. But that is what I am. I could sell the sheep, and the farm, but there's still you two. I wasn't ruthless, I just wasn't! I wanted him to sort his marriage out properly, without rushing off and just abandoning Sue, but when he was ready I wasn't. And he didn't wait. He was off.'

— * —

I remember it ending in the same weather it began in, in the yellow-grass days of summer. Jenny still dressed the way she had for him, elegantly, in long skirts. She wore sunglasses all the time; behind them her eyes were red. She pored over his letters, and wrote, and walked the sheep, and took us on trips to the reservoir, where they had had their happiest day. And though she noticed everything, as she always had, her gaze did not seem to linger: it slid to the side, stared off, away somewhere. She tried hard to be gay with us, and to worry about the sheep, to be brave and to hold it and hide it. 'I'm just fine,' she would say. 'Just fine!'

But she carried a desolate silence with her, cradled and covered, half hidden, but never not there. And so it was not hardship, or poverty, or Mad Bombers, or illness which finally undid her hold on the hill. It was not the misbehaviour of children, our needs and demands, nor the death nor the agony of animals. It was not the weather, nor the isolation, nor the state of the house which ultimately drove us away.

It was love, and the terrible beauty of the place, its heartbreaking view and its sky. It was all the wonder of the mountain that did for us, its colours and wild bright days.

'It was the end of the farm for me, really,' she said. 'After he went, I couldn't stay there. It wasn't the loneliness or even the winters. It was having been there with him.'

We began to look for somewhere else in earnest. Jenny thought about a little terraced house on the edge of town, but it was too near people and traffic. She was tempted by a little cottage further down the valley, halfway up the hillside, and we looked at a farm up a hill above our school, but nowhere we saw had anything to replace or compensate for the magic that we knew. There was also the question of whom we should sell to: Jenny was determined that whoever came after us should farm the land, not break it up or fertilise it to death.

Too quickly, it seemed, a couple were interested, and they fitted all her criteria. They would farm, they would not fertilise, they said; they would plant trees, and have cattle as well as sheep. It fell to me to walk them around the land, and I did so, feeling like a traitor. As we came to badger setts there was a noise just under our feet. We stopped. There, just beneath us, were three tiny squeaking cubs. I watched as the husband and wife looked at each other, their faces delighted and amazed. This is how it was for my parents, I thought, as the land cast its old spell again. I was jealous and forlorn, we all were – what would be left of us, in exile from our right place?

In the end we found a large old house, half derelict, half comfortable, which had not been much messed around. It had the thick walls and the old ship feeling of the farm. It had an old apple orchard, and there were kind neighbours nearby. Jack's cottage was just across the garden.

'We'll be able to wave to you, Jack,' Jenny said. 'It will be wonderful!'

But Jack was ill, sunk, and rarely smiled now. 'Don't know if I'll see the cuckoo,' he said.

'Oh of course you will,' she said. 'You always say that, and you always do!'

Before we made the move he died; he succumbed to the rule
of threes. He had pneumonia; his relatives did not tell Jenny when
his condition worsened; and 'they', the doctors, did not help him.
'I could have saved him,' Jenny wept, 'if I'd only got there in time
and made a fuss . . .'

Jack's funeral was in the chapel. Higher up the valley, under a
swell of the mountains, the chapel stands in a coomb above a dark
stream. Its situation lifts your eyes up to the hills behind it, and
in the sharp line of the highest horizon, and in the nearby sky,
which starts at the top of the steep fields above the graveyard, you
feel the presence of an austere and watchful God. The chapel was
full of men in dark suits and smart overcoats; their shoes shone
brighter than water. Women and children went upstairs, into the
gallery. The singing was high and strong; thinned voices raised
the notes in a tribute that was honouring and acknowledging and
bleak all at once; old men saluting one of their own and the end
of a life of their time.

We followed the coffin down the lane to the graveyard, which
is on a steep slope, and climbed up through the tussocks and
headstones. There were sheep cropping the field above; the farmers looked them over as the minister said the last words, instinctively making sure they were all all right.

David Hughes was there: he looked up at the mountain, its
high prow forging on, always, across the clouds. He squeezed
Jenny's arm. 'Lucky Jack,' he said, quietly. 'Yes,' Jenny nodded.
'Lucky Jack.'

When she knew we were leaving Jenny walked around the
fields with her camera. It is an autumn afternoon. The mountain
is on the turn; brown die-back showing through the green. In the
distance the hills are hazy, over the tops of trees still heavy with
fading leaves. By the Far Meadow gate the rose hips are blood
bright in the hedgerow, and as she walks through the fields, taking
pictures, the sheep turn towards her and stare.

Moving day passed in a haze, frantic and unreal. As we boxed
our things, all our books and bits, the walls were revealed, stripped

bare. As we exposed the collapsing plaster and the rotting boards, the mouseholes and cobwebs and centuries of dust, the old house seemed to age and shrivel. We packed, stuffed and carried, hurrying madly, trying not to take it in. Jenny hit the same peak of adrenalin and desperate matter-of-factness with which she sent old sheep to the slaughter. We copied her, working like mad. It was as though we were trying not to acknowledge what we were doing; refusing to hear the voices of the farm and the mountain; too miserable to attempt a proper farewell.

I wrote a note, like a short love letter, and stuffed it into the space behind the wallpaper of my bedroom, where no one but the mice would find it.

A friend came with a circular saw to liberate the fridge from the sideboard. He cut straight through the work-surface, as my brother watched him, transfixed. It was, Alexander says, as though his childhood ended there: common sense, efficiency and a snarling machine slicing through the heart of the house.

'Well, goodbye little farm,' Jenny said, as the removal men struggled to shut the back doors of their van. It sounded strange and unconvincing, as though neither she nor the place really believed she was leaving.

When we reached the new house she handed one of the men the sledgehammer, and asked him to batter down a blocked-up door.

'Are you sure?' he said.

'Quite sure,' she replied. 'It's going to be the new way in.'

'Well, I never saw anyone move into a new house like this,' he said. 'Stand back!'

That night, our first in our new home, I plugged in the television. The great compensation of civilisation delivered three channels of fuzz and one quite clearly.

'Mum! Television! It works! One channel does, anyway.'

'Oh really,' she said, tiredly. 'What's on?'

'*Death on the Nile.*'

'Oh. Peter Ustinov. Jolly good.' It was the tone she used when things were not jolly good, and we sensed the film was a hoary old repeat even then. But we all sat on boxes of books, jammed between sofas, and stared at it nevertheless.

With time, Jenny cast her spell over the house. It is a simple system of tolerance and consideration, of not destroying things, not cutting things down or meddling unless there is absolutely no choice. Swifts nest in the eaves, butterflies hibernate on the windowsills, and there is – despite my protests – an ant colony in the kitchen. Swallows and house martins come annually to the yard, and robins and wrens live in the garden. Sometimes a sparrowhawk ambushes the crowd around the bird table.

A hedgehog used to appear in the kitchen, scoop up slugs and slurp away at the milk bowl, to the bemusement of the cat. On the ridge of the roof is a starling which does a perfect imitation of a buzzard. Every spring the jackdaws fill the chimney with twigs and wool, rear their young there and depart, leaving a pillar of sticks blocking the flue. In the autumn the chimney sweep comes and pulls it all down, advising Jenny to have the birds shot. But then there would be no chatting voices in the chimney, and no bright pale eyes watching her comings and goings, and she would have to gather kindling for winter fires herself. In her relationship with nature is a minute appreciation, born of attention and observation of its details, coupled with a passionate engagement with its great patterns. Her stance is political as much as spiritual: behind the simple creed of live and let live is the belief that 'let live' is an active process, involving effort, sacrifice and love.

Jenny and Guy are great friends and barely ever meet.

She is philosophical about it. 'It was a good thing I didn't marry him, really,' she says. 'Trouble is, he's ruined everyone else for me. No one will ever compare.'

'You were lucky to have had those times,' I say, as we watch two greenfinches attacking the bird feeder.

'Yes,' she says, 'I was.'

'When you met him, you said it was the first time you had been in love for fifteen years – since Dad?'

She shakes her head.

'I don't think I was ever in love with Robert. I loved him, but I wasn't in love with him.'

That strange feeling comes over me again, a kind of shock without surprise.

'So why did you marry him then?'

'Because he has a wonderful, golden side to him, and I was very fond of him, and because he wanted to, really,' Jenny says. She is smoking cigars now, like a retired pirate.

'When you were here and he was in London you must have realised it wasn't going to work – so why did you keep going back there? Why were you surprised when it ended?'

'Well, I used to say to Ursie perhaps it will be better in our forties. I thought we might just settle into it.' She looks rattled now, and I know this is unfair, but I can't resist one more question. 'But how could it have got better when you didn't love each other?'

'I don't know! Maybe I thought that's what marriage was, because my parents' marriage was so rotten and miserable. I think I thought that was what it was supposed to be like!'

Part of the answer I had been seeking is there. Having wrestled for so long with the idea that the rupture in our childhood stemmed from my father, and having been so puzzled that he could not keep loving my mother, though she seemed to me so loveable, it is a kind of relief to hear that it was mutual; that her behaviour was as singular, wilful and yet will-less, as his. It makes them seem more compatible, somehow, and since even now I cannot escape the urge to push them together, perhaps I have finally found a way of joining them: they were perfectly, heroically, mismatched. They were doomed, and everything they had and did was miraculous, a romantic defiance of their fate. When they meet now there is a gentleness between them that could be an acknowledgement of that; an ease, a kind of fondness for the other's humour and strangeness, and a respect for their steel. They are both romantics, and though I have learned of the dangers which attend and await romantic people, that bipolar breed, the certain failure, the heartbreak – theirs and others' – and the loneliness, I cannot quite wish they, or I, had been otherwise. If life is hills and valleys, then let the hills be high.

We came down from our mountain, but we did not quite let it go. We kept one field, the Far Quoiker which adjoins the hill. Eleven acres of hummocky ground, with a spring, and anthills, and gorse. Green woodpeckers live there, probing the humps for insects, and there is a family of kestrels in the ash. There are squirrels' drays, and a March hare and a hundred miles of view.

From certain parts of the field you can see the farm. It is much changed now. All the sheds have been incorporated into a large, comfortable house. The green lane is gone. The spinney was cut down, the gorse bushes ploughed up and the great ash tree behind the house was felled. The fences do not sag, there are businesslike sheds in the First Meadow and there are fewer animals in the fields. It has all been rebuilt and smartened up, transformed into a fit and conventional dwelling for twenty-first century tenants. It had to happen, of course. Without a great deal of money and work everything would simply have fallen down.

But the wonder of existence on the edge of that ruin, the fragile and reverent way we lived, patching up rather than replacing, in slow step with time and weather, imprinted by them rather than proofed against them, preserved mysteries and a particular magic of which only traces remain.

Only the Quoiker has not been improved in any way. The gate at the top leads to the mountain, and Mum still puts a few sheep through. In the summer she follows along behind them, high-hearted, up ridges like a giant's stair, just as she used to, as all the tenants before her did, following the animals to their grazing under the great wide air. Near the gate there is an ancient stone wall, constantly collapsing, which she has repaired for years. She says it makes the perfect therapy, if she feels troubled, to unearth and sort the stones. You cannot hurry, you have to try things, let the parts show you how they join. In the weight of the rocks, in their shapes and relationships, are patterns as old as time. You enter a kind of reverie, she says, as you lift them and fit them together.

# Acknowledgements

All thanks to Tif Loehnis, without whom I would still be on a slush pile. Thank you, Roland Philipps and Rowan Yapp, for your amazing backing, patience and judgement. Thank you, Howard Davies, and all at John Murray for your trouble and time.

I am hugely grateful to David, Anna Rose, Merlin and Elizabeth Hughes, for putting me up, and putting up with me, with such love and encouragement.

Thanks to all my friends and mentors in and around BBC Radio Arts, and especially Julian May, Mohit Bakaya, Allegra McIlroy, Rob Ketteridge, Aasiya Lodhi, Lawrence Pollard, John Wilson, Ian McMillan, and Peter Blegvad.

I have been especially blessed with the great friendship and support of Robin Jenkins, Toby Lynas, Jane Matthews, Chris Kenyon, Fliss Morgan, Roger Couhig, Mike White, Kevin Bohnert, Claire Paterson, Richard Coles and Alison Finch.

Very special thanks to Sally Spurring, for everything. And to Dad, Mum and Alexander, for your love, forgiveness and faith. This is for you.